T0267937

Small, Medium, Large

Small, Medium, Large

How Government Made the U.S. into a Manufacturing Powerhouse

COLLEEN A. DUNLAVY

polity

Copyright © Colleen A. Dunlavy 2024

The right of Colleen A. Dunlavy to be identified as Author of this Work has
been asserted in accordance with the UK Copyright, Designs and Patents Act
1988.

First published in 2024 by Polity Press

Polity Press
65 Bridge Street
Cambridge CB2 1UR, UK

Polity Press
111 River Street
Hoboken, NJ 07030, USA

All rights reserved. Except for the quotation of short passages for the purpose
of criticism and review, no part of this publication may be reproduced, stored
in a retrieval system, or transmitted, in any form or by any means, electronic,
mechanical, photocopying, recording, or otherwise, without the prior
permission of the publisher.

ISBN-13: 9781509561735

A catalogue record for this book is available from the British Library.

Library of Congress Control Number: 2024931591

Typeset in 11 on 14pt Warnock Pro
by Cheshire Typesetting Ltd, Cuddington, Cheshire
Printed and bound in Great Britain by CPI Group (UK) Ltd, Croydon

The publisher has used its best endeavors to ensure that the URLs for external
websites referred to in this book are correct and active at the time of going to
press. However, the publisher has no responsibility for the websites and can
make no guarantee that a site will remain live or that the content is or will
remain appropriate.

Every effort has been made to trace all copyright holders, but if any have been
overlooked the publisher will be pleased to include any necessary credits in
any subsequent reprint or edition.

For further information on Polity, visit our website:
politybooks.com

To
Lena Andersson-Skog
Linda Gordon
Jürgen Kocka
and
Merritt Roe Smith
for your inspiration and support
over the years

Contents

Illustrations

Preface and Acknowledgments

Every historical study has its own history. Sometimes an alert historian detects contradictions in previous studies that cry out for further research. Other times, a research project springs from the historian's personal experience or identity. In yet other instances, contemporary issues (e.g., climate change) raise questions that previous generations of historians have not considered. Occasionally, one research question, through engagement with evidence, morphs into a quite different question. And sometimes sheer serendipity – the chance encounter – provokes fruitful new questions.

Serendipity sparked this study of standard sizes and the government's role in pushing manufacturers toward mass production from the Great War (1914–18) through the 1960s. When I was engaged in research on another topic altogether, I came across a paragraph in a published primary source that startled me. "Hmmm," I thought, "that's weird." In a brief passage, the writer reported that manufacturers, under pressure from the War Industries Board during the Great War, had reduced the diversity of products they made in order to shift to mass-production methods. But, when the war ended, they reversed course and re-diversified their product lines – "return[ing] to the old uneconomic conditions of over-diversity,"[1] as the writer put it. He then described a federal government initiative to get them back on track toward mass production by forging nationwide agreements on standard sizes. Thanks to research that my students had done over the years on surgical instruments and agricultural implements,[2] I knew about government officials' efforts during World War I to shift manufacturing to a mass-production basis. But, having learned how to mass produce, manufacturers reversed course? Reducing the scale of production to make a greater variety of products on a smaller scale? As a historian of business and technology, I knew full well that history is not linear, that economic history has been full of branch points and alternative paths, that the benefits of mass production are context-dependent. But, still, trying and then rejecting mass production? Reversing course altogether? And a government program to entice them back to mass production? I was startled. Thus began the research presented in this little book.

The history of standard sizes presented here may startle some readers, too. Those who are not well acquainted with the history of government and the American economy may regard it as an aberration, a striking departure from long-term trends. As decades of research suggest, however, the government's role in pushing American business toward mass production is fully consistent with the long sweep of U.S. history. Also, those who discern the novelty in the history presented here might assume that it is grounded in newly discovered archival sources. Not so, for this is a history that has been hiding in plain sight – in the wealth of published primary sources that form the foundation for this study.

My original intention was not to publish a book at all. Initially, I envisioned a journal article on U.S. Secretary of Commerce Herbert Hoover's Division of Simplified Practice and its push for mass production in the 1920s, a stand-alone piece that would alert business historians to this pivotal but overlooked episode in American history. As the 1920s story took shape, however, I realized that I needed to deepen the context on both the front and back ends – by exploring product diversity before the war and World War I efforts to reduce diversity, as well as the long-term durability of the initiative, visible all around us today in a plethora of familiar standard sizes. And so it grew beyond the confines of a journal article.

To keep the book sharply focused on the origins of standard sizes in the U.S., I have left it for others to place this story in comparative perspective. As a comparative historian myself, I was sorely tempted to compare the American story with experience elsewhere – in Britain, which was at the forefront of standardization in other ways, but not this one; in Germany, where World War I launched a similar standardization movement that included product sizes; and in France, always a fascinating outlier in industrial history. Sweden would likely make a fruitful addition to the mix. And then there is the intense competition in the 1920s over whose national standards would prevail in which markets around the globe. As a moment's reflection on the diversity of bed sizes or electrical outlets from nation to nation confirms, competitive forces won out; such products were never standardized globally. But I have resisted those temptations and kept my focus squarely on the U.S. Commerce Department project, which did what "market forces" could not do – turned the United States into a manufacturing powerhouse.

Pursuing the project in fits and starts over the past decade and a half, I have benefited from the insights and generosity of a host of colleagues and students with congruent interests in political economy. The story first took shape in my lectures on the history of American capitalism at the University of Wisconsin–Madison, in a newspaper article some 15 years ago, and then as a conference paper presented at the annual meeting of the Business History Conference in June 2015. I am grateful to my fellow panelists Stephen Mihm, Laura Phillips Sawyer, and David F. Weiman and to the session attendees for helpful and encouraging comments. Thanks, also, to Caitlin Rosenthal and Espen Storli for inviting me to present the lumber portion of the story to a stimulating mix of American and Norwegian scholars at the University of California, Berkeley, in November 2015. Although I ended up using Commerce Department files at the National Archives and Records Administration in College Park, MD, I am obliged to archivist Craig Winter for his willingness to review selected folders for me at the Herbert Hoover Presidential Library and Museum during the Covid pandemic. Over the years, my thinking about simplified practice has been shaped by fruitful conversations with a host of others: Leslie Abadie, Idit Ben Or, Regina Blaszczyk, Alexia Blin, Suzanne Desan, Pierre-Christian Fink, Barbara Forrest, Walter Friedman, Pierre Gervais, Linda Gordon, Allen Hunter, Camden Hutchison, Kenneth Lipartito, Bethany Moreton, Marina Moskowitz, Daniel Raff, and Steven Usselman. For thorough readings of the manuscript and ever astute comments, I owe an eternal debt to Florence Bernault, Pamela Laird, Jürgen Kocka, Mary O'Sullivan, Merritt Roe Smith, and Kathleen Thelen. Any errors of fact or interpretation are, of course, my own. To Ian Malcolm and staff at Polity Press, my gratitude for their enthusiasm and expert support. And, finally, to my beloved partner in life's adventures, Ron Radano, many thanks for your patience with this and all else.

1

The Puzzle of Standard Sizes

"Standard sizes" are familiar, ubiquitous, taken for granted in modern consumption. Consider bed frames and mattresses. Shoppers today know without thinking that both bed frames and mattresses are offered in the same small number of standard sizes and that, say, an American queen-sized mattress will fit an American queen-sized bed frame.[1] Consumers need only decide which standard size is right for them. Likewise with electrical plugs and outlets: American consumers share the tacit knowledge that the plug on an electrical device bought in the U.S. will fit into the electrical outlets of an American home (though not necessarily into outlets in another country). And they can comfortably assume what was not always the case: a randomly purchased roll of toilet paper will fit (in width at least) their toilet paper holder. Many everyday goods from batteries to printer paper are commonly available in a limited number of standard sizes, lending an extraordinary homogeneity to modern consumption. Behind the scenes, rarely visible to the ultimate consumer, lie even more standard sizes – in factory fittings, building materials, plumbing fixtures, and the like.

What makes standard sizes "standard" is that dozens, if not hundreds, of different firms manufacture everyday products in the same, limited set of sizes and shapes. In other words, they are standardized across firms. This means that competing firms carry the same sizes and shapes "in stock," readily available, while other sizes or shapes must be special-ordered and cost more, if they are available at all.[2] Leaving out of consideration those consumers who preferred or needed something other than the standard sizes, mass producers, distributors, and retailers, in effect, as a notable expert put it, "standardized the customer."[3]

How did it come to be that competing mattress manufacturers – some 400 establishments in the U.S. as of 2019[4] – all offer consumers the same small number of "standard" mattress sizes? Once a collective agreement on standard sizes has been achieved, of course, firms have strong incentives to focus their production on those standard sizes so that customers can easily find a mattress to fit their bed frame and bed sheets to fit their mattress. But how and when did industry-wide standard sizes come to be established in the first place?

Collective agreements on a national scale do not arise spontaneously or naturally; they must be forged.[5] An individual manufacturer, to be sure, had to limit its production to a few sizes or styles in order to produce those few sizes or styles in large volume. (Thus, the U.S. War Department's first step in developing the keystone of mass production, interchangeable-parts manufacturing technology, after the War of 1812 was to decide which single musket to produce.[6]) If a firm enjoyed a position of overwhelming market dominance, its standard sizes or styles, decided upon unilaterally, might become de facto nationwide standards. But, in general, an individual manufacturer's "standard" products were unlikely to be identical to those of their competitors. Indeed, they were quite likely to be different, if differentiating products in size or style was a way of avoiding price competition with one's competitors. In the 1920s, standard sizes, the National Industrial Conference Board observed, were "confined almost entirely within the limits of the individual establishment. . . . [I]n the absence of combination, the tendency to standardization does not reach beyond the bounds of the several producing organizations."[7] A bed manufacturer concurred: "Individual bed manufacturers did not lack standards for themselves. That wasn't the trouble at all. But they were all individual standards, perfectly useless so far as other bed manufacturers were concerned."[8] Reducing product variety *across firms*, in other words, required "combination," a collective agreement among many competing firms. It did not happen naturally. Quite to the contrary, collective action posed formidable challenges in fragmented industries, marked by many buyers and many sellers, all the more so if their suppliers and customers also had to be brought on board.[9] How, then, did direct competitors – companies all producing or selling the same line of goods – set aside often intense competitive pressure (not to mention legal constraints) and forge collective agreements on standard sizes?

The mystery deepens when one considers the speed with which standard sizes emerged in the 1920s. In 1919–21, surveys showed, some 900 American manufacturers made bedsteads, springs, and mattresses in 78 different sizes,[10] a diversity that seems unimaginable today. In 1922 an industry-wide agreement reduced those 78 sizes to 4 standard widths and 1 standard length.[11] Within a decade, some 90 percent of the nation's output of beds, mattresses, and springs conformed to the new standard sizes.[12] In the meantime, this "simplification" of household mattress and bed sizes, as it was called, spurred nationwide agreements to simplify hospital beds (from 33 lengths, 34 widths, and 44 heights to 1, 3, and 1, respectively) and blanket sizes (from 78 to 12).[13] By the end of the decade, standard sizes had been established for more than 100 commodities – from sterling silver flatware, writing paper, jelly jars, shovels, grocery bags, and milk bottles to bank checks, warehouse forms, restaurant checks, and a variety of tools and building materials.[14]

How did this nationwide transformation – the simplification of everyday goods that we now take for granted – come about so swiftly and thoroughly? As a starting point in working out this puzzle, it would be helpful to know more about the diffusion of mass-production techniques among smaller manufacturers after the turn of the twentieth century. But, despite reams of research on the history of mass production and distribution, it remains a mystery, for historians have neglected to ask how those techniques, after Henry Ford's remarkable achievements with the Model T in the 1910s,[15] were taken to the next level, diffusing throughout the American economy over the middle decades of the twentieth century.

Historians' inattention to the diffusion process stems from the narrative framework that has guided scholarship in American business history for decades. This framework is anchored in a dichotomy between small-scale producers of luxury products and large-scale manufacturers producing low-priced goods in "landmark factories," to borrow Joshua Freeman's term.[16] In her now-classic study of the Great Merger Movement, Naomi Lamoreaux put the dichotomy succinctly: "In the United States during the late nineteenth century, most firms adopted one of two basic strategies. Either they manufactured small quantities of carefully differentiated, high-quality products, or they mass-produced a cheap homogeneous output."[17] There is no room in this interpretive framework to ask how mass-production techniques might have diffused among middling manufacturers.

Structured by this framework, business historians confined their attention to one or the other side of the dichotomy. Under the sway of Alfred D. Chandler, Jr.'s influential studies of mass production and distribution, they initially focused on "big business" – on leading manufacturers and retailers in the late nineteenth and early twentieth centuries. The Chandlerian narrative centered on the growth of large integrated firms and salaried managers exploiting growing national markets.[18] Then, in the 1980s, scholars turned to the other end of the spectrum, to small business and specialty production in the age of mass production – what Philip Scranton termed the "other side" of Chandler's story.[19] Scranton's pathbreaking empirical studies explored specialty or batch production, which entailed small runs of a diversity of products made by networks or clusters of specialty firms. Such firms, he showed, constituted a vibrant element of the American manufacturing landscape through the turn of the twentieth century.[20] In *Endless Novelty*, moreover, he blurred the line between large-scale, mass-producing firms and small-scale, specialty firms by showing that specialty production was associated not only with small firms but also with "giant enterprises making the 'big stuff' of America's infrastructure (locomotives, heavy machinery)."[21] Scranton rightly dates the decline of specialty production in the U.S. to the 1920s and attributes it both to government policies that valorized price competition over product diversity and to changing distribution practices,[22] an interpretation consistent with the fuller story told here. But neither Scranton nor other scholars who pushed back against an excessive focus on big business have explored the diffusion of mass-production techniques among middling manufacturers,[23] a process that would have required them to standardize – "simplify" – their own product lines and might conceivably have laid a foundation for nationwide standard sizes.

As the twenty-first century opened, business historians could be forgiven for thinking that little remained to be discovered about the history of mass production and distribution. "Big business" no longer elicited a frisson of excitement; the literature on its counterpoint, flexible specialization, had matured. Research interests, increasingly inflected by social and cultural history, turned to a host of other topics such as finance and fraud, insurance, family firms, slavery, and race and gender.[24]

Looking in other directions, we might seek help in understanding the origins of standard sizes from scholars who have

studied the broader standardization movement or the career
of Herbert Hoover, who, as we will see, was pivotal in pushing mass-production methods as Secretary of Commerce in
the 1920s. For most students of the standardization movement, however, standard product sizes and styles constitute
little more than a footnote to the larger story, which concerns
technical standards (e.g., weights and measures, screw threads,
electrical units).[25] The most recent studies, moreover, focus
not on the standards themselves but on professional engineering associations and prominent engineers as the key actors
in the standardization movement and on the development of
consensual processes for establishing technical standards.[26]
JoAnne Yates and Craig N. Murphy's *Engineering Rules*, for
example, while impressive for its international sweep, categor-
izes standards in terms that seem to exclude product sizes and
shapes.[27] Most studies of Herbert Hoover's tenure as Secretary
of Commerce, meanwhile, offer only brief descriptions of
the simplification initiative as one piece of his larger "war on
waste."[28] One exception is William R. Tanner's more in-depth
study of Hoover's simplification initiative, and he does note,
in general terms, that it "encouraged the increased use of new
technologies for mass production."[29] On the whole, however,
studies of Hoover offer little insight into the diffusion of mass-
production techniques, whether as a prelude to his initiative or
as a consequence.

As it presently stands, historians, with their passing references to the "uniform products" or "standardized consumer
goods" pouring out of factories,[30] leave us with the impression that the diffusion of mass-production techniques in the
1920s – the making of the U.S. into a "Fordist" nation of mass
producers and consumers – was a natural process of emulation and learning, set in motion by Henry Ford's astonishing
accomplishments. The foremost historian of the technology
underlying mass production, David Hounshell, is explicit
about this. "As a consequence of Ford's openness," he writes,

"Ford production technology diffused rapidly throughout American manufacturing. . . . The Ford Motor Company educated the American technical community in the ways of mass production."[31] He bases this assertion, which has worked its way deeply into the historical literature,[32] not on case studies of firms adopting Ford's methods – actually putting his lessons into practice – but on the widespread attention that Ford's accomplishments attracted in trade journals. There is no denying that Ford's methods garnered widespread media notice, but what did American manufacturers do with that knowledge? Lacking direct evidence of diffusion, scholars rely on statistics and inference to discern its outlines in the 1920s. "That other industries also adopted the assembly line was evident from a startling statistic," David Nye writes in *America's Assembly Line.* "[D]uring the 1920s the number of [factory] workers remained static," he notes, while manufacturing "output soared."[33] Clearly, something changed in the 1920s.

Assume for a moment that Hounshell is right: American manufacturers did indeed learn how to mass produce by reading reports in the press on Ford's accomplishments or by touring his factory. Once individual manufacturers learned to mass produce, one might be tempted to assume, they simply took the logical next step, moving *collectively* to limit their product lines to the same set of "standard" products. Indeed, a contemporary observer described the process in just these terms – as a natural, rational evolution toward nationwide product standards. "These examples of standardization – of lamp bases and of lighting voltages," General Electric's M. D. Cooper observed in 1923, "are typical of the normal course of development and perfection of an industry." Increasing product diversity, with its added costs, uneven quality, and logistical challenges, prompted what he characterized as "a general demand for standardization." Manufacturers rose to that challenge, agreeing to produce the same limited number of product sizes and shapes for the convenience of all.[34] A truly heroic achievement, if it happened that way.

But did it? There is more to Cooper's story than evolving knowledge and manufacturers stepping up to meet "a general demand for standardization." Electric lamp manufacturing was dominated by his company, General Electric (GE), which put it in a market position to set nationwide standards for electric lamp bases. By 1900, some 70 percent of lamps had GE's Edison screw base.[35] Which meant, of course, that some 30 percent of lamps had other types of bases. Even in this special case – an industry dominated by a single manufacturer – achieving the full standardization of lamp bases to which we are accustomed today required a boost from the federal government in its role as a large consumer. In 1907, after negotiations with electric lamp manufacturers and various federal agencies, the U.S. Bureau of Standards issued detailed "specifications" to cover the federal government's purchases of electric lamps. The first edition specified the Edison screw base.[36] As a recounting of this history in a Bureau publication in the 1920s noted, "The great variety [of electric lamps] then in use was promptly simplified to a moderate number adequate for all needs."[37] The editor of *Scientific American* concurred: "Once upon a time there were over 150 different styles of electric-lamp sockets. In buying a new bulb it was almost necessary to take your socket out and carry it to the store, to be fitted with a bulb. Today a lamp bought anywhere fits, automatically, a socket bought anywhere else."[38]

If even a monopolistic industry needed an assist from the federal government to establish nationwide standards, how did fragmented industries manage to do so in the 1920s? A multitude of middling concerns – established companies accustomed to manufacturing a diversity of everyday commodities in modest volumes, often tailored to their customers' specifications – surely pondered the risks of emulating Ford's model.[39] The basic question was whether they, individually, should radically reduce the variety of products they made in order to scale up for mass production, as Ford had in the first decade of the twentieth century, and risk losing customers to competitors who continued to offer just what the customer wanted.

The history recounted in the following chapters shows that the key to the puzzle of standard sizes lies neither in learning nor in manufacturers' voluntary response to a "general demand for standardization," but in the interplay of economics and politics in the diffusion process itself. As a wealth of commentary in trade journals and the like makes clear, formidable market forces blocked the diffusion of mass-production techniques among smaller manufacturers. It was only under the cover of nationally agreed-upon standard sizes that they broke free of market forces and transitioned to mass production. And, as we will see, it was initially the Great War and, in the 1920s, Secretary of Commerce Herbert Hoover and his Division of Simplified Practice that provided the impetus and the necessary cover, an achievement that would arouse interest worldwide.

Our starting point is the incredible diversity of everyday commodities in the U.S. on the eve of the Great War and the strategic dilemma that this posed for middling manufacturers contemplating mass production (chapter 2). This dilemma was resolved abruptly, if temporarily, by the United States' entry into the war (chapter 3). In a forceful campaign, wartime officials, led by Arch Wilkinson Shaw of the War Industries Board's Conservation Division, pushed manufacturers of diverse products to simplify their product lines so that they could shift to mass-production methods and thus conserve materials, labor, and transportation for war uses. The pivotal moment came when the war ended – a brief interlude that exposed the unnaturalness of the wartime push for mass production (chapter 4). With wartime controls lifted and manufacturers facing consumer resistance in a "buyer's strike," followed by the sharp depression of 1920–1, many wartime mass producers set aside what they had learned in the war and reverted to their old ways, re-diversifying their product lines as a tried-and-true competitive strategy to capture the reluctant consumer's dollar. It was this reversal that prompted Secretary of Commerce Herbert Hoover to revive the wartime program in a form tailored for peace (chapter 5). Under the protective umbrella of government-sanctioned collective agreements among competitors to limit product diversity, mass-production techniques diffused rapidly and broadly across the American economy from the 1920s through the 1950s (chapter 6). Had the federal government not enabled American business to push back against market forces, the story of standard sizes suggests, mass-production techniques would not naturally have diffused as far and as fast as they did in the United States. Absent, in the words of a British admirer, "Hoover's fostering hand,"[40] the twentieth-century American variety of capitalism would have looked markedly less "Fordist."[41]

2

"A Profusion of Styles" on the Eve of the Great War

Conveying a sense of the diversity of products[1] available to American consumers on the eve of World War I is difficult. Prewar data are anecdotal and thin, largely because the diversity of American products attracted widespread comment only after the Great War brought widespread attention to it. "Certainly the public was never aware," a post-war report observed, "of the extent to which duplication of common varieties of manufactured goods had been carried."[2] Reports on reductions in product diversity during World War I provide ample evidence of the range of products affected but describe the wartime limits only in general terms. Paper products, for example, underwent "[s]tandardization and simplification"; shapes and sizes of straw hats were "limited"; "[s]pecific limitations on size and style for all kinds of furniture" went into effect. And so on.[3] Or wartime reports listed the number of sizes and styles permitted during the war, but not the numbers prevailing before the war.[4] Also, the available data are sometimes less clear cut than one would like. Metal beds, for example, were reportedly made in 600 styles before the war,[5] but "style" in this tally included more than size, so the number of bed sizes (both metal and wood) cited earlier – 78 shortly after the war – is not comparable.

Laying out the available data, moreover, would likely overwhelm the reader with minutiae. And the broader question would remain: How does one assess their significance? Washing machines, for example, could be purchased in 446 styles and sizes before the war, while automobile tires were manufactured in 287 types and sizes. Files and rasps were offered in 1,351 varieties, trace chains (for harnessing draft horses) were available in 504 varieties, and tanners made 81 colors of shoe leather.[6] Do those numbers, on their face, convey the diversity of prewar commodities?

With the benefit of hindsight, however, observers who had their eyes opened in wartime testified to the pervasive product diversity of the prewar years, roundly condemning it with colorful descriptors. Government officials, for example, thought the paint and varnish industry, in allowing its product types, colors, and sizes to proliferate, had become "too subservient to the dictates of whim and caprice."[7] Bed and mattress manufacturers, according to Secretary of Commerce Herbert Hoover, were caught in "a snarl of heterogeneity" as bed frame sizes proliferated and mattress manufacturers scrambled to keep up with them.[8] "[T]he mattress men," he observed, "have been engaged, not in a business but an adventure in tailoring!"[9] Shoe styles, officials believed, were not only too numerous but "involved excessive and wasteful uses of material."[10] Shoe manufacturers were also accused of indulging in "extremes in color repertoire" and "color extravagance."[11] An "excessive multiplicity of styles" was said to characterize men's and boy's clothing.[12] Many plow bolt sizes on the market before World War I were deemed "superfluous."[13] Government officials even lamented the proliferation of "freak varieties of American flags."[14] Although presidential executive orders in 1912 and 1916 had established 12 standard flag sizes for government use, a large flag manufacturer was reported in 1922 to offer "289 varieties, not one agreeing with any of the twelve standards."[15]

Businesspeople, too, regarded the variety of products available before the war to have been excessive and burdensome. Manufacturers, the director of Harvard's Bureau of Business Research believed, "were glad to be rid of most of the styles, varieties, and sizes of products that were limited [during the war]. In every trade wasteful practices had crept in which it was mutually advantageous to stop."[16] The president of the Philadelphia Chamber of Commerce, Ernst T. Trigg, lauded the wartime "elimination of useless styles and sizes."[17] Tire manufacturers, *Printers' Ink* reported, were well aware that they suffered from "a profusion of sizes and styles."[18] Paint and varnish manufacturers, according to an industry expert, had long been "conscious of the fact that they were 'carrying too many lines.'"[19] When manufacturers of stoves, ranges, and furnaces were requested to reduce the styles they offered during the war, a *Printers' Ink* writer heard "a mighty sigh [of relief] in stovedom."[20] Manufacturers of electric railway tools, too, deemed "many sizes and styles" of the forges they made to be "entirely useless."[21] In the furniture business, a trade journal reported, "[i]t has long been recognized that the extremely wide variety of sizes in bedsteads, with the resultant excess variety of sizes in springs and mattresses, is unreasonable if not ridiculous."[22] Lamenting the "vast multitude of sizes of various gages, grades and finishes" in which steel sheets were made, an industry insider, writing under the pseudonym "Millman," issued a resounding call in the trade journal *Iron Age* to "[e]liminate the shoddy, the gaudy and the unnecessary items" that American manufacturers were producing.[23] And so on.

Initiatives by some trades to reduce diversity on their own, though with little success, also signaled business disgruntlement with product diversity. Perhaps the best-known case was the effort, beginning in the 1860s, to standardize screw threads

– a daunting challenge because so many different trades had
vital interests at stake. The Sellers or "United States Standard"
thread came to be "widely used in New England and by railroads," Bruce Sinclair's classic study concluded. But, even
though endorsed by the U.S. Navy, it did not become a nationwide standard.[24] Indeed, persistent diversity of screw threads
in American metalworking industries hampered munitions
manufacturing during World War I, prompting Congress to
establish the National (or U.S.) Screw Thread Commission in
1918.[25] The Society of Automotive Engineers (SAE) established
several hundred standards, many of which reduced the variety
of automotive parts before the war, but industry-wide standardization remained elusive. SAE standards were observed
mainly by smaller manufacturers, while large manufacturers
forged their own, internal standards.[26] Among Cincinnati
machine tool manufacturers, Scranton notes, "standardization
of screws, bolts, and terminology had stalled [on the eve of
the war], despite repeated association resolutions and scores
of prescriptive articles in the trade press."[27] Since the early
twentieth century, paint manufacturers, too, had sought collectively to reduce the number of can sizes they offered and to
standardize their dimensions, but they were unable to achieve
the unanimity required for effective "concerted action."[28]
Proposals to establish a limited number of "fashionable" ready-
mixed paint colors annually also went nowhere.[29] Wooden bed
manufacturers and metal bed manufacturers, "independent of
each other," a trade journal reported, "made some attempt at
standardization with fair success." But this left mattress manufacturers unable to reduce the variety of sizes they made, since
they had to "follow the sizes made by both metal bed and wood
bed manufacturers."[30] In the farm implement sector, notorious
for its product diversity, trade associations had sought since
the early twentieth century to standardize their products, but,
likewise, proved unable to do so before World War I.[31] Lumber
interests, too, repeatedly sought to standardize their products

collectively. The National Lumber Manufacturers Association was organized in 1902 in part to set lumber standards, a goal it pursued intermittently without success for some 20 years.[32] Paving brick manufacturers had long perceived the advantages of standardized products, but, despite having organized nationally in 1905, the industry made no progress in forging an industry-wide agreement before the war.[33]

Writing shortly after the end of World War I, a government economist, Homer Hoyt, offered a vivid portrait of the product diversity – the "profusion of styles and brands of goods" – that seemed endemic to the United States before the Great War:

> The variety of design in ordinary articles gave full opportunity for the satisfaction of the most fastidious tastes; the discriminating judge of chairs had 518 patterns of piano stools and a countless legion of ordinary chairs from which to make his choice; the connoisseur of plows and cultivators could undoubtedly find the style dictated by his own individualistic notions from the varied assortment displayed by the agricultural implement dealers; and anyone who was particular about the appearance of the interior of his house could spend his lifetime in examining samples of wall paper. From the cradle to the grave, from the many varieties of cribs and baby carriages to the profusion of styles in burial shrouds and coffins, the American consumer has been unrestricted in his choice.[34]

Despite his rather benign characterization of product diversity, Hoyt went on to condemn, in economic terms, the "extravagant pleasure display" inherent in rampant product diversity.[35]

Why such a diversity of products?

Why did product sizes and shapes proliferate with abandon in the U.S. in the early twentieth century? When one considers the array of forces that encouraged product diversity at that time, the outcome seems overdetermined – though fundamentally, the evidence suggests, it reflected the intense competition that plagued fragmented industries and could doom efforts to consolidate them.[36]

An obvious source of product diversity lay in the strategies of manufacturers themselves. Specialty manufacturers, by definition, produced a variety of products in smaller lots, and, as Scranton shows, they persisted well into the era of mass production, accounting in 1923 for "the same one-third of value added" as in 1909.[37] Older industries, in particular, were thought to be susceptible to "the fallacy in over diversification."[38] Mature mass producers also enhanced product diversity when they continued, as in textile manufacturing, to produce bulk goods but added specialty goods to their product mix.[39] Large companies that integrated forward into sales and marketing contributed another increment of diversity when they used their existing resources not only to handle new product lines (product diversification) but also to offer what Susan Strasser terms "'line extensions': new models, sizes, or flavors of an existing product, using the existing brand name."[40] In the absence of industry-wide coordination, moreover, an increase in the number of firms transitioning from specialty to mass production did not necessarily reduce the variety of products on the market. This was because, as noted earlier, firms that reduced their own product lines in order to mass produce usually made their core products distinctive in some way to avoid direct (price) competition. Innovation plus inertia, meanwhile, contributed its own increment of diversity: as manufacturers introduced new product sizes and styles, they were slow to eliminate older sizes and styles, resulting in an expansion within product lines.[41]

Also integral to product diversity was the business practice of "hand-to-mouth" or "current" buying – that is, placing small, frequent orders for quick delivery, rather than placing

large orders seasonally for future delivery ("forward ordering"). According to a detailed study published by the Brookings
Institution in 1929, the term "hand-to-mouth buying" first
appeared in reports on the dry goods trade in 1868. The practice was the norm in dry goods to 1897, after which forward
ordering became "more common."[42] But in the 1910s, and then
with a vengeance in the immediate post-World War I years,
hand-to-mouth buying resurged, becoming entrenched in the
1920s.[43] Traditionally, the practice had been viewed as a sign of
business caution in hard times – hence its prevalence during
the long price decline in the last quarter of the nineteenth
century. But by 1914 the *Magazine of Wall Street* discerned
a more fundamental transformation under way: "The swift
changes of fashions, the demand of the consumer for fresh
goods, the increased facilities of transportation, any and all of
these are ascribed as the factors more efficient than hard times
in bringing about this change in the methods of the buying
world."[44] While forward ordering provided a pillar of support
for the mass production and distribution of a narrow, stable
line of products, retailers' and wholesalers' frequent purchases
in small lots created incentives for manufacturers to expand
the variety of products they offered, which in turn made hand-
to-mouth buying all the more attractive.[45]

A third factor encouraging product diversity was the fragmented American political structure. Despite the much-lauded
growth of a national market by the turn of the twentieth century, the division of economic policymaking powers among the
federal government, the states, and municipalities persistently
fragmented markets and business practice well into the twentieth century.[46] Consider the matter of commodity container
sizes. As the flow of business transactions across state borders
grew in the early twentieth century, the U.S. Congress came
under pressure to legislate nationwide standard sizes for commodity containers.[47] Although the basic units of measurement
(pound, yard, gallon, bushel) were virtually uniform throughout

the states by this time, commercial practice regarding the gallon and bushel diverged. Some states defined gallons of specific commodities in terms of weight, rather than volume, and some states defined special – and different – bushels for specific products. The "charcoal bushel," for example, equaled 2,748 cubic inches in Connecticut, 2,500 cubic inches in Colorado, and 2,571 cubic inches in Pennsylvania. For some commodities, meanwhile, Congress had established its own – different – definitions for customs purposes. "This diversity causes confusion in the commerce between the different States," the Bureau of Standards dryly noted in 1912, as it published a 564-page compendium of state and national laws governing weights and measures.[48] By 1926, its compendium had grown to more than 900 pages.[49] Food marketing was particularly complex because municipalities, too, established their own commercial standards.[50] Building codes also differed at all levels of government. In the words of *Electrical World*'s commercial editor, the "great diversity of state and governmental requirements result[ed] in a baffling absence of uniformity" in hardware and contributed "a further impulse to the increase of varieties and stocks."[51]

For some observers, a fourth factor, American "individualism," promoted product diversity. Economist Homer Hoyt, in describing "a profusion of styles and brands of goods" before the war, portrayed it as an aspect of "prewar individualism."[52] The president of the American Society for Testing Materials agreed: "Consumers are willing to pay for selection and for the gratification of their individualistic tastes as to style, color, form, etc. It is this fact which, in a very great measure, has resulted in the enormous number of commodities, differing in only slight degree from each other, now being offered on the market."[53] The steel industry insider "Millman" quoted earlier also saw manufacturers' proliferating products as a response to "the variety of tastes and extravagances of the public."[54] An automobile dealer, Regina Lee Blaszczyk reports in *The Color*

Revolution, discerned distinctive socio-demographic preferences for automobile colors in the 1920s.[55] One commentator,
noting that men's overalls were produced in 64 lengths, discerned regional preferences: "as a general rule, the Middle West
clamors for regular lengths, the South for long lengths and the
East and far Southwest for short lengths."[56] Individual or local
preferences also generated a profusion of farm wagon gears.
"For a hundred years wagon manufacturers had been adding
to their assortments, inventing and devising new styles, kinds,
and varieties," a report on World War I mobilization noted.
"One kind is popular in one locality; in another the farmer will
have none of it, but demands something entirely different. It's
a big country, and it has a thousand local conditions, prejudices, likes, and dislikes; and the manufacturer, during times of
peace, finds it profitable to cater to local taste and opinion."[57] A
prominent wartime official voiced a similar opinion, attribut-
ing the excessive variety of agricultural implements to "[t]he
habits and prejudices of localities and individual farmers" and
to manufacturers who catered to their every demand.[58] Other
commentators, meanwhile, attributed product diversity in part
to the "idiosyncrasies" not of consumers, but of manufacturers.[59]

The root cause of product diversity, however, was seen in a
fifth factor – competition for the consumer's dollar.[60] Drawing
an analogy with the Tower of Babel, the U.S. Chamber of
Commerce's Domestic Distribution Department condemned,
as a "wart upon business," the "useless competition" that led
"variety [to be] piled upon variety."[61] An *Electrical World*
editor put it this way:

> Steadily comes the growing conviction that at the bottom of it
> all is an uneconomic excess of competition – too many manu-
> facturers producing duplicating lines in too great variety and
> too small volume, too many jobbers stocking and selling too
> many lines of too many articles and both buying and selling
> them in too many small shipments, too many contractors and

retailers doing each so small a part of the available business that too few can prosper.[62]

Likewise, a *Printers' Ink* writer attributed the prewar proliferation of automobile tire sizes and styles to "competitive rivalry [that] had built up to huge proportions."[63] Even economist Homer Hoyt, seeing American "individualism" reflected in "the medley of patterns" available to consumers, discounted consumer preference as its root cause and pointed his finger at "cutthroat" competition: "While the psychic satisfaction derived by the consumer in the enjoyment of something different from the ordinary staple has contributed to create and support the multiplication of brands," he maintained, "the chief driving power has been excessive competition among manufacturers."[64] A survey of paint manufacturers during the war found that "most manufacturers had been led into the practice of making an excessive variety of grades and colors on account of competition."[65] A wartime official, reflecting back on the prewar period, cited most of the factors noted above but, as "[t]he chief reason for the multiplicity of styles, varieties and sizes," singled out competition.[66]

In the hot competition for customers before the war, offering an enticing diversity of products had become entrenched as the dominant business strategy among middling manufacturers. "When the United States entered the European conflict," a business professor explained, "the policy among American manufacturers was to produce a multiplicity of styles, sizes, shapes and finishes. In most circles, it was the commonly accepted belief that competition compelled every producer to turn out commodities different from every other producer."[67] A U.S. Chamber of Commerce official saw the prewar mentality of manufacturers in similar terms:

In the years just preceding the war there was a very noticeable tendency to multiply in commodity manufacture the variety of kinds and sizes in response to a demand, fancied or real, from distributors and consumers. "The Customer is Always Right" almost became a slogan in industry in carrying such service to the extreme. Factories were fast becoming custom shops in some lines through a competition which was permitting the buyer not only to depart from recognized standards but to specify such variations as his fancy might dictate.[68]

When "it was supposed that 'The customer was always right,'" a business writer noted in the *Paint, Oil and Drug Review*, "[n]aturally, the customer became somewhat tyrannical."[69]

Even the Ford Motor Company initially adhered to the prevailing strategy of product diversity. It began as a small-scale assembler catering to customer demand. "We had the usual idea of the times that the way to get business was to offer a variety to choose from," Ford's former business manager, James Couzens, recalled. "It was thought that selling started with the customer and worked back to the factory – that the factory existed to supply what the customer asked for." Then, in 1909, having achieved a degree of brand recognition and a strong market position, the company took the truly radical step of cutting its product line to a single model, which, from 1912, it offered only in black. In effect, Ford broke the tyranny of the consumer. "What the Ford company really did – although not in so many words – was to reverse the process," Couzens explained. "We worked out a car and at a price which would meet the largest average need. In effect, we standardized the customer."[70]

But, for companies that lacked Ford's stature in their markets, consumer sovereignty prevailed, and product variety remained their principal competitive tool. "[A]s any manufacturer will corroborate," a writer in *Industrial Management* observed in 1925,

this production of numerous varieties of a single commodity, is almost a necessity so long as competition is the "life of the

trade." Each manufacturer is after business, and the more styles
he shows the more business he gets. One is always fearful lest
the next one will display the "latest" style, and this is a direct
cause for a large variety of styles.[71]

Electrical World's commercial editor agreed: "That such
excesses exist in many lines is recognized freely, but fear of
competition interposes many obstacles to action. Many believe
that if they 'cut out' this type or that, some other firm will spe-
cialize upon it and profit at their expense."[72] A paint industry
expert concurred: "the paint manufacturers . . . knew that they
were producing tints and shades in unprofitable profusion. But
so long as the trade demanded and competitors continued to
supply, the competition must be met."[73] Stove manufacturers,
too, "wanted to cut down their lines" before the war, *Printers'
Ink* reported, "but it was hard for any one of them to take
the radical step alone."[74] Competitive pressures in fragmented
industries, in short, drove what one post-war expert termed
"the 'diversificationists' [*sic*] dominance" before the war.[75]

The principal vector of competitive pressures, observers
maintained, was actually not consumers but salesmen and
jobbers.[76] The editor of *Factory* magazine, for example, was
convinced that sales staff pushed product variety that consumers did not actually want. "The selling end of the business is far
more to blame for high manufacturing costs due to overspe-
cialization than is the consumer," he maintained. "It is not the
consumer who puts variety into a line. It's true the consumer
asks to be offered goods with certain modifications from a
standard, but his wishes have a long way to go to get back
to the factory." Instead, he blamed the "many intermediaries between the ultimate consumer and the factories which
make what the ultimate consumer buys. Each of these intermediaries is prone to believe the product must be made in this
or that added style or variety, or with this or that additional
adornment."[77] The director of Harvard's Bureau of Business

Research, citing competition as "[t]he chief reason for the multiplicity of styles, varieties and sizes," agreed: "The excessive variety originated far more commonly in the sales department than in the production department."[78] This was also what the pioneer sanitaryware manufacturer Thomas Maddock's Sons concluded in getting to the root of production troubles in 1912: its sales department was "asking almost impossible things of the factory: [it] wanted highly special articles and not very many of each; they must be of high quality, reasonable in cost, and [it] demanded quick delivery."[79] A paint manufacturer, too, believed that sales pressure, or what he termed "dealer psychology," spurred the proliferation of products:

> The most common reason a manufacturer gives for handling a great variety of styles, sizes, patterns, and the like, in a particular line of goods that might very well be simplified, is that "the dealer wants them." . . . "Great stuff, this simplification," declares the manufacturer. "I'd like to put it into effect. But our customers [dealers] wouldn't stand for it. They like variety." And every whim of the customer is satisfied.[80]

When the Scott Paper Company decided to cut its products from 2,000 to 3 brands in 1910, it reportedly had to go around its own jobbers: "They were the dictators," and they demanded a diversity of products to offer retailers.[81] A World War I official likewise singled out salesmen as the vector of competitive pressures. Excessive manufacturing costs, he maintained, "are often due to competitive demands, real or assumed. Many salesmen, in order to please the whims of particular customers, will insist upon the manufacture of new styles or new shapes of articles."[82] Such examples could be multiplied many times over.

On the eve of the Great War, in short, competitive pressures pushed American manufacturers to multiply their product offerings as they catered attentively to their consumers' diverse wants, whether real or imagined. "A profusion of styles and brands" was the result. A few manufacturers, such as Henry Ford, were in a market position to "standardize the consumer," but competition prevented the vast majority from doing so. Such manufacturers, as one observer explained, "were practically helpless. If the trade could not get what it wanted from one manufacturer, there was someone else who could fill the order."[83]

Yet, even as products proliferated, enthusiasm for standardization, efficiency, and the elimination of "waste" in American life grew by leaps and bounds. This was driven partly by media attention to Henry Ford's one-model policy and prodigious output, which took mass production to new heights of productivity.[84] It also reflected the extension of Frederick Winslow Taylor's efficiency methods into virtually every corner of American life in the early twentieth century.[85] And it built on several decades of energetic efforts by professional associations and the Bureau of Standards to standardize measurements and terminology, first in scientific fields and then in industrial engineering.[86] In 1910, the efficiency craze even prompted the Carnegie Foundation to enlist an industrial efficiency expert to study the efficiency of American colleges and universities, prompting a sardonic response in New York newspapers.[87] The high point of enthusiasm for efficiency, Jennifer Karns Alexander argues in *The Mantra of Efficiency*, came in the years immediately before the outbreak of the Great War in Europe, stimulated by widespread public attention to attorney Louis Brandeis's claim before the Interstate Commerce Commission in 1910 that American railroads, if run more efficiently, could save a million dollars a day.[88] "By 1915," she writes, "the word *efficiency* was plastered everywhere – in headlines, advertisements, editorials, business manuals, and church bulletins."[89]

As the Great War raged in Europe, American manufacturers thus found themselves in a perplexing situation, caught in the crossfire between their tried-and-true strategy of product diversity and Ford-inspired enthusiasm for efficiency. *Printers' Ink* captured their dilemma in a 1916 article highlighting the contrasting product strategies of two large firms: the Ford Motor Company, which by then offered a single model of its automobile in five versions; and the Burroughs Adding Machine Company, which offered "nearly a hundred kinds of adding-machines and some six hundred combinations of styles." Although the writer came down on the side of those trying to reduce "these almost limitless variations" and produce in larger volume, they acknowledged the dilemma facing their readers: "When two well-known sales organizations build big successes, one on a standardized product and the other on 'built-to-measure' goods, it is hard for the average sales or advertising executive to know which way the wind does blow."[90]

But, for middling manufacturers in competitive, fragmented industries, product diversity seemed to be the only viable alternative to the ruinous ("cut-throat") price competition and economic concentration that had marked the turn of the twentieth century. Ford's advice to "the little man" in manufacturing and retailing – "get big" – was simply untenable.[91] Reaching a consensus on collective action to limit product variety proved a daunting challenge for those industries that tried, and in any event the United States' strong antitrust tradition looked on collective action with suspicion. Product diversity at least allowed them to shift competition, as economist Homer Hoyt explained, "from the plane of price to that of quality by splitting up the standardized product into many brands that are distinguished from each other by slight differences in size, shape, color or design."[92]

If competition for the consumer's dollar may serve as a proxy for "market forces," then the proliferation of products in pre-World War I America seemed to be a natural consequence of market forces. "[M]any sizes and styles of material and devices have come into use," the director of the U.S. Bureau of

Standards concluded in 1921, "not through any real demand for such a variety of equipment but through the undirected natural expansion of the business."[93] A National Industrial Conference Board report also saw a natural process at work: "The unregulated unfolding of the competitive economic process tends to evolve a wasteful multiplicity of goods which serve essentially the same purpose."[94] Historian David F. Noble, commenting on product diversity at the turn of the twentieth century, likewise attributed it to "the rapid and uncontrolled growth of modern industry."[95]

The effect of market forces, in short, was to push middling manufacturers deeper into product diversity, not toward mass production. If the results of market forces are understood as "natural," then the diffusion of mass-production techniques was decidedly unnatural and required a concerted, collective pushback against market forces. That pushback came when the U.S. began to mobilize for the Great War. As "standardization fever" took hold,[96] government policies abruptly tipped the balance from consumer sovereignty to industrial efficiency – at least temporarily.

3

Suppressing Product Diversity in the Great War

E fficiency became paramount when the U.S. Congress declared war on Germany in April 1917, following the sinking of the USS *Housatonic*, revelation of the infamous Zimmermann note, and ongoing submarine attacks. Although war had broken out in Europe nearly three years earlier, deep divisions over U.S. neutrality had hobbled military preparedness. American participation would prove to be brief, but no one knew beforehand when the war would end. For 19 months from the U.S. declaration of war to armistice in November 1918, wartime officials scrambled to retool and ramp up the American economy in support of its expanding military forces.[1]

Although key individuals in early efforts to mobilize the American economy for war were strong proponents of standardization and scientific management,[2] what ultimately became a concerted push to simplify American commodities grew out of a decidedly pragmatic approach to conserving resources for the war effort. Having rejected a contentious proposal to declare certain lines of business "non-essential" and prohibit them altogether,[3] the Council of National Defense (CND) and, later, the War Industries Board (WIB) under the

chairmanship of New York financier Bernard Baruch[4] sought
to enhance the technical efficiency of all businesses by working
with them to streamline their operations and free up economic
resources for the war effort. As the man who headed their
"conservation" efforts later explained, "we adopted a policy
of eliminating the *non-essential uses* of labor and capital and
material and equipment from all types of industry."[5] What
wartime officials – usually at the suggestion of the affected
businesses – categorized as "non-essential uses" were deemed
"waste," and this waste-focused approach meant that wartime
policies affected American businesses across the board. A
post-mortem on the mobilization of the economy likened the
effort to transforming trees into lumber: "War, the apotheosis
of all things practical and utilitarian, approached our business
tree with an intensely practical eye. It was soon evident that we
should have to do a terrific amount of lopping off before the
lumber could be made most useful for war purposes."[6] Others
portrayed it as cutting the fat out of American business.[7]

The Council of National Defense's conservation unit, the
Commercial Economy Board (CEB), was created in March 1917
at the suggestion of Chicago manufacturer and publisher Arch
Wilkinson Shaw (figure 1), who was promptly appointed its
chair.[8] With his flagship publications *System: The Magazine of
Business* and *Factory: The Magazine of Management*, Shaw was,
in Walter Friedman's estimation, "perhaps the most influential
publisher of magazines and books on sales management."[9]
Shaw, working with the dean of Harvard's new Graduate
School of Business Administration, economic historian Edwin
F. Gay, while he was a lecturer there in the early 1910s, played a
key role in inaugurating scholarly studies of the distribution of
manufactured goods. Harvard's Bureau of Business Research
was created at his suggestion and with his funding. Focused
on distribution, it collected data on business practices to be
used in the classroom, giving rise to the "case study" approach
for which the Harvard Business School is still well known.[10]

Figure 1.   Arch Wilkinson Shaw, 1917. Photographers: Harris & Ewing – Library of Congress, www.loc.gov/item/2016867915.

Shaw himself published an article in the *Quarterly Journal of Economics* in 1912 that is regarded as a pioneering study in the field of marketing.[11] The impressive efficiencies achieved in industrial production, Shaw argued, had "outstripped the existing system of distribution." He urged American businesses to address the "chaotic condition" of distribution, which, he maintained, "act[ed] as a check upon further development of production" and generated "a tremendous social waste."[12] The Bureau of Business Research first studied shoe retailing and, by the time war broke out in Europe in 1914, had launched a second project on grocery retailing.[13]

During the early years of the war in Europe, Shaw had become convinced that American business would face formidable European competition after the war if it did not enhance its efficiency and learn, as Europeans were learning, "the priceless lesson of nationally associated business effort." He characterized France and England as rapid learners, noting that "Germany, of course," with its history of strong cartels, "had only a little way to go in this respect. But now it has come about that democratic France and England are by way of outdoing Germany at her own game."[14] Indeed, what he witnessed in Europe had prompted him to approach the CND about creating a commercial economy board.[15] To enhance U.S. competitiveness, the federal government, he believed, should aid American industry by gathering, analyzing, and circulating systematic information on business practice and "working out still better methods than are found in the best of actual business."[16] As chair of the CND's new Commercial Economy Board, Shaw was well placed to put these ideas into effect, and early reports suggested that the board intended to do just that.[17] In filling out the board, Shaw recruited his colleague at Harvard, economic historian Edwin Gay, who fully supported Shaw's scholarly interests in distribution.[18]

In line with their professional concerns, the Commercial Economy Board initially focused on the distribution of goods; only tangentially were economies in production mentioned among its goals.[19] The first problem the board tackled was the conservation of wheat for military use and exports.[20] This initiative ferreted out wasted resources in the distribution of that everyday staple, bread. Alerted by large wholesale bakers themselves, the board's investigations centered on the bakers' long-standing practice of allowing retailers to return unsold bread without charge. In what would become its usual procedure, the board first collected data, a step that was rapidly becoming standard practice in business and policy circles in this era.[21] In this case, the data concerned bread returns, gathered from more than 200 bakers nationwide. Its survey revealed that returned bread amounted to nearly 5 percent of daily bread production and was disposed of either to the poor at reduced prices or to farmers for use as livestock feed.[22] The culprit behind this practice was reported to be competition. "It was not by [the bakers' and retailers'] wish that this waste existed," a wire story noted, "but was the result of competition and accommodation to the public demand."[23] Based on the survey results, the board, in consultation with bakers, issued a circular asking bakers across the nation to stop the practice of bread returns altogether by July 1917.[24] Large wholesale bakers welcomed the board's assistance in ridding the industry of the costly practice, though smaller bakers and retailers were less enthusiastic.[25]

Compliance with the board's conservation projects – at least at this early stage – was entirely voluntary, bolstered by mobilization of the state-level councils of defense, exhortations in trade journals, and broader publicity.[26] The board disseminated notices relating to the study of bread returns and its recommendation to stop them in the *Official U.S. Bulletin*.[27] It enlisted journalist Ida M. Tarbell, who served on the CND's Committee on Women's Defense Work, to publicize the new no-returns policy to women via newspaper articles.[28] Master bakers, meanwhile, advertised the new restrictions directly to their customers, reprinting the board's request and urging housewives to cooperate by ordering bread a day ahead.[29] Overall, the initiative to eliminate bread returns was estimated to have saved about 1.2 million pounds of wheat flour annually.[30]

The board also found ample room for economizing in the broad spectrum of services that retailers, driven by competitive pressures, offered to shoppers by this time.[31] "Customers had demanded 'service,'" a wartime report explained, "and merchants had competed with one another in rendering it until it had grown to enormous proportions."[32] Retail stores routinely offered their customers three or four deliveries a day as well as "special" deliveries. Retailers were also accustomed to letting shoppers return purchases virtually at will, a practice

that CEB member Henry S. Dennison portrayed as "a luxuri-
ous outgrowth" of competitive pressures.[33] By one estimate,
20 percent of department-store merchandise was returned to
retailers. Following a conference organized by the National
Retail Dry Goods Association and the collection of data from
some 1,500 retailers around the country, the CEB issued its
formal recommendation: it asked retailers to stop all special
deliveries, to restrict their routine deliveries to one per day, to
establish cooperative delivery systems in smaller towns, and to
limit returns to three days.[34] In the words of a retail merchants'
association, the new policies amounted to a "revolution in the
delivery system."[35] The savings in labor – critical to the war
effort as the draft got under way – totaled an estimated 25
percent for department stores and 50 percent for retail grocery
stores, not to mention additional savings on delivery vehicles
and fuel.[36]

Here, too, extensive publicity – by the state councils
of defense and in movie theatres, stores, newspapers, and
magazines – was used to sell the wartime restrictions to consumers.[37] Washington, DC, department stores, for example,
addressed a newspaper advertisement "To the Shopping
Public," announcing the new restrictions on deliveries and
returns.[38] Ida Tarbell of the CND's Women's Committee
authored a letter on "Reduction of Deliveries" that was distributed to the state councils for their use in mobilizing support for
the campaign.[39] The WIB's chairman Bernard Baruch appealed
directly to women in the pages of the *Ladies' Home Journal* for
support of this and other conservation measures.[40] "The people
of this democratic country are used to getting what they want,"
Printers' Ink noted in late 1917. "It is not easy to get them to
accept a curtailment of their privileges or of their demands."
But the Commercial Economy Board's experience with cuts
in delivery service showed that, "when the reasons for the
curtailment are fully explained to them [via advertising], they
are only too glad to do their share."[41] Indeed, with the new

"carry your own" policy, shoppers carrying their own packages came to signify patriotism.[42] By mid-1918, the Council of National Defense claimed, its "campaigns" to eliminate returns of unsold bread and to curtail retail deliveries "ha[d] wholly eliminated both types of wastage in nearly every State."[43]

The drive to streamline American manufacturing

When a crisis-driven reorganization strengthened the WIB's powers in March 1918 and the CEB became the WIB's Conservation Division, also headed by Arch Wilkinson Shaw, conservation efforts shifted from the distribution of commodities to their production.[44] This was when a comprehensive drive to simplify American commodities got under way. The economies achieved by the Commercial Economy Board in distribution, a CND official later observed, were "but a scratch on the surface compared with the deep cuts into the mountain of waste of energy and material effected by the reorganization of industrial processes and practices." When the board turned its attention to production, he continued, "[i]t was found that almost all industries were encumbered with an unbelievable amount of unexamined tradition, that resulted in duplication of effort, waste of material, and unnecessary expenditures of energy. . . . Everywhere was found the superfluity of luxury and taste and the impedimenta of custom."[45]

For marketing expert Arch Shaw, who continued to lead the nation's conservation efforts as head of the WIB's Conservation Division, a closer look at American manufacturing practices must have been eye-opening, as it was for so many others. In his prewar writings, Shaw had contrasted the "chaos" of the nation's distribution system with the vaunted efficiencies achieved in industrial production. Product diversity he portrayed not as a hindrance to efficient production and distribution but, from a marketing standpoint, as a valued means of

satisfying consumer demand. "The more highly differentiated
the scale of commodities is, the more accurately will it be possible for the individual consumer to satisfy his material wants.
For true value is not objective, but subjective," he wrote. "The
practical basis of exchange is the extent to which the article
will satisfy the desire of the purchaser. The price you can secure
depends on the intensity of this desire, not on the material
value of the finished product, such as its calories of food value
or its wearing qualities." Thus, his textbook encouraged future
business leaders "to intensify the demand for your goods, to
add to the material value a psychic value in the gratification
the customer experiences in its color, flavor, design, or style."[46]
And American manufacturers, especially those of the middling sort in hotly competitive industries, had indeed excelled
in adding "psychic value" as product variety proliferated in
the prewar years. But, viewed against the backdrop of urgent
wartime needs, resources devoted to enhancing the psychic
value of commodities suddenly became wasted resources. "It
is probable that not even Mr. Shaw, before he got well into his
work," a post-war report noted, "had any idea of the lengths to
which conservation could go in the elimination of sizes, kinds,
and styles in almost everything manufactured."[47]

Under Shaw's leadership and with increasing urgency, conservation officials pursued a wide-ranging set of initiatives to
"discipline" American industry, as WIB chairman Baruch put
it,[48] and push manufacturers toward mass production. They
did not necessarily expect manufacturers to emulate Henry
Ford's model of ultra-efficient mass production, associated
above all with the assembly line.[49] As an engineer noted
after the war, there are "many grades of mass production."[50]
Conservation officials took a pragmatic stance, simply seeking
maximum output using less skilled labor and a minimum of
materials – all as soon as possible, please. The critical first
step was getting manufacturers to limit the variety of products
they made so that, with minimal changes to their equipment,

they could produce that limited set of products in much larger volume. "[W]e did not go to Washington with a definite program of standardization," Shaw explained after the war, "but . . . simplification seemed to be the only way in which, and by which, we could release from the resources of the nation those resources necessary for the conduct of the war."[51] By eliminating "every non-essential motion, and all unnecessary use of material, equipment or working capital," Shaw later explained, and limiting production to a small set of standard products, manufacturing operations could be streamlined, production runs could be lengthened, increasing output and reducing the relative amount of labor needed; manufacturers as well as their suppliers and dealers or retailers needed to carry less inventory; and transportation costs could be minimized. The aim, in Shaw's words, was "for the bulk of the industry of the country, even its smaller concerns, to take full advantage of the economies of mass-production technique, and to achieve the efficiency of the repetitive process, resulting in continuity and speed of operation."[52]

In aggregate, the wartime conservation measures "scarcely permit of a tangible analysis because of their number and their variety," a post-war report concluded. Its author then proceeded to offer a comprehensive overview of the tactics employed, aimed squarely at the production and distribution of commodities. The watchwords were reducing, eliminating, standardizing, economizing:

Conservation . . . was generally effected by securing a maximum reduction in the number of styles, varieties, sizes, colors, or finishes of the product; eliminating the number of styles and varieties that took more than the amount of material strictly necessary . . . ; eliminating features or accessories which used materials for adornment or convenience but which were not essential to the utility of the product; eliminating patterns and types of products which were less essential to the civilian needs;

substituting materials which were plentiful in the place of those which were not plentiful and were needed for the war program . . . ; discontinuing the use of certain materials for unnecessary purposes . . . ; standardizing sizes, lengths, widths, weights, thicknesses, and gauges of materials, parts and sections; reducing the excessive waste of materials in manufacturing processes . . . ; securing economy in samples used for selling products; securing economy in containers by eliminating boxes or cartons which required excessive shipping space. . . ; securing economy in packing by increasing the number of units per package.[53]

As an alternative measure of the scope of World War I conservation measures, he offered this *partial* list of the industries affected:

the agricultural implement, automobile tire, barrel goods, bedding, bicycle, book cloth, bottle, boys' clothing, camera, chain, chandelier, chinaware, clock, composition roofing, corset, delivery service, electric appliance, fabric glove, felt shoe, furnace, furniture, gas range, hand stamp and marking device, hardware, harness and saddlery, hosiery and underwear, household wringer, leather glove, mackinaw, men's clothing, metal bedstead, motorcycle, moving-picture machine, office appliance, oil refining, oil storage tank and pump, oil stove and heater, optical goods, overall, paint, pencil, plumbing supply, radiator, railroad machinery, range, refrigerator, rubber clothing, rubber footwear, rubber goods, safe and vault, shoe, steel pen, steel pipe, stove, straw hat, sweater, talking machine, thread, tin, tin plate, traveling bag, trunk, typewriter ribbon, vacuum cleaner, vehicle, waist, washing machine, weatherstrip, wholesale dry goods, wooden container, wool felt hat, and women's clothing industries.[54]

The conservation program was truly breathtaking in its sweep. "All down the line of American industry," a journalist reported, "one could find some reorganization effected or about to be effected through 'agreement' with the Conservation Division of the War Industries Board."[55] As a post-war analysis put it, conservation measures "invaded all of America's manufacturing life."[56]

In working out agreements across the United States' manufacturing landscape, Shaw's Conservation Division built on the template forged by his Commercial Economy Board in limiting bread returns and retail deliveries.[57] The division first gathered information on needs and requirements from government and industry sources, either on its own initiative or at the request of the industry itself. Leading plow manufacturers, for example, enlisted the division's help in their campaign to eliminate left-handed plows, while buggy makers approached the division with their own standardization plan in hopes of retaining access to economic resources.[58] The division then held a series of conferences with industry representatives to explain the government's needs. "This is what you can do," Arch Shaw would tell the industry representatives. "You can go carefully over your practice and tell me what you can eliminate without absolutely crippling your industry and working actual hardship to the public. Disregard what people want merely because they want it. Tell me what they have to have and what they can get along without."[59] Industry representatives then formulated specific recommendations for economies, which division officials refined, circulated widely, discussed with critics, and finally issued as detailed conservation "schedules." These "schedules of self-denial," as historian Frederic L. Paxson termed them, were published in the *Official U.S. Bulletin* and in trade journals.[60] Since the Conservation Division initially had no enforcement powers, its objective in this cooperative or collaborative procedure was to enhance compliance by achieving a maximum of consensus. The goal, as Baruch later explained, was "to get as complete unanimity as possible."[61]

In negotiations between the trades and conservation officials, trade associations served as the lynchpin, as they did for
most aspects of World War I mobilization.[62] Since the 1880s,
national or regional trade associations had become, in Alfred
Chandler's words, "the normal way of doing business in most
American industries."[63] A "fairly complete" tally by the U.S.
Department of Commerce and Labor in 1913 counted some
230 commercial organizations of international, national, or
interstate scope in the U.S.[64] These included a peak association or national association of associations – the Chamber of
Commerce of the United States – formed the preceding year
in response to a call by President William Howard Taft and his
Secretary of Commerce and Labor for an organization to serve
as a communications channel between the national government and American business as a whole.[65] As the U.S. geared
up for war, existing trade associations appointed "war service
committees" to represent their trade in negotiations with government officials.[66] From the Fall of 1917, the U.S. Chamber of
Commerce, which, in Paul A. C. Koistinen's estimation, had
stood "in the vanguard" of the economic preparedness movement,[67] oversaw the process and certified the committees. If
a trade was unorganized, then the Chamber worked with it
to organize a national association and appoint a war service
committee.[68] By the war's end, the U.S. Chamber of Commerce
had "formally certified" hundreds of war service committees
"as ready and able to speak for their respective industries."[69]
The war service committees worked closely with the WIB's
57 commodity sections, which were devoted to products as
diverse as steel and woolen goods. The commodity sections,
which Baruch regarded as "the backbone of the [WIB's] whole
structure," supported the Conservation Division by collecting
industry data, organizing consultations with industry, and
administering the conservation schedules.[70]

But collaborative procedures and widespread business
enthusiasm for government aid in reducing product diversity

did not ensure full compliance with conservation schedules. Since conservation officials lacked explicit enforcement powers, they turned to a variety of indirect measures to enhance compliance. The abrupt decline in foreign competition during the war undoubtedly eased this task. "To American manufacturing industries," economist F. W. Taussig observed, the Great War "served as protection more effective than any tariff legislation could possibly be."[71] Quelling domestic competition, therefore, was the core challenge for conservation and other WIB officials. A credible enforcement policy – one that ensured that all firms followed the rules – was essential to the division's success, as Arch Shaw recognized early on: "under competitive conditions it will naturally be impossible for one merchant to economize extensively without giving his competitors an unfair advantage."[72] Setting a specific date on which a conservation schedule took effect industry-wide helped to reduce the risk. But those who cooperated with the wartime restrictions needed firmer assurance that their competitors would not gain a market advantage by skirting the restrictions.[73]

By the war's end, conservation officials had forged a credible enforcement policy marked by increasingly severe sanctions. Two were social in nature. In the first instance, they appealed to manufacturers' patriotism – asking for their "patriotic cooperation" in drawing up and abiding by conservation schedules.[74] "Although the board, of course, had no power to compel observance of its recommendations by process of law," the Council of National Defense explained, "it has been able to secure the desired results through voluntary cooperation of business men," thus enhancing a "spirit of national unity."[75] A second level of sanctions – also social in nature – took the form of public pledges. Individual firms were required to pledge in writing not only that they themselves would abide by the recommendations but that they would do business only with firms that also complied. "Most American business men will observe a pledge when once given and they need not be vigilated," Baruch maintained. Requiring pledges "gave confidence to each business man that all his fellows in trade would observe like practices with himself."[76]

When the WIB's powers were strengthened in early 1918,[77] its Conservation Division finally gained the leverage it needed to enforce cooperation if it could not be elicited by social means. The lever was the board's priorities power – as Baruch later put it, "the iron fist in the velvet glove."[78] This was the WIB's power to establish priorities for access to economic resources, which entailed assigning individual purchase orders a priority ranking that suppliers were obliged to observe in filling orders.[79] "As the priority power began to show its effectiveness," Baruch explained, "there appeared a method of enforcing rules of conservation."[80] The board's priorities commissioner not only controlled the allocation of critical raw materials but, working with other WIB agencies, "could also withhold, for the purpose of bringing recalcitrants into line," access to fuel and transportation.[81] Companies that declined to cooperate with conservation measures, in other words, faced the very real threat that they would be denied the resources they needed to continue in business during the war.

All told, from mid-1917 to the end of the war in November 1918, the Conservation Division and its predecessor, the Commercial Economy Board, working through trade associations, drew up conservation "schedules" for some 250 lines of business.[82] Indeed, the division became one of the most visible agencies of the WIB. "Ask the average merchant or manufacturer what the War Industries Board did," former CND official Grosvenor Clarkson wrote after the war, "and nine times out of ten he will refer to functions of the Conservation Division."[83]

The Conservation Division's efforts to simplify American commodities were amplified, finally, by other wartime agencies. When the U.S. Food Administration under Herbert Hoover took over the wheat conservation program, it designated a "standard loaf" of bread, reducing loaf sizes from some

38 to 4 standard sizes and abolishing small loaves because they cost more to bake.[84] The General Medical Board's Committee on Standardization worked with manufacturers to speed up production and lower the cost of medical and surgical supplies by minimizing the number of sizes and styles they produced.[85] The WIB's Price-Fixing Committee quickly realized that it was exceedingly difficult, if not impossible, to fix product prices when products were not standardized. The agricultural implements industry had learned this before the U.S. entered the war: "Variation in types of machines and their equipment as made by different manufacturers has always been a marked characteristic of the farm-machinery industry," noted a Bureau of Corporations report in 1915. "This lack of a common type has rendered impossible any satisfactory statistical treatment or comparison of prices."[86] (Indeed, offering a diversity of products was intended to hinder direct price comparison.) If products were not uniform, a post-war report explained, citing the example of common bricks, price was not a good indicator of value: "A common result of price fixing is standardization. It is essential in fixing a uniform price that the grade and quality upon which the price is fixed does not vary, for otherwise the value received will vary in spite of the fixed price."[87] Thus WIB officials responsible for fixing prices also worked to reduce product diversity, easing the way for uniform cost accounting.[88] In another instance, the War Department's Standardization Committee, as part of a broader effort to standardize electrical supplies, worked with the Bureau of Standards, the War Industries Board, and battery manufacturers to reduce the diversity of battery sizes on the market, cutting large cells from 10 to 3 sizes and flashlight batteries from some 40 to 6. "In limiting the number of sizes," a post-war report explained, "the Bureau [of Standards] had the cordial cooperation of the manufacturers who had been more or less compelled in the past, for trade reasons, to manufacture a large variety of shapes and sizes for which there was comparatively little use."[89] The thrust

of wartime simplification, in short, extended well beyond Arch
Wilkinson Shaw's Conservation Division.

Results of wartime simplification

What concrete results did this forceful and sweeping, albeit
brief, push to reduce product diversity and to diffuse mass-
production techniques yield? No comprehensive account has
been published, although some historians give examples, in
passing, of the specific reductions that were achieved or agreed
upon before the war ended.[90] As with the description of prewar
product diversity in chapter 2, conveying a sense of the breadth
and depth of reductions without overwhelming the reader with
minutiae is a challenge. But at least in this instance, unlike with
measures of prewar product diversity, yardsticks are available
to help in gauging the significance of the reductions, since,
when concrete reductions were cited, they were sometimes
given in the form of "before" and "after" data.

A table prepared by the U.S. Chamber of Commerce
(figure 2), for example, listed pre- and post-reduction numbers
for a series of commodities and helpfully calculated the percentage reduction in variety.[91] All of the reductions captured in
this table were achieved during World War I, with the exception of paving bricks and fruit containers.[92] The table includes
two major clusters of commodities – farm implements (nine
types plus Total) and paper (seven types) – together with a wide
range of other articles, from hammers and hatchets to pencils,
piano stools, and wheelbarrows. The reductions achieved in
farm-implement varieties averaged 87 percent overall,[93] while
reductions of the other articles in the table ranged from 43 percent (Book Papers) to 97 percent (Linen Papers).

The Chamber's table offered just a sampling of the wartime reductions in product diversity chronicled in wartime
and post-war reports,[94] and further examples help to convey

ARTICLE	FROM —	TO	PER CENT
Berry Boxes	17 —	3	82
Bond Papers	105 —	7	93
Book Papers	35 —	20	43
Ceramic Tile			75
Chain—Malleable	2044 —	820	60
Cover Paper	22 —	5	77
Cultivators	45 —	8	82
Disc Harrows	33 —	14	58
Disc Plows	11 —	9	18
Dry Cells	17 —	6	65
Fertilizer	100 —	17	83
Flashlight Batteries	30 —	8	73
Grape Baskets	31 —	3	90
Hammers, Hatchets	2752 —	761	72
Interior Tile	735 —	115	87
Ledger Papers	40 —	5	88
Linen Papers	98 —	3	97
Paving Brick	66 —	7	89
Pencils	700 —	250	64
Piano Benches	34 —	11	68
Piano Stools	15 —	1	93
Pipe and Fittings	17000 —	610	96
Planters and Drills	791 —	29	96
Pocket Knives	1500 —	300	80
Reversible Harrows	9 —	6	33
Riding Plows	27 —	15	45
Rubber Sponges	7 —	3	57
Shells—Smokeless			85
Shells—Black Powder			72
Small Tools			50
Stalk Cutters	16 —	6	62
Stoves and Ranges	2982 —	364	88
Till Baskets	30 —	5	83
Total Implements	1092 —	137	87
Tractor Plows	13 —	9	31
Typewriter Paper	37 —	11	70
Walking Plows	147 —	41	72
Water Bottles	20 —	5	75
Wheelbarrows	42 —	16	62
Writing Papers	40 —	5	88

Figure 2. Great War era reductions in variety:
"Current Editorial Comment: Sidelights on Standardization,"
Industrial Management 65, no. 1 (January 1923): 33.

their breadth and depth. Styles of horse collars were reduced from 60 to 15 and riding saddle styles from 200 to 36.[95] Shoe leather colors were reduced from 81 to 3 (black, white, and one shade of tan), while shoe manufacturers and retailers agreed to reduce their product styles by two-thirds.[96] Washing machine sizes and styles were reduced from 446 to 18, and metal bed styles from 600 to 24.[97] Styles and sizes of automobile tires were cut from 287 to 32 with an agreement to reduce them to 9 within 2 years.[98] Varieties of files and rasps were reduced from 1,351 to 619.[99] Ready-mixed house paint colors were reduced from as many as 100 to 32, and, to conserve tin, small container sizes were eliminated altogether – something that the industry, as noted earlier, had tried to do on its own without success.[100] Typewriter ribbon colors were reduced from 150 to 5.[101] As Bernard Baruch himself noted in his post-war report on the War Industries Board, "It would be wearisome to catalogue at length all the schedules which were issued and all the savings effected."[102] Taken together, the reductions in product diversity negotiated during the war reshaped the landscape of American manufacturing.

Although not all schedules had taken effect when the war ended in November 1918, their impact was felt for some time afterwards in certain lines of business because of the lag time between the design of products and their ultimate sale. Further reductions in styles and sizes of automobile tires, agreed to during the war, were in place by 1919.[103] The restrictions on ready-mixed house paint colors and can sizes were postponed twice to allow the industry to reduce its stockpiles of manufactured products (civilian house paint sales declined sharply during the war) and did not take effect before the war ended,[104] but paint manufacturers had already taken the restrictions into account in preparing products for the 1919 painting season.[105] Likewise, as the *Business Digest and Investment Weekly* noted a month after armistice, "the roster of limitations imposed upon shoes and ready-made clothing will survive for, say six months,

principally because goods now in process of manufacture conform to the 'recommendations' for standardization."[106]

The "slim silhouette" in women's fashions

For women's fashions, the long-term effects of World War
I measures to simplify commodities were nothing short of
extraordinary. The "slim silhouette," so characteristic of wom-
en's attire in the 1920s, became the dominant fashion trend
during the war not only for the reasons that fashion historians
have emphasized – women's wartime experience and acceler-
ating cultural and political changes.[107] It was due as much, if
not more, to a U.S. government campaign to conserve wool for
military uses.

Launched in early 1917, the project to conserve wool for use
in uniforms and blankets was one of the Commercial Economy
Board's first, alongside bread returns and retail deliveries.[108]
As Shaw later recalled, the wool project marked "the beginning of simplification."[109] From June through October 1917, the
CEB held a series of conferences with the various branches of
the garment industry.[110] Out of these meetings came an initial
agreement to reduce the number of fabric styles that textile
manufacturers offered as well as the number and size of fabric
samples (which saved both cloth and salesmen's baggage space).
The garment trades were also encouraged to minimize their
use of virgin wool and to substitute silk and cotton for wool as
much as possible.[111] In menswear, this had longer-term effects,
according to historian Victor S. Clark. The restrictions gave rise
to a "vogue for woolens," rather than the traditional worsted,
which "hung on from season to season despite the refusal of
manufacturers to believe it more than a passing fancy."[112]

In the meantime, CEB officials also pursued ways of saving
wool by "simplifying styles" – that is, as the CND's annual
report explained, eliminating "style features which took up

cloth needlessly."[113] In menswear, one result, despite considerable trade resistance, was elimination of the belted coat.[114] For women's wear, the CEB moved to simplify styles more comprehensively. Having quickly "discovered," the *Ladies' Home Journal* explained, "what any woman could have told [them] – that styles came from Paris,"[115] the board turned to the French ambassador and the French government for help in securing the cooperation of Parisian clothing designers. Called to a meeting at the Ministry of Commerce in August 1917, French couturiers promised to abide by the American restrictions on wool use and redesigned their American models for the Fall 1918 and Spring 1919 seasons.[116] The result, when French models reached the American market, was the "slim silhouette." As the Fall 1918 season opened, the *Ladies' Home Journal* explained the backstory:

> the Paris dressmakers were brought together [in 1917] for the purpose of creating new models which would satisfy the demands of taste and style, and yet at the same time result in less cloth being used in their reproduction by American garment makers. Out of this came what is now familiar as the "slim silhouette," the type for all models sent over from Paris, and made possible by the agreement of the Paris couturières to use not more than about four yards and a half of fabric in any one garment.[117]

In persuading French designers to alter designs for the American market, U.S. conservation officials upended, for a time, the traditional power relations between Parisian and American purveyors of fashion. "Just imagine a few years ago," a garment man remarked, "an American sending a message to French couturiers making suggestions as to what they must do if we are to adopt or to follow their fashions!"[118]

The arrangement with French designers was the first step. Having secured their cooperation in reducing yardage, the

Commercial Economy Board then pursued, as a trade association representative put it, a "harmony of action" in the women's garment trades. In November 1917, it held a meeting in New York of representatives from all branches of the American trade – from cloth and clothing manufacturers, importers, wholesalers, and retailers to dressmakers, catalog companies, and fashion publishers.[119] Well in advance of the meeting, the CEB had sent out a letter outlining the proposed new measures to conserve wool.[120] Following speeches by trade association presidents and a member of the CEB, the several hundred attendees gave their unanimous approval.[121]

In concrete terms, what the attendees endorsed at the meeting was a multi-part resolution aimed at women's and children's clothing.[122] It committed them to reduce the woolen fabric in outer garments by at least 25 percent, to "advocate" the use of non-wool fabrics, and to combine wool with other fabrics, pledging to "use their influence in advertising and exhibiting to popularize the use of these other materials."[123] The resolution also imposed specific limits on woolen fabric used in coats, suits, and dresses: optimally 3 yards of 54-inch fabric "and in no event more than 4½ yards." Finally, even though conservation officials disavowed any intention to influence design,[124] the resolution committed the garment trades to "mak[ing] garments of a definite character, featuring the slim silhouette." Immediately after the resolution was approved, according to the fashion magazine *Vogue*, the president of the Paris designers' syndicate, the Chambre Syndicale de la Couture Parisienne, "cabled [its] endorsement" of the American wool conservation program.[125]

For this initiative, portrayed by *Women's Wear Daily* as a "country-wide campaign to popularize [the] slim silhouette,"[126] the full array of compliance mechanisms came into play.[127] In this instance, however, some observers deemed publicity aimed directly at the final consumer to be less important. A *Vogue* writer thought the endorsement of French designers would suffice to sell the program: "When Paris is behind this move-ment there can be no doubt of its being fashionable and no fear that the narrow silhouette will not be thoroughly modish."[128] A participant in the November garment-trades meeting agreed that French endorsement would be sufficient: "it is within the power of a dozen or more of the prominent costume houses with influential French affiliations to sway the style tendency in whatever direction they desire."[129] Others simply thought that women would follow the lead of designers. "One point emphasized" at the November meeting, the *American Cloak and Suit Review* reported,

> was that it would be best not to take this discussion to the public in general, but to bend our efforts among ourselves as retailers, manufacturers, woolen mill owners, jobbers, and fashion writ-ers to use less wool, taking it for granted that women in general will be content to accept as "good style" the modes of lesser yardage offered for her selection.[130]

The writer and social reformer Charlotte Perkins Gilman regretfully agreed. Conservation officials had approached the garment trades, rather than women directly, she noted:

> Because women do not choose what they shall wear. It is chosen for them, decided by those clothing interests and other interests more obscure, and issued as a mandate from season to season. Women look eagerly for these authoritative bulletins, not to find what they want, but what they must have. If the mandate . . . offers a short and skimpy coat, half cotton, as what "they" are wearing, then we need not ask the woman anything at all. She wears what she is told.[131]

Still, the garment trades had accepted a mandate to sell the new restrictions to consumers, and, as *Printers' Ink* noted a few days after the November meeting, the consumer would need to be educated: "The average man or woman doesn't know about the wool shortage. Why it is short and why it has to be saved must be convincingly advertised or the garment manufacturers will have a disgruntled clientele on their hands."[132] After an initial news embargo to prevent the current season's fashions from becoming unsaleable,[133] advertisements in the fashion press began to highlight the new fabrics and the slim silhouette. "A glance through the women's magazines and the Sunday supplements of that period," Arch Shaw later wrote, "shows that they all devoted pages to the 'slim silhouette.'"[134]

Consider, for example, mentions of the slim silhouette as a wool conservation measure in *Vogue*, the leading American fashion magazine of the era.[135] A January 1918 article entitled "Save Wool and Serve the Soldier" portrayed acceptance of the slim silhouette as a matter of patriotism: "If a woman is slender as to silhouette, if her coat ends in the neighborhood of her hips, if her skirt is as short and as scanty as her stature will permit, then one may know that she is truly patriotic and that she is doing her bit in the conservation of wool."[136] Another set of fashion illustrations in the same issue echoed the theme: "It looks as though our national silhouette were about to become patriotically slim," the text began. "Of course, you know the reason for this, – we are Hooverizing on wool." ("Hooverizing" referred to Herbert Hoover's widely publicized food conservation measures.) A caption in bold letters at the top of the page brought home the main point: "Every bit of wool that your suit denies itself goes to keep a soldier's shoulders warm; that's why it is most patriotic to affect the slim silhouette."[137] In early February, *Vogue*'s "Spring Fashion Number" heralded "a new phase in fashion" prompted by the need to conserve wool and signified by "absolutely new" costumes that "use as little material as possible."[138] The February issue also reported news from Paris that the designer Cheruit was emphasizing "the slim silhouette" and shortening the length of coats "[i]n the interest of wool conservation."[139] An article on corsets in the same issue noted: "The concentrated efforts of both Paris and America to conserve wool have established a slender silhouette and a mode of dress which quite frankly reveals the lines of the figure."[140] In mid-February 1918, *Vogue's* "Seen in the Shops" column continued the theme: "Fashion and the government have joined forces this spring to promote the conservation of wool," one result of which was new suits that were "[s]cant of skirt and short of coat."[141]

To be sure, the Commercial Economy Board did not invent the slim silhouette. Fashion trends in Paris were already emphasizing, in Marlis Schweitzer's words, a "simplification and streamlining of the female silhouette" before the war.[142] In the early 1910s, the American press took note of the trend in scattered references to "the slim silhouette."[143] In October 1916, a caption on a *Good Housekeeping* illustration of French designs for the winter season characterized "the slim silhouette" as "[t]he mode of tomorrow."[144] A "barrel" silhouette, introduced in the Fall of 1916, had reduced yardage significantly, but the "toothpick" silhouette went further, according to *Women's Wear Daily*, eliminating fullness around the knees.[145] In early 1917, a *Vogue* writer reported that Gabrielle Chanel, whose models were "much in demand," was making a new tailored suit with a skirt only 2 meters wide.[146] In Paris, a *Harper's Bazaar* writer reported in September 1917, "the slim silhouette" (or "the 'toothpick' silhouette") characterized the season's dresses and coats as well as suits.[147]

But there were opposing trends. In November 1915, *Vogue* portrayed two silhouettes in active contention, that of "yesterday" emphasizing fullness, and the other, the "slender and graceful lines" of "to-day."[148] In early 1917, *Women's Wear Daily*, too, noted stylistic tensions between "the ample lines which are just leaving us and the narrower lines which are appearing on the horizon."[149] Yet, just before the CEB's intervention, according to one fashion scholar, European trends favored skirts with "a flamboyant display of yardage."[150] The popular "war crinoline" skirts could require as much as 8 yards of fabric.[151] With European markets in turmoil, French couturiers began designing models specifically for the lucrative American market.[152] As figure 3 shows, the designs that French couture houses sent to a "Fête Parisienne," a combined charity–marketing event organized in New York in 1915 by *Vogue* and a French fashion magazine, featured full skirts.[153] A postwar report maintained that French designs initially planned for

Figure 3.   French models for the American market, 1915: *Le Style Parisien*, November 1915 (Gallica, Bibliothèque nationale de France), reproduced in Kurkdjian, "Jeanne Paquin, Jeanne Lanvin, Jenny, and Gabrielle Chanel, 1914–18," 335.

the 1918 American market would have used "an abundance of materials."[154]

In a fashion environment in flux, the CEB's close collaboration with French designers did what it was intended to do: effectively propelled the "slim silhouette" to prominence in American fashion. Shortly after the war ended, *Good Housekeeping* reported that the trend persisted: "Although there are no startling changes to be found [in the newest Paris dresses], the slim silhouette becomes so much slimmer that it makes a change in itself."[155] Because of the lag time between the design and final sales of apparel, wartime restrictions constrained the design of women's fashions at least through the spring of 1919. And even when the restrictions were lifted, the slim silhouette persisted. "[F]or the practical purpose of saving twenty-five per cent of the material used in women's frocks and gowns," a former CND official quipped in 1924, "the Conservation Division brought it about that woman in 1918 should emulate Diana rather than Juno. The fashions thus set have since evolved alarmingly in the three dimensions, and now have passed from the realm of economics to that of manners."[156] The slim silhouette – or, as *Vogue* termed it in connection with Coco Chanel's fashions in 1921, "severe simplicity" – became the hallmark of women's fashion in the 1920s.[157] Indeed, in the mid-1920s, *Vogue* made an explicit aesthetic link between Chanel's fashions and the standardized, simplified products required for mass production. A 1926 illustration of her little black dress (figure 4) characterized it as "[t]he Chanel 'Ford' – the frock that all the world will wear."[158] In fact, the more relaxed fit of the slim silhouette lent itself much better to mass-production methods than did the fitted bodice of earlier fashions.[159] This, together with the Conservation Division's role in catapulting the slim silhouette to prominence in the U.S. as it worked to streamline production and distribution methods across the wartime economy, made the analogy with Ford entirely fitting.

Figure 4. The Chanel "Ford," model "817." Imported by Saks Fifth Avenue: *Vogue* (American ed.), October 1, 1926, 69 (ProQuest *Vogue* Archive).

Women's wear was just one of a multitude of products and practices that underwent wartime simplification in an intensive learning process that left a deep impression. As the editor of Shaw's *Factory* magazine observed, "That period of war's white-heat, when all that was unessential melted away until the underlying, surprisingly simple, skeleton of industrial necessity was revealed, has left its impress everywhere in manufacture."[160] WIB chairman Bernard Baruch deemed the economies achieved by reducing product diversity "one of the great lessons learned from the war."[161] The former director of the CND, Grosvenor Clarkson, also believed that manufacturers had "learned a lesson under the tutelage of the Conservation Division" and had gained "the knowledge and experience" to thrive in the perilous post-war years.[162]

But lessons learned during the war, as the next chapter shows, would prove no match for the forces of competition that resurged when the American economy abruptly demobilized. In the extraordinary competition for the consumer's dollar after the war, most manufacturers set aside what they had learned about mass production and reverted to the strategy of product diversity that had dominated the prewar years.

4

Product Diversity Resurgent, 1918–1921

With the signing of the armistice on November 11, 1918, the question whether American manufacturers would retain in peacetime the "lessons" in mass production that they had learned in war took on sudden urgency. Key government officials certainly thought that, in some form, the wartime lessons *should* be translated to peacetime. Among the "dollar-a-year men" who headed the WIB's 57 commodity sections, "the most universally recommended proposal" in the immediate aftermath of the war, historian Robert D. Cuff concludes, was that the conservation program be continued.[1] In his weekly news conference just a few days after armistice, War Industries Board chairman Bernard Baruch concurred: the work of conservation and standardization – "a matter of necessity" in wartime – should be turned into "a matter of advantage" in peace.[2] He reiterated the point in his official report on the WIB's wartime activities three years later: "We may well draw from this war experience a lesson to be applied to peace, by providing some simple machinery for eliminating wasteful trade practices which increase prices without in the remotest degree contributing to the well-being of the people."[3] Arch Wilkinson Shaw himself, although non-committal during the war,[4] remained an enthusiast after the war – among other things, energetically advocating reduction in product variety as "the next big step in management" through his magazines *System* and *Factory*.[5]

Broad swaths of the business world shared officials' enthusiasm for continuing the conservation measures in peacetime. One proponent was the New England paper goods manufacturer Henry Dennison, who straddled the worlds of government and business during the war.[6] As early as 1917, while a member of the Commercial Economy Board, he expressed hope that the elimination of wasteful practices under the pressure of war would prove permanent – that "after this experience a great many of the mushroom practices that have grown up in the moist air of American competition may be permanently eliminated."[7] Shortly before the war ended, the textile trade press featured, in Scranton's words, "nationalistic appeals to extend wartime simplification."[8] Shortly after it ended, the optical industry's war service committee pressured government officials to maintain their support, announcing that the industry had agreed on "a voluntary program of conservation and standardization" and requesting that the Conservation Division "approve, publish and enforce this program as already voluntarily adopted."[9] In early 1919, paint manufacturer Ernest T. Trigg, president of the Philadelphia Chamber of Commerce, argued for a continuation of the "revolutionary" wartime program. He was concerned both about the ability of American business to compete in foreign markets and about its ability to reabsorb war workers and returning soldiers. "The war showed the necessity for the exercise of every economy," he declared, "and this should be the aim in peace times. Intelligent cooperation should exist among those engaged in similar industries to prevent the doing of things through motives of competition which are extravagant and wasteful and benefit no one." The WIB's "good work" in "the elimination of useless styles and sizes in manufactured products," he maintained, "should be perpetuated and extended to many industries which were not covered during the war."[10] The president of the American Society for Testing Materials, citing the wartime reductions and savings achieved, saw "wonderful possibilities in this direction" in peacetime, though he wondered whether consumers would be willing to forgo "the gratification of their individualistic tastes as to style, color, form, etc."[11]

Enthusiasm for a continuation of the government-organized conservation program was not limited to specific industries or firms, however. In the estimation of a *Printers' Ink* writer, "regret" that the conservation measures were ending was, "if anything, more widespread in business circles than in the Government environment."[12] The writer reported that "business men are making appeals to Washington by mail, telegraph and personal visit, not to be over hasty in abolishing the conservation schedules." Even those not directly involved "in formulating the schedules . . . would regard it as a positive catastrophe if Uncle Sam, in his haste to give business a free hand, should allow business to slip back into all the old, wasteful, illogical habits from which it has so recently been lifted."[13] A five-day congress of the war service committees, convened in December 1918 by the U.S. Chamber of Commerce and drawing an attendance of some 5,000, declared itself in favor of carrying forward cooperation in the interests of conservation: "The war has demonstrated that through industrial cooperation great economies may be achieved, waste eliminated, and efficiency increased," the congress resolved. "The Nation should not forget, but rather should capitalize, these lessons by adapting effective war practices to peace conditions through permitting reasonable cooperation between units of industry under appropriate Federal supervision."[14]

The Conservation Division's collaborative process of crafting conservation schedules surely heightened business enthusiasm to retain wartime economies. Manufacturers now had first-hand experience with the impressive economies that reducing product diversity enabled them to achieve – as the economist Homer Hoyt put it, they had "tasted the fruits of the economies of standardization."[15] But it also mattered that the economies sought were ones that they themselves had proposed to the Conservation Division.[16] As the editor of *Factory* pointed out, this essentially gave them what we would call "buy-in" today: "They do not think of it [simplification] as merely a Governmental war-time regulatory expedient, but consider it a practical measure they themselves helped apply in order that their country's needs might be met when materials, men and money were at a premium." Now, in the throes of the 1920–1 depression, he pointed out, "there is a new taskmaster – price instead of patriotism."[17]

But demobilization came quickly and most WIB restrictions were abruptly lifted. Bernard Baruch resigned as WIB chair in late November 1918, and all WIB restrictions lapsed at the end of the year.[18] "By and large," the *Business Digest and Investment Weekly* noted a month after the armistice, "the entire conservation structure is scrapped, so far as government is concerned."[19] Secretary of Commerce William C. Redfield, an ardent proponent of trade associations and standardization, had the WIB's Conservation Division transferred to his department, where it became the Industrial Cooperation Service, its transition to the Commerce Department overseen by Arch Shaw.[20] Redfield and Shaw immediately reached out to electrical manufacturers with a proposal that their "well organized" industry participate in "a trial" of continued government–industry cooperation in peacetime.[21] But Congress, in what Redfield termed "a fit of alleged economy," declined to provide further funding and the service was dissolved after six months.[22] When *Printers' Ink* asked a WIB official about "the continuance of the conservation programmes that have brought about temporarily the simplification of styles, the reduction in the number of models, and the elimination of slow-moving lines," he responded bluntly: "It is squarely up to the trades – more specifically to the trade associations."[23]

Would American trade associations be able to sustain the initiative in peacetime? Having nearly tripled in number between 1913 and 1919, many were young, war-forged organizations.[24] And they faced fierce economic and political headwinds in the immediate post-war years. War-induced overcapacity plagued many lines of business. Rapid demobilization brought economic turbulence. Consumers, forming "Buy Nothing" clubs, resisted high prices in the 1919–20 "buyers' strikes."[25] In the 1920–1 depression, the U.S. experienced its steepest price decline since the Civil War.[26] Hand-to-mouth buying, which enabled and encouraged product diversity, intensified.[27] Competitive pressures and unsavory business methods surged, prompting business leaders to establish the Commercial Standards Council in 1922, principally to combat commercial bribery.[28] The Wilson administration's firm policy of rapid disengagement left little hope that the federal government would facilitate collective action in peacetime. Baruch's call for "some simple machinery for eliminating wasteful trade practices" went unheeded, even though, as Laura Phillips Sawyer notes, "many prominent economists, business leaders, and regulators urged that the lessons of wartime government–business cooperation be sustained through peacetime."[29]

Individual firms might be able to hold the line, particularly if they dominated their line of business, but industry-wide retention of the wartime conservation measures, as business leaders were well aware, depended on concerted action.[30] And, despite some optimism that the war experience had disciplined free-riders,[31] concerted action in pursuit of economies in production and distribution faced legal hurdles. Thus, the thousands of businesspeople who attended the U.S. Chamber of Commerce's "reconstruction" congress in early December 1918 came out forcefully in favor of buttressing trade associations' capabilities. They resolved to press for federal legislation that would remove "all obstacles to reasonable cooperation" and committed themselves to preserving the war service committees under the Chamber's supervision. They also endorsed efforts to organize trade associations in any industries that were not yet organized, encouraging "every dealer, jobber, manufacturer, and producer of raw materials" to join and support "the national organization in his trade."[32] In the meantime, however, as government support for collective action lapsed, American firms found themselves, in economist Hoyt's words, caught "between the whirlpool of ruinous competition and the sharp rocks of the Sherman [Antitrust] Act."[33]

Notwithstanding the uncertain legal status of cooperation to reduce product diversity in peacetime, contemporary observers thought a few of the better-organized trades would be able to hold the line. "[T]he farm equipment industry, which eliminated more dead wood from its catalogs than any other industry – cutting out hundreds of styles, sizes, etc., for which there is only limited demand – stands pat for the perpetuation of the revised program," the *Business Digest and Investment Weekly* reported a month after armistice, and it had the institutional strength to do so: "No doubt whatever is expressed that the trade is sufficiently well organized to put over this plan."[34] For at least a couple of years, according to a government official, the industry's wartime reductions remained "effective, though here and there an obstreperous buyer or a weak-kneed salesman has again secured some useless variation with the resultant expense carried all through office records, catalogues, jigs, machine set ups, stocks, workmen's and salesmen's education."[35] The shoe industry, too, seemed poised to retain the wartime restrictions, because, "as a result of the war," *Printers' Ink* noted, "the different branches of the shoe trade are more completely organized than ever before."[36] Anecdotally, the director of Harvard's Bureau of Business Research reported, he had heard of "numerous instances in which the conservation schedules still are being observed in whole or in part."[37]

Paint manufacturing was one of the industries that succeeded only "in part." At least into 1922, Philadelphia paint
manufacturing executive Ernest Trigg reported, ready-mixed
paint manufacturers had informally retained the wartime
limitations on numbers of house paint colors. His own company and, he believed, most of its competitors continued
to restrict their output of house paint to a maximum of 32
colors.[38] Paint catalogs and price lists confirm that mass retailers Sears, Roebuck and Co. and Montgomery Ward, as well
as The Sherwin–Williams Company, limited their colors into
the mid-1920s.[39] But, where container sizes were concerned,
the industry had relapsed. "When the armistice came," Trigg
explained, "a number of [paint] manufacturers, convinced that
the fewer sizes plan had paid, again made an effort to have it
voluntarily made a permanent feature of the industry's distribution." This time, trade association surveys showed that even
paint dealers and retailers, who had opposed prewar efforts
to eliminate smaller containers, were now on board: "once
having tried it," they favored retention of the wartime limits on
container sizes. But unanimity across the industry remained
elusive: "For the same reason as before the war, we failed to
get unanimous agreement and the old line of package plan was
restored."[40]

In another industry – automotive tire manufacturing –
product innovation undermined the wartime achievements.
Styles and sizes of automobile tires, as noted earlier, had been
reduced from 287 to 9 by 1919. But those were pneumatic
tires, and in 1923 the new low-pressure or balloon tire was
introduced.[41] Balloon-tire sizes quickly proliferated, increasing
from 4 to 40 within five years and leaving tire dealers, in the
words of a U.S. Rubber Co. official, "bewildered."[42] Graphically
illustrating the profusion of tire sizes at a meeting of automotive engineers in 1928, a B. F. Goodrich Co. plant manager
quipped: "[I]t is necessary to consider the question humor-
ously, as the sizes had been developed in such a haphazard

way. . . . If a Friday passes in the factory without a rush order for a new size of tire to be built over Sunday, the production department thinks something is wrong."[43] Despite the industry's earlier history of interfirm standardization,[44] it struggled throughout the 1920s to standardize balloon tires.[45]

Most industries, however, succumbed to competitive pressures, abandoning simplified product lines, and reverting to product diversity as the strategy of choice. Like a one-two punch, consumer resistance to high prices and the sharp depression of 1920–1 brought the prewar tensions between producer-oriented industrial efficiency and consumer-oriented product diversity back to the surface. Manufacturers, as one observer noted, found themselves caught "between the devil and the deep blue." Their distributors wanted "new styles and models with which to stimulate buying," while their production people were "asking for fewer numbers in the line so that various factory economies may be taken advantage of."[46] As sales pressure mounted, product diversity began creeping back in. "'This coming year the factory is going to make whatever the sales department wants, standards or no standards, simplicity or no,' is the way one executive put it to me," *Factory's* editor reported in the midst of the depression. He urged his readers to resist the "creepage" and warned of the consequences: "this depression may open the door to overspecializations and complexities which it will be difficult to uproot later on. So if we don't watch sharply, most of the simplification steps which the war taught us may be lost."[47] As a later report summed it up, "A hungry sales force and a factory running on part time combine to influence policy in favor of producing anything that anyone can be induced to buy."[48] And once some manufacturers began to re-diversify their product lines, competition ensured that others followed suit.[49] The result, in the words of a key figure in post-war efforts to revive wartime practice, was once again a "wild-orgy of diversification," driven by a "cult of diversification" whose "creed" was to "give the buyer what he wants."[50]

Anecdotal evidence suggests that product diversity did indeed resurge after the war. Manufacturers of builders' hardware for dwellings "discarded" wartime restrictions on sizes and styles once the War Industries Board lifted its conservation schedules.[51] Varieties of steel reinforcing bars had been reduced in sizes and grades during the war, but, when the government restrictions were removed, the "discarded sizes" were offered again. "[T]he former confusion," an industry statement noted, "has returned to disconcert producers, distributors, and users."[52] Once the War Industries Board stepped back, varieties of grinding wheels (for grinding machines, a type of machine tool) proliferated. "Hundreds of thousands of wheel shapes, sizes, and types had insinuated themselves into factories and industrial plants," a mid-1920s report noted.[53] Files and rasps, having been reduced during the war from 1,351 varieties to 619, trended upward again after the war, reaching 661 by 1923.[54] In mid-1922, the products of shoe, clothing, and furniture manufacturers were said to be "running to the bizarre in an effort to stimulate sales."[55] Indeed, a mid-1920s statistical study of boot and shoe manufacturing found a "marked decline in productivity since 1921," which it attributed to a "great increase in demand of retailers for varied and fancy styles." Despite being better organized as a result of the war, boot and shoe manufacturers were producing lot sizes in the "hundreds or even dozens, each lot differing from the others by some insignificant variations of stitching or perforation."[56] In mid-1921, one shoe manufacturer, though fully aware of the advantages of a simplified product line, was reported to be offering 700 styles because "[h]is customers demand something 'different,' and his own salesmen declare that they cannot sell the goods unless he yields to the demand." For this manufacturer, a *Printers' Ink* writer noted, competitive pressure posed "a concrete business problem" that made firm-level simplification impractical.[57]

Data snapshots collected by the Commerce Department in the 1920s likewise suggest that product diversity reigned again after the war. American buyers had a choice, for example, of 66 varieties of paving brick, 700 varieties of hotel chinaware, 552 varieties of woven-wire fencing (sold in 2,072 varieties of packaging), 49 shapes and sizes of milk bottles, and 29 styles of milk bottle caps. Slate blackboards for wall installation were available in 90 heights. Plumbers or homeowners could choose from 1,114 varieties of brass lavatory and sink traps. Toilet paper rolls came in 13 sizes, loaded shells in 4,076 varieties, bank checks in thousands of sizes, and salt in 35 package sizes.[58]

Widespread appreciation of wartime achievements in streamlining American business, growing alarm that wartime economies were being abandoned, economic depression, nationwide labor strife – this was the context in which a disturbing study of American business practice appeared in 1921. Entitled *Waste in Industry*, it came from a new umbrella organization of engineers, the Federated American Engineering Societies (FAES), formed in 1920 in an intellectual milieu that envisioned a unified public role for engineers – and engineering methods – in what was widely anticipated to be the post-war "reconstruction" of American society. The FAES's first president was Herbert Hoover, who would soon become the U.S. Secretary of Commerce. The FAES's first action was to approve a proposal by Hoover to appoint a committee of engineers to study waste in production.[59]

A month before he took office as President Warren G. Harding's Secretary of Commerce in 1921, Hoover summarized the study's rationale and preliminary results for the FAES executive board. Its overarching goal, in his words, was "to visualize the nation as a single industrial organism and to examine its efficiency towards its only real objective – the maximum production." As Hoover saw the world, "[t]he primary duty of organized society is to enlarge the lives and increase the standards of living of all the people – not of any special class whatever." And increasing the national standard of living hinged on enhancing "national productivity."[60]

Focused on six industries and completed in five months' time, the study – a rapid-fire study that Hoover termed a "reconnaissance report" – highlighted four sources of waste in industry, all centered on production: low production, interrupted production, restricted production, and lost production.[61] The most important causes, as Hoover summarized them, were business cycles and seasonal fluctuations, labor strife, and "a too high degree of individualism in certain basic products and tools."[62] Quantifying waste of resources to two decimal points, the report estimated that it ranged from 28.66 percent in the metal trades to 63.78 percent in men's clothing manufacture. The study attracted widespread notice, not least for its controversial conclusion that the bulk of the responsibility for waste ("over 50%") lay with management rather than labor.[63]

The FAES committee's study, in highlighting product diversity as a major source of waste in American industry, echoed rising concern in the business world as product varieties proliferated again in the slump of 1920–1. This set the stage for Herbert Hoover, as Secretary of Commerce, to revive and reinvigorate World War I efforts to suppress the market forces that spawned product diversity and blocked the diffusion of mass-production techniques.

5

Hoover's "Fostering Hand": Simplified Practice in Peacetime

When Herbert Hoover took office as President Warren G. Harding's Secretary of Commerce at the age of 46, he had already acquired a string of distinguished sobriquets – "The Great Engineer," "The Great Humanitarian," "Master of Emergencies."[1] Orphaned in rural Iowa, raised by Quaker relatives in Oregon, a member of Stanford's first class in 1891, he had achieved an international reputation – and considerable wealth – first, as a manager (later, partner) in a British mining company with global interests and, from 1908, as an independent consultant – work that took him to Australia, China, Burma, and Russia. Hoover retired from mining in 1914 (while retaining mine investments), and then, as war broke out in Europe, turned his formidable energies to humanitarian work. From 1914 through the war, he organized private food relief for German-occupied Belgium, an extraordinary feat that won him international acclaim. When the U.S. entered the war, he put his expertise to work as head of President Woodrow Wilson's U.S. Food Administration, while continuing to chair the Commission for Relief in Belgium. After the war he focused again on humanitarian work, this time organizing economic relief for war-ravaged Europe as

Figure 5. Herbert Hoover, 1918. Photographers: Harris & Ewing – Library of Congress, www.loc.gov/item/2016868991.

head of the American Relief Administration. Barely into his forties, Hoover (figure 5) had already demonstrated, in the words of a biographer, "inexorable energy and the drive of a locomotive,"[2] qualities that he would bring to bear in his efforts as U.S. Secretary of Commerce to revive the World War I push for mass production.

By the time he took office as Commerce Secretary in March 1921, Hoover had developed firm ideas about how the U.S. should "reconstruct" its political economy in the aftermath of world war, ideas that he articulated in a *Saturday Evening Post* article in 1919, followed by a series of newspaper and magazine articles and culminating in a 1922 pamphlet entitled *American Individualism*.[3] The "ism" in his pamphlet's title signaled Hoover's strident opposition to social movements stirred up during the war – socialism, communism, syndicalism, and "capitalism in the sense that a few men through unrestrained control of property determine the welfare of great numbers."[4]

In the competition for hearts and minds, he believed, the United States' essential weapons were equality of opportunity and a rising standard of living, the latter resting, in Kendrick A. Clements's words, on two pillars: "increasing productivity and the broadest possible distribution of its fruits throughout society."[5] To broaden the distribution of wealth, Hoover favored high wages, a progressive federal income tax, and the federal estate tax; increasing productivity, for Hoover, meant working closely with trade associations and labor unions to eliminate waste in all its forms. He also saw the elimination of waste as essential to American firms' ability to compete in post-war foreign markets.[6]

To his position as Secretary of Commerce, Hoover thus came armed with a comprehensive agenda to eliminate waste in the American economy and with a template furnished by the war experience.[7] (Hoover preferred the term "elimination of waste" over "efficiency," because the latter term, he explained, "'has come to imply in the public mind a certain ruthless inhuman point of view.'"[8]) Increasing "national productivity," as noted earlier, meant ridding the economy of those sources of waste outlined in his FAES committee's 1921 study, *Waste in Industry*. Hoover's guiding premise in this endeavor was that government should serve, in a Hoover scholar's words, "primarily as a coordinator, mediator, and information-dispenser, not as a coercive or restrictive force."[9] Thus, in its pursuit of increased productivity, the Commerce Department would support business, as Hoover put it, "on a basis of cooperation," which he portrayed as "an entirely new departure" in American government–business relations.[10] Given the extensive government–business collaboration that had marked the recent war effort, he might better have said "an entirely new departure *in peacetime*."

Viewed against the backdrop of the war experience, Hoover's reorganization and expansion of the Commerce Department clearly built upon and expanded wartime practice.[11] Just after the war, Secretary of Commerce Redfield, as noted earlier, had tried to reconstitute the War Industries Board's Conservation Division within the walls of the Commerce Department but failed to gain congressional backing (i.e., funding).[12] By virtue of what a business writer called Hoover's "galvanic influence" in the very different political-economic circumstances of 1921,[13] he succeeded where Redfield had failed – securing a 32 percent increase in Commerce's budget as its staff expanded by 20 percent over his eight years as secretary.[14] That Hoover saw the WIB – and, more specifically, the WIB's Conservation Division – as the template for his campaign against waste in American business is suggested by the fact that his first choice to serve as his assistant in reorganizing the department was Arch Wilkinson Shaw, the World War I conservation czar.[15] In staffing the FAES's Committee on the Elimination of Waste, Hoover had relied on engineers, and, as Clements notes, he "regarded engineers as uniquely qualified to point the way to waste reduction."[16] Nevertheless, for assistance in reorganizing the Commerce Department and launching his cooperative waste-elimination program, he turned not to an engineer but to the marketing expert Shaw, who, by the war's end, had worked out impressive collaborative procedures for reducing waste in American business. Indeed, it was Shaw's signal success in working with bakers to eliminate bread returns, according to a wartime official, that inspired Hoover's enthusiasm for voluntary cooperation.[17] When Shaw declined his offer, Hoover recruited Shaw's colleague Frederick Feiker, an electrical engineer by training who, like Shaw, worked in business publishing, among other things, as editor of Shaw's magazines *System* and *Factory* before the war.[18] Shaw provided critical background support for Hoover's initiative, however, by serving on an advisory committee and showcasing simplification repeatedly in his publications.[19]

One of Hoover's first steps in strengthening the Commerce Department – creating "a real Department of Commerce," as he put it[20] – was to restructure it in the image of wartime agencies, though not in so many words.[21] This he did by creating commodity divisions in the Bureau of Foreign and Domestic Commerce, which became, in Clements's words, "the core of the department."[22] The commodity divisions, 15 in number by 1922, were headed, like the WIB's commodity sections, by individuals drawn mainly from the relevant industry. The commodity divisions worked closely with private-sector committees whose members, like those of the war service committees, were generally nominated by the relevant trade association and were able to speak for their industry. Hoover's commodity divisions sought principally to gather and disseminate information on business practice and conditions for their respective commodities, with special emphasis on export markets in the early years.[23] Despite the divisions' initial focus on foreign markets, their resemblance to WIB's commodity sections was crystal clear to a contemporary observer. "The [WIB's] commodity section plan has been adapted to peacetime needs in the Bureau of Foreign and Domestic Commerce," former CND director Grosvenor Clarkson reported in 1924. "All of the lessons in the advantages of cooperation learned during the war are not being forgotten. The new commodity sections . . . deal with essentially the same commodity production groups as the War Industries Board assembled."[24]

Hoover's second – and, for his campaign to eliminate industrial waste, the key – structural change was to create a new division that mirrored the WIB's Conservation Division. This was the Division of Simplified Practice (DSP), created in the Commerce Department's Bureau of Standards toward the end of Hoover's first year as secretary.[25] In announcing its creation and outlining its mandate, Bureau of Standards director Samuel W. Stratton linked the new division explicitly to World War I conservation efforts: "The experience of this country during the war, followed by the report Waste in Industry, . . . proved conclusively the urgent necessity of utilizing standardization, of eliminating freak varieties, and of concentrating the processes of manufacturing and distribution upon articles of the greatest interchangeability." The new division, Stratton explained, was part of "a general program for eliminating industrial and commercial wastes, for stabilizing employment, developing our foreign commerce, increasing the quantity of American products, and, in general, securing for every American citizen a higher standard of living."[26] Stratton and his technical experts at the Bureau had opposed housing the new division in the Bureau of Standards because simplified practice, as we will see, was based on commercial rather than scientific or technical data, but Hoover overruled them and the Bureau remained its home for decades.[27]

The key to achieving a higher standard of living, Hoover believed, was streamlining American business and pushing it toward mass production and distribution, as the Conservation Division had done during the war. Hoover's Foreword to the division's 1924 publication *Simplified Practice: What It Is and What It Offers* laid out the basic idea succinctly: eliminating "these endless variations" in manufactured products would reduce costs all along the line from manufacturing through distribution, lower costs would "eventually" be reflected in lower prices for consumers, and lower prices would increase real wages, thus raising the standard of living.[28] He also believed that lowering the price of manufactured goods offered the only viable solution to post-war farm problems.[29] Candidates for simplification included industrial as well as consumer products – virtually anything that might profitably be mass produced. Although the ultimate goals – raising the American standard of living rather than winning the war – differed, the new division, as journalist and Hoover aide Edward Eyre Hunt pointed out, was "continuing in time of peace the war work of the Conservation Division of the War Industries Board."[30] Writing in 1927, economist Rexford G. Tugwell saw Hoover as "[t]he sole representative of the War Industries idea in Washington today."[31]

To head the new division, Hoover recruited another electrical man, William A. Durgin, portrayed in a trade journal as "well known and highly esteemed in the electrical fraternity." With a degree in electrical engineering from MIT, Durgin had worked for the Commonwealth Edison Company and its predecessor, Chicago Edison, since 1904, and had published not only technical articles but also a popular book on the history of electricity. In late 1921, in an echo of World War I practice, Hoover requested that Commonwealth Edison allow Durgin, at that time its director of public relations, to take "an indefinite leave of absence" so that he could come to Washington and "give his services to the government" as head of the simplification initiative.[32] Hoover recruited Durgin at the suggestion of his assistant Frederick Feiker, who had likewise taken a leave of absence from his position as vice president of the publishing firm McGraw-Hill.[33] An experienced public speaker, Durgin, long before the age of slide projectors or PowerPoint, liked to leaven his pitches for simplified practice with humor and lantern slides (figure 6).[34] When Durgin

Figure 6. William A. Durgin's lantern slides.
Illustrations in Durgin, "Alice in Modernland," 14–15.

returned to Commonwealth Edison in 1924, he was succeeded as chief by Ray M. Hudson, who had joined the division as a technical assistant with training in mechanical engineering, work experience with an Illinois manufacturing company, and World War I service with the Emergency Fleet Corporation. A former member of the Taylor Society's board of directors, Hudson was particularly attentive to organized labor's views of standardization.[35] Like Durgin, Hudson would use dry humor to sell simplified practice, once quipping to an audience of automobile tire engineers that he would be brief because "the longer he spoke, the greater the tire."[36] In 1927, when Hudson was promoted to the Bureau's assistant director for commercial standardization, he was succeeded by Edwin W. Ely, who had served with the Sixth French Army in the war and worked in engineering and marketing in the U.S. and Asia. Ely served as head of Simplified Practice (later, Commercial Standards) for some 30 years.[37]

The Division of Simplified Practice's specific charge, spelled out in its name, was to enable American industries to engage – in peacetime – in collective reductions of product diversity. The more familiar term "standardization" they sought to avoid because of its popular connotations. "Why do we talk of Simplified Practice instead of Standardization?" Durgin asked in the pages of *Nation's Business* as the initiative was gaining momentum. "Well, largely because to the average man or woman 'standardization' has come to have a restrictive, compelling, Prussian sound which at once arouses all their opposition." The government's role in promoting it also raised hackles. "So under Secretary Hoover's inspiration we have carefully avoided talk of standardization, and emphasized solely the advantages of Simplified Practice."[38] To the International Milk Dealers Association, Durgin admitted that simplified practice was, "if you please, a form of standardization, but such an everyday commonsense form that it should arouse none of the opposition felt to standardization in general."[39]

The companion term, simplification, occasionally used in connection with conservation during World War I,[40] also came into wider use after the war. Shaw's publications *System* and *Factory* claimed credit for coining the term "simplification" to name a broader movement to reduce complexity in all aspects of American business, and they publicized the movement widely under that name, beginning with the February 1921 issue of *Factory*, shortly before Hoover took office as Secretary of Commerce.[41] In a 1924 handbook for managers, Durgin's successor, Ray M. Hudson, endorsed the distinction: simplification was "that policy of management which seeks to conduct all activities, and perform all functions, of an enterprise in least elaborate manner consistent with any given purpose," while simplified practice meant the "specific application of simplification to manufacture of goods" – that is, "reduction of variety in sizes, dimensions, and immaterial differences in everyday commodities."[42] Usage shifted, however, over the decade. For a time in the mid-1920s, "group simplification" came into use to describe industry-wide, as opposed to firm-level, reductions in variety.[43] By the 1930s, DSP staff reserved "simplification" for firm-level reductions in product variety and "simplified practice" for industry-wide reductions.[44] For simplicity, I use the terms "simplification" and "simplified practice" interchangeably and try to make clear whether the reference is to firm-level or industry action on products or processes.

The new division's key challenge was to solve the collective-action problems that made industry-wide reductions of product diversity so challenging in peacetime. In his welcoming remarks to the first simplified practice conference, Hoover highlighted the problem the division would address: the collective inefficiency of American manufacturing revealed by the Great War. Individual manufacturers showed "remarkable efficiency," he noted. What concerned him was "the very considerable inefficiency of collective industry." "If we had the same native efficiency collectively in this country that we have individually," he believed, "we would have no difficulty in maintaining our own in foreign or international commerce, of maintaining the high wage levels and the high standards of living." Manufacturers in various industries had been persuaded by their war experience "that there was something of permanent value" in simplification and had sought to forge agreements on their own after the war. But they were hamstrung, he maintained, by antitrust strictures, on the one hand, and by the need to reach a consensus with their suppliers and customers, on the other. Thus, Hoover offered "the friendly help of the Government" in surmounting both obstacles.[45] "The law makes it illegal for manufacturers to agree among themselves to effect these saving simplifications," he explained in a 1922 interview, "but we solve the problem by getting each manufacturer to agree with us to do it."[46] A clever move, but, as we will see, antitrust concerns lingered. For the daunting task of reaching industry-wide consensus, he offered the Division of Simplified Practice "as a center point around which their own cooperative action could take place."[47] Very quickly, "centralizing agency" became the preferred term of art to describe the DSP's role in negotiating collective agreements up and down the chain of production and consumption as well as across the trades.[48] Those with a stake in the simplification of a particular product line, a DSP publication explained, had "sometimes divergent and possibly antagonistic" interests and were "unwilling to meet except through some unbiased third party or on some neutral meeting ground."[49] The DSP would serve as that unbiased third party and the Department of Commerce, where simplified practice conferences were usually held, as the neutral – and legally safe – meeting ground.

As articulated time and again by the Division of Simplified Practice in the 1920s and beyond, the advantages of simplification in peacetime were essentially the same as in war, although the overall goal was quite different. A newspaper article during the war, for example, alerting consumers to

expect fewer product varieties in shops, had explained that
the Conservation Division's reductions in variety would lower
the cost of production, increase its speed, and reduce "the
amount of materials and capital tied up in the manufacturers'
and dealers' stocks throughout the country," thus freeing up
resources for the war.[50] The Division of Simplified Practice,
too, highlighted the production gains, lower costs, and reductions in inventories wrought by simplified practice, typically
outlining distinctive benefits for three groups – manufacturers,
distributors (jobbers, wholesalers, retailers), and consumers.[51]
Those unfamiliar with the wartime achievements could find
ample testimony to concrete results in Arch Wilkinson Shaw's
magazines, which showcased the productivity gains achieved
by individual manufacturers and distributors (figure 7).[52] From
the mid-1920s into the 1960s, DSP publications routinely
included a succinct but detailed summary of the benefits for
all three groups (figure 8).[53] Of all the cited benefits, only one

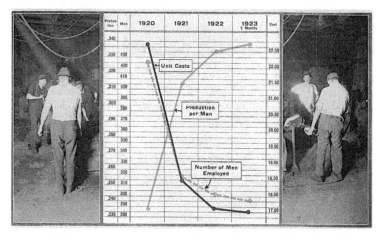

Figure 7.   Increase in productivity at the firm level:
August H. Landwehr, "Simplification Lowers Production Costs
$1,000,000 for Eight Plants, I. How We Got 50% More from Every
Dollar of Wages," *Factory* 31, no. 1 (July 1923): 21. Landwehr was
treasurer and manager of the Holland Furnace Company.

To the Producer and Manufacturer

1. Less capital tied up in slow-moving stocks.
2. More economical manufacture due to simplified inspection requirements, longer runs with fewer changes, less idle equipment, less stock to handle, reduced clerical overhead, etc.
3. More permanent employment as contrasted with present seasonal employment.
4. Larger units of production and less special machinery.
5. More prompt delivery.
6. Less chance of error in shipment.
7. Less obsolete material and machinery.

To the Jobber, Wholesaler, and Retailer

1. Increased turnover.
2. Elimination of slow-moving stock.
3. Staple line, easy to buy, quick to sell.
4. Greater concentration of sales efforts on fewer items.
5. Decreased capital invested in stocks and repair parts on hand.
6. Less storage space required.
7. Decreased overhead, handling charges, and clerical work.

To the Consumer

1. Better values than otherwise possible.
2. Better service in delivery and repairs.
3. Better quality of product.
The trade associations and the individuals prominent in this industry have employed their time and thought, together with the combined services of the Division of Simplified Practice of the Department of Commerce, the Chamber of Commerce of the United States, and the American Engineering Standards Committee to lay out a simple and definite plan to reduce waste and thereby give better service at less cost. It rests with you to make the plan a success by giving your cooperation.

Figure 8.   The benefits of simplified practice: U.S. Department of Commerce, *Simplified Practice Recommendation No. 15: Blackboard Slate, issued by the Bureau of Standards, Original Draft, July 1, 1924* (Washington, DC: Government Printing Office, 1925), frontispiece.

– "Greater concentration of sales efforts on fewer items" – had somewhat more salience in peacetime than during the war, when government policy had sought to reduce civilian consumption. Merchandising continued during the war, of course, and simplification eased marketing problems even in wartime.[54] But simplification in war and in peace served fundamentally different purposes, which Arch Shaw summed up this way: "The philosophy of simplification in war time is to cut down demand. ... In peace time the philosophy of simplification is practically reversed, because in peace time the purpose of simplification is to lower costs, so that demand can be increased."[55]

Even before Hoover had recruited a chief for the new division, Commerce staff took two steps reminiscent of Shaw's methods during the war. First, they gathered systematic, nationwide information on the status of "standardization" in American industry. In mid-1921, a survey went out under Hoover's name to business editors across the country, asking them to report on industries and companies that were already standardizing "materials, processes, and methods." The editors were also encouraged to suggest lines of business where standardization might be pushed further.[56] The second step was to convene a national conference to simplify paving bricks. Held in November 1921 and led by Hoover's assistant (and Shaw's colleague) Fredrick Feiker,[57] this first peacetime simplification process could be organized so expeditiously, one suspects, because Commerce staff did not need to work out a process from scratch: they, like American firms, were already quite familiar with Shaw's wartime model of collaboration.

The paving-brick conference, the first of more than 100 simplified practice conferences in the 1920s,[58] established Hoover's peacetime template for the simplification process (figure 9).[59] It began with an informal meeting or "preliminary conference," in this case instigated by the National Paving Brick Manufacturers Association (NPBMA). At the association's request, Department of Commerce staff and representatives of the U.S. Chamber of Commerce, a vocal advocate of simplification,[60] met with NPBMA representatives to assess the prospects for industry-wide cooperation and to draw up plans for a survey of current products. The NPBMA then surveyed paving brick manufacturers to gather firm-level data on the kinds and styles of brick they were producing and in what quantities. Based on this data, the NPBMA drew up a

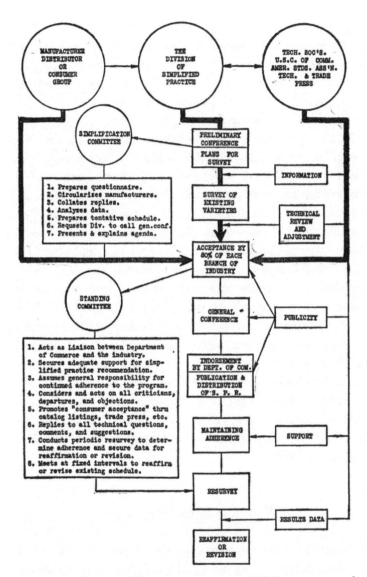

Figure 9. The simplified practice process: U.S. Department of Commerce, Bureau of Standards, *Refrigerator Ice Compartments: Simplified Practice Recommendation R109-29 [issued February 27, 1930], Effective Date, October 1, 1929* (Washington, DC: Government Printing Office, 1930), 9. A similar diagram was included in Brady, *Industrial Standardization*, 130.

proposal to eliminate those varieties of brick that were being produced in smaller volumes. The Department of Commerce then invited all interested parties to a formal meeting ("general conference"), which was held at the Department of Commerce and featured a keynote address by Hoover himself. The general conference brought together Commerce Department officials, representatives of the manufacturers, War and Navy Department officials, and the industry's "consumers" – in this instance, federal, state, and city highway engineers. The conference approved unanimously the elimination of 55 of 66 varieties of paving brick and created a standing committee to consider further reductions. (Subsequent reductions brought the number of standard sizes down to 7 in 1922 and 4 in 1925.)[61] The Commerce Department then mailed the final recommendation and conference minutes to all interested parties, along with an acceptance form.[62] Once a sufficient proportion of manufacturers, distributors, and consumers had returned signed forms accepting the recommendation, the Department of Commerce issued *Simplified Practice Recommendation No. 1*. This basic peacetime process, used to simplify an array of commodities, varied little over the years.[63] It was, in the judgment of political scientist E. Pendleton Herring, Hoover's "outstanding achievement" in his efforts to encourage industrial cooperation.[64]

Parallels in war and peace

In multiple ways, Hoover's process mirrored that of the Conservation Division during the war.[65] First and foremost, *collaboration* with trade associations was at the core of both, the collaborative process encompassing the array of economic interests that spanned the long chain of production and consumption. Just as the Conservation Division had galvanized the entire business world of fashion, from textile manufacturers to clothing designers and fashion editors, to conserve wool during the Great War, the Division of Simplified Practice sought to involve in the post-war deliberations all economic actors with a stake in a particular commodity. Trade associations, which again tripled in number to some 2,200 between 1919 and 1931,[66] served as critical intermediaries, as they had in the war. The simplification of bank checks, for example, involved not only the multitude of state and national banks but also suppliers of printed checks and major users of bank checks. The banks were represented by the American Bankers Association (ABA), which had launched its own simplification initiative in 1921. When its process stalled, the ABA enlisted the DSP in 1925 to help in negotiating agreements with the lithographers and printers that supplied blank checks. Representing the lithographers and printers at the general conference were the United Typothetae of America, the Association of Bank and Commercial Stationers, the Lithographers Cooperative Association, and the National Association of Employing Lithographers. Major users were represented by the National Association of Manufacturers, the National Association of Purchasing Agents, the Railway Accounting Officers Association, the Railway Treasury Officers Association, and federal agencies.[67] What has come to be called "associationalism" was in the air before, during, and after World War I, and Hoover's collaborative process served to amplify the importance of trade associations in the 1920s.[68]

As had been true during the war, however, there were boundaries around the collaboration process, at least initially. Retail consumers were expected to benefit from simplification, they were becoming organized for other purposes in the 1920s,[69] and consumer advocates such as Stuart Chase enthusiastically endorsed Hoover's simplification initiative.[70] But in the deliberations that produced simplified practice recommendations (SPRs) through the 1920s, "consumers," in practice, meant intermediate consumers, not retail consumers.[71] In the aftermath of the buyers' strike of 1919–20 and as the modern consumer movement began to coalesce, manufacturers, distributors, and perhaps government officials were reluctant to include retail or "ultimate" consumers in simplified practice conferences. "It was felt by certain individuals," the home economist Alice Edwards noted obliquely, "that their [consumers'] presence might be disturbing to some of the other representatives and, therefore, that simplification programs would be best served if representatives of ultimate consumers were absent."[72] Beginning in 1923, however, one organization – the American Home Economics Association (AHEA) – did participate in the formulation of several simplified practice recommendations.[73] Representatives of the AHEA attended a preliminary conference to simplify bed blankets, conducted their own survey "to learn how individual consumers felt in the matter of sizes of blankets," and participated in the general conference in 1924 that produced *Simplified Practice Recommendation No. 11*.[74] The AHEA, which would later work with the American Engineering Standards Committee on quality standards,[75] also took part in DSP-organized agreements to simplify steel lockers, sterling silver flatware, tinware, and ice cake sizes.[76] In the mid-1920s, at the Division's suggestion, the AHEA formed a permanent committee to solicit ideas for the simplification of household commodities and to work with the Division on a simplified-practice "program as relates to the home."[77] By 1940, Edwards reported, organizations such as the AHEA, the General Federation of Women's Clubs, and the American Association of University Women were routinely invited to participate in the deliberations "when the proposal is of interest to them."[78]

Neither initially nor later did workers or trade unions participate in the simplification process. Hoover supported an array of labor-friendly policies and had included unions in the President's Conference on Unemployment, which he organized in the Fall of 1921.[79] The FAES's 1921 report *Waste in Industry*, moreover, devoted more than 100 pages to labor problems such as unemployment, strikes and lockouts, and industrial accidents, and, as noted earlier, it placed responsibility for waste largely on management.[80] But the simplification of products, like scientific management, was evidently seen as the province of management, not labor, in the United States. In 1925, William Green, president of the American Federation of Labor, a union of skilled workers, endorsed the work of the Division of Simplified Practice, despite the fact that it reduced demand for skilled labor, because reductions in product variety were intended to lower the cost of living.[81] A few years later, he did express reservations about "standardization," both within firms ("mass production") and across firms ("simplified practice"), highlighting the decline in manufacturing jobs since 1919, inadequate distribution of the fruits of rising productivity, and the lack of opportunities for workers to "be educated to an understanding of the production process as a whole and to share in directing policies which affect their daily work." But he did not suggest that unions should have a seat at the table in industry-wide decisions to adopt simplified practice recommendations.[82] A 1926 *Primer of Simplified Practice* acknowledged concerns that simplified practice was "automatizing workers," but maintained that the worker enjoyed higher productivity, higher wages, increased buying power, and in some cases a shorter workday, all of which "compensates him in a measure for the monotony of repetitive process."[83] Only after World War II – and for a different audience – did a list of the benefits of simplified practice include a section "To the Employee." This appeared in a 1951 pamphlet prepared for the European context, where unions were more powerful, and highlighted four benefits for labor: "1. Steady work ... 2. Steady earnings. 3. Sustained earning or buying power. 4. Less time spent 'in training' for new jobs." These benefits, an editorial note declared, unions "generally understood and accepted."[84] Be that as it may, collaboration, in practice, was limited to government, business, and the occasional consumer representative.[85]

In peace as in war, secondly, the simplification process was *data driven*. Proposals to eliminate specific product varieties were invariably grounded not in technical data but in a survey of recent production or sales. (Hence, the Bureau of Standards' objections to housing the new division.) The survey was carried out by industry representatives, one of whom was designated "Secretary Hoover's representative" to encourage firms to furnish proprietary data and probably to allay concerns about the legality of doing so.[86] The survey data often startled industry participants, the division reported: "it is a common experience to find the groups themselves amazed at the possible combinations of sizes, types, etc., that have been produced."[87] Very quickly, an empirical rule emerged, which DSP staff regarded as "axiomatic" by the mid-1920s: 20 percent of product varieties usually accounted for some 80 percent of

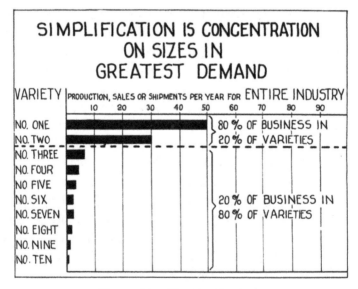

Figure 10. The 80–20 axiom:
Priest, *A Primer of Simplified Practice*, 14.

sales (figure 10).[88] The results of a survey of bed-blanket production in 1920–2, for example, very roughly conformed to the
80–20 axiom. It found that, of a total of 78 sizes of blankets on
the market, 4 sizes accounted for 75.62 percent of the production of wool or wool-mix blankets, while 7 sizes accounted for
80.12 percent of the production of cotton blankets. *SPR No. 11*
reduced the overall number of bed blanket sizes from 78 to 12
standard sizes.[89] As a 1930 management textbook explained,
in terms reminiscent of Ford's success in "standardizing the
consumer," firms that simplified their products were "catering
to the tastes and needs of the *average* buyer, leaving those
who fall outside their field of specialization to the special-order
manufacturer."[90] And in those cases where production or sales
of large firms dominated the data, this procedure meant that
the selected standard sizes would be those of the large firms. In
any case, the collective decision to elevate 20 percent of product varieties to the status of standard or "stock" sizes rested
securely on detailed sales data, a stage in the simplification
process that the DSP termed "fixing the facts."[91]

Analyzing the survey data and preparing the supplemen-
tary materials necessary to garner industry-wide support for a
recommendation was occasionally a huge task. The simplification and standardization of the capacity of paper grocers' bags,
for example, entailed engineering studies to figure out how to
change over existing machinery to manufacture the proposed
standard sizes, preparation of an instruction manual that
was mailed to all manufacturers of grocery bags and makers
of bag manufacturing machines, and design of a Commerce
Department-approved emblem to be used on standard-size
bags (figure 11). The Bureau also agreed to maintain a set of
standard bags for reference and to inspect sample bags submitted by manufacturers. In all, two years elapsed between the
preliminary and general conferences.[92] To support the simplification of pocket knives, the Pocket Knife Manufacturer's
Standard Catalogue was prepared, illustrating the 140 "basic

This emblem certifies standard size

and this label **will guarantee standard size, full count, & uniform packing.**

Members Of The Grocery Bag Manufacturers Service Bureau.

Look for the orange-and-blue Label

THE GROCERY BAG MANUFACTURERS SERVICE BUREAU 53 Park Place, New York

Figure 11. Standard-size emblem:
Priest, *A Primer of Simplified Practice,* 38.

dies" that were designated as standard. Copies could be obtained from the Division of Simplified Practice.[93] In another instance, unanimous approval of a recommendation to reduce grinding-wheel sizes from 715,200 varieties to 255,800 rested on five years of research.[94]

A solid foundation of data provided critical support for Hoover's efforts, like Shaw's, thirdly, to *maximize consensus* as a means of enhancing adherence. Time and again, attendees at simplified practice conferences were reminded that unanimity was crucial.[95] In some cases, this limited the scope of the eliminations initially adopted. At the general conference in 1923 to simplify milk and cream bottles, for example, one group proposed reducing bottles to a single variety (i.e., height) for each size, but, the minutes reported, "the majority felt that the intent and purpose of the conference would be defeated if they attempted to go so far in the initial step." So, to achieve "unanimous action," the conference set 3 standard heights each for half-pint, pint, and quart bottles (previously available, respectively, in 14, 13, and 12 varieties) and a single-diameter cap.[96] The general conference to simplify paper endorsed standard paper sizes, including today's standard American "letter" size (8½ in. × 11 in.), but postponed other measures because of concerns that they "would have resulted in an attempt to revolutionize the industry."[97] It was a testament to the solid groundwork laid by trade associations and DSP staff that a single "general conference" was usually sufficient to achieve unanimity on simplified practice recommendations. With very few exceptions, the SPRs opened with the words "In accordance with the *unanimous* action of the joint conference ..." (figure 12).[98] Backed by unanimity in the general conference,

SIMPLIFIED PRACTICE RECOMMENDATION NO. 7.

FACE BRICK AND COMMON BRICK.

In accordance with the unanimous action of the joint conference of representatives of manufacturers, distributors, and users named on the opposite page, of face brick and common brick, the United States Department of Commerce, through the Bureau of Standards, recommends that recognized approximate dimensions of the above types of brick shall conform to the following:

Approximate Dimensions Expressed in Inches.

Types.	Length.	Thickness.	Width.
Common brick...........	8	2¼	3¾
Rough face brick........	8	2½	3¾
Smooth face brick......	8	2½	3½

GEORGE K. BURGESS,
Director, Bureau of Standards.

APPROVED, June 21, 1923, subject to regular annual revision by similar conference.

HERBERT HOOVER,
Secretary of Commerce.

Figure 12.   Consensus: *SPR No. 7: Face Brick and Common Brick* (1924), 3.

recommendations were then circulated to the industry for acceptance. In the acceptance process, the DSP defined consensus as acceptance by 80 percent (by volume) of each of the interested groups – manufacturers, distributors, and consumers.[99] As DSP Chief Edwin W. Ely later explained, 80 percent was "merely an arbitrary figure," "just . . . something positive to talk about," a number that seemed "a fair basis" for judging industry acceptance.[100]

Only rarely did a proposed simplified practice recommendation fail to achieve industry acceptance once it had been approved by a general conference. The paint business was one of the more intensely competitive lines of business and, given the industry's difficulty in achieving a consensus before and after the war, it is not surprising that a simplified practice recommendation for paint and varnish colors and containers ran into trouble.[101] Initiated by the National Retail Hardware Association (NRHA) and endorsed by a general conference, a simplified practice recommendation was accepted by 80 percent (by volume) of distributors and consumers, but not manufacturers. In the face of manufacturers' resistance, a set of "limitations" was approved in 1924, with the NRHA, which favored a greater reduction in house paint colors, abstaining. The paint and varnish limitations were not codified in an SPR until 1932.[102] Other initiatives that were approved by a general conference but failed to gain industry acceptance included the simplification of boxed elastic webbing and a proposal to eliminate polished finishes on shovels, spades, and scoops, the latter case necessitating a second general conference.[103] Also, a handful of SPR numbers were assigned to specific commodities and then reassigned to others, which likely indicated a failure to gain industry-wide acceptance.[104]

In some cases, consensus was achieved but only after herculean efforts. The most challenging, second only perhaps to garment sizes,[105] was the simplification of lumber sizes and grades.[106] Lumber markets were highly fragmented with strong regional differences and interests; from a technical standpoint, lumber was exceptionally difficult to standardize; and the standardization of lumber touched on a wide array of economic interests, from manufacturers, wholesalers, and retailers (of lumber as well as wooden products) to architects, engineers, general contractors, and government agencies. Lumber interests had pursued nationwide standardization since the early twentieth century, as noted earlier, and after World War I, the effort resumed at the American Lumber Conference in 1919, which enlisted the National Lumber Manufacturers Association (NLMA) to undertake studies in conjunction with the U.S. Forest Products Laboratory. Again, progress proved elusive. But by this time lumber was facing not only the traditional regional and inter-firm competition, but also the "new competition" from substitute building materials such as cement, which put a premium on concerted action to defend lumber markets.[107] So the NLMA turned to Secretary Hoover and his new Division of Simplified Practice for help in standardizing lumber sizes and grades. For Hoover, simplifying lumber was especially important because it would reinforce his broader goal of enhancing the American standard of living, which, he believed, rested in part on better housing.[108]

Lumber simplification entailed a marathon of meetings and Hoover's personal intervention merely to reach a second-best solution. First came a series of preliminary meetings, followed by *four* general conferences between 1922 and 1924, each attracting more than 100 attendees. At the third general conference, which approved standard lumber sizes, Hoover intervened personally to broker a compromise when manufacturers and retailers found themselves at loggerheads over ⅟₃₂ of an inch. The difference evidently mattered most for freight rates and thus affected interregional competition.[109] When the manufacturers and retailers could not reach an agreement, Hoover convened an evening meeting with five representatives of each.[110] The result was a double standard: the minimum thickness of a "standard size" surfaced 1-inch-thick board was set at $^{25}/_{32}$ of an inch, while $^{26}/_{32}$ of an inch was set as the minimum for the "extra standard" surfaced 1-inch-thick board (later called the "industrial standard").[111] The new standard sizes (plural) were unanimously approved, along with an array of other standards regarding lumber grading, nomenclature, etc., at the fourth general conference in 1924. Even though the industry had failed to agree on a single standard thickness, Hoover touted lumber simplification, the NLMA later reported, as "'Exhibit A' of what an industry, with able leaders and sincerity of purpose can achieve for itself, without governmental interference or restraint."[112] What the NLMA could also have noted is that the lumber industry, after decades of futile efforts, was only able to move toward consensus because of the critical assistance lent by Hoover and the DSP. The dual standards proved durable; they were not replaced by a single standard until 1970.[113]

Once 80 percent of manufacturers, distributors, and consumers had accepted a recommendation, fourthly, the Commerce Department published it as an official "Simplified Practice Recommendation," the equivalent of the War Industries Board's *conservation schedule*. The imprimatur of the federal government was clearly expressed on the title page – in the words "United States Department of Commerce" emblazoned across the top, in a graphic depiction of the department's seal, and in the words "issued by the Bureau of Standards" (figure 13). The introductory text, moreover, invariably described the SPR as the official recommendation not of the industry or trade associations but of the Department of Commerce itself. Published by the Government Printing Office, each SPR bore the explicit approval of both the director of the Bureau of Standards and the Secretary of Commerce (see figure 12). "It is one thing to set up simplified standards and another to carry them out," *The Furniture Index* observed in 1922. "To make a program of standardization 'stick' it is

Figure 13. The federal government's imprimatur.

necessary that . . . advantage [be] taken of the great educational force which is exerted when the government stamp of approval is given to a program of simplified standards."[114] The DSP sent free copies to those who had formally accepted an SPR or wished to consider doing so, while the Government Printing Office sold copies to others (totaling nearly 300,000 by the end of 1926).[115]

Like the World War I conservation schedules, moreover, the SPRs included measures to dampen competitive pressures.

Recommendations almost always took effect industry-wide on a specific future date. For individual firms, as World War I officials had recognized, transitioning to a simplified line was risky in the short term, when they stood to lose customers to their competitors while waiting for lower costs and advertising to stimulate sales. "[F]rom the standpoint of the individual manufacturer," a *Printers' Ink* writer warned in June 1921, "it takes too long for low production costs and selling prices to stimulate sales. In the meantime his competitors will be out with 'new and snappy styles,' and how will the salability of his goods fare during that interim? That is the real question."[116] The DSP's answer was the same as the Conservation Division's: the SPR included an effective date on which concerted action would begin, thus offering individual companies some protection by eliminating the risky transition period. And the effective date was usually set far enough in the future to allow firms to sell off their non-standard products.[117] Standing committees were also appointed by the general conference to meet annually and consider revisions of the standards, based on the latest sales data. This opened up opportunities for new standard sizes when sales data warranted. In 1924, the paving-brick standing committee, for example, adopted "a guiding formula" for revisions of its list of recognized sizes: if a standard brick size accounted for less than 2.5 percent of total shipments for three successive years, it was dropped; if a new brick size accounted for 5 percent or more of shipments, it was added; and, taken together, the standard types should represent at least 75 percent of total shipments.[118] The DSP also conducted periodic resurveys of sales to estimate adherence to the SPRs, which enabled individual firms to gauge the extent to which their competitors were abiding by the recommendations.[119]

As with World War I conservation measures, fifthly, getting Americans to accept the new standard sizes took sustained *persuasion*. The 1921 report *Waste in Industry* recognized as much in recommending that men's clothing manufacturers reduce their lines, manufacture "for stock," and then "adopt vigorous, positive selling methods, backed up by effective national advertising," to induce their customers to buy stock items.[120] Individual manufacturers who simplified their product lines testified – frequently in the pages of Shaw's magazines – that simplification posed daunting merchandising challenges. The president of a pharmaceutical house that had cut its product lines drastically summed up the dilemma this way:

> First, the actual volume of sales on the 65% of the items eliminated was a worth-while percentage of our total volume. We were throwing away business. Would we be able to make it up on the remaining items, and that quickly, without suffering a slump? Second, what would be the attitude of the jobbers, the retailers, and the doctors – the three classes we were serving, now that we were unable to give them everything they wanted? How would that affect us in the race for business?[121]

The company's answer was "a new selling policy" – "active salesmanship" – that altered relations with their salesmen and their customers. They held a convention of their salesmen "to sell them on our new policies," furnished them with scripts of selling points, and had them take a salesmanship course. "As I look back on our experience," the president reported, "I should say that a definite selling program is a necessary accompaniment to a program of elimination."[122] Tire manufacturer Harvey S. Firestone agreed. "People have become too accustomed to having every passing fancy satisfied without thought that others as well as themselves must pay the bill." His conclusion: "Simplification is largely a matter of education"; consumers had to be taught that standardized products were cheaper and of better quality.[123] And convincing consumers that standardized products were "truly better and cheaper," consumer advocates F. J. Schlink and Robert Brady noted, was a "long and difficult process."[124] The American Multigraph

Figure 14.   American Multigraph Sales Co. advertisement, 1924:
"Buyers Will Change Bad Buying Habits," *System* 46, no. 6
(December 1924): 802–3.

Sales Company offered manufacturers and distributors its services in educating consumers on the value of simplified products: "Buyers Will Change Bad Buying Habits," a 1924 Multigraph advertisement (figure 14) promised, "If Sellers Will Show Them I low." The General Electric Company moved cautiously, trying to nudge its customers toward the new "staple" items without losing those who preferred specialized products. "While the General Electric Company is prepared now – as in the past – to furnish a variety of Wiring Devices for every electrical requirement," its 1924 catalog declared, "it joins the Division of Simplified Practice of the United States Department of Commerce in urging customers to adjust their requirements to the use of staples devices regularly carried in stock."[125]

For some manufacturers, the main challenge was to persuade their own salesmen and jobbers to accept simplified product lines. "Sales departments, as a rule, like to give

customers what they want," a prominent loom works manager observed, "and a sales department is apt to think that
the variety that has been built up today represents, in large
measure, customers' desires in their field." So salesmen and
jobbers had to be persuaded that customers would see the
value in a simplified line.[126] This perception accorded with the
experience of the Walworth Manufacturing Company, when
it reduced its catalog of pipe fittings, valves, and tools from
17,000 to 610. "Salesmen and dealers used to catering to every
wish and whim of the customer," its president reported, "are
at first inclined to protest. . . . To counteract this, education
is necessary." While it found "a general argument on standardization, the big subject of the day," to be persuasive with
its customers (i.e., engineers), the company emphasized the
bottom-line benefits of faster turnover to its sales force.[127] A
manufacturer of hand tools reported that it took "some two
or three years" to overcome the opposition of its salesmen to
a simplified line and that jobbers, too, had to "be educated by
the manufacturer . . . The whole proposition must be sold and
sold hard."[128] When the American Writing Paper Company
reduced its grades of paper by more than 80 percent between
1917 and 1921, it dropped jobbers altogether and designated
local merchants as its agents, sent the agents' salesmen on
plant tours to educate them, and established a "service department" to deal directly with printers, its main customers.[129]
The Scott Paper Company used a similar strategy to break the
resistance of jobbers to a simplified product line. After reducing its product lines from 2,000 private brands to 3 of its own
brands in 1910, Scott Paper stopped working with jobbers altogether and turned directly to retailers, extending them credit,
establishing a chain of warehouses, and engaging in national
advertising to build consumer demand for its brands. Once it
had established a national name for its brands – and jobbers
were therefore willing to handle its limited line of products –
Scott Paper dismantled its retail operation (with its attendant

costs and risks) and again relied on jobbers to distribute its products.[130]

The Division of Simplified Practice recognized, too, that simplified practice recommendations would have to be actively "sold." Those who signed the standard SPR acceptance form, like manufacturers in World War I, pledged to "use our best effort in securing general adoption of the simplified list."[131] When bank checks were simplified in 1926, the general conference anticipated consumer resistance. "[D]ifficulties will arise," the minutes noted, "with the few bank customers who desire checks or voucher checks to suit their own ideas or forms which are intended primarily to be advertisements and only incidentally serve as checks." Printers and lithographers were encouraged to contact banks before filling an order for nonstandard checks, and banks, in turn, would need to explain to their customers "the unnecessary costliness of handling checks nonstandard either in size or form."[132] In general, the DSP's chief noted in 1924, "[p]roducts, however meritorious, do not 'sell' themselves." Once adopted, standards had to "be thoroughly and persistently advertised and demonstrated."[133] By the mid-1920s, the division used the term "cross-acceptance" to refer to the acceptors' broad obligation to promote simplified lines in all phases of their business – purchasing, production, and sales.[134] "Interlocking of acceptances," *A Primer of Simplified Practice* explained, "is the leaven which works throughout the entire mass."[135]

In efforts, as consumer advocates Schlink and Brady put it, "to break down the resistance" of consumers to simplified product lines,[136] advertising took on new importance. Consumer education on a scale to match mass production meant mass advertising – a relationship that a 1923 McGraw-Hill Company advertisement spelled out succinctly: "Simplification presupposes mass production. Mass production necessitates mass selling. That means advertising."[137] Advertising surged in the 1920s,[138] and Hoover's push for simplification both enhanced the size of the wave and gave rise to a novel use of advertising. As a *Printers' Ink Monthly* writer explained, companies that engaged in simplification, many of which had never advertised before, were now using advertising to *quash* demand for their eliminated products and redirect it to their simplified line – "us[ing] advertising," in other words, "to lead demand instead of drifting with it."[139] Even more so than in the Great War, effective advertising was an essential element of a simplification strategy. "In each case of simplification, whether by a manufacturer or an association," the *Printers' Ink Monthly* writer concluded, "it has been followed by advertising to create a known-in-advance demand for the simplified line."[140]

Like the Commercial Economy Board members who mobilized the women's fashion industry in their wool conservation efforts during World War I, finally, Secretary Hoover and DSP officials disavowed, time and again, any intention to interfere with *style or taste*. The potential constraints imposed by simplification loomed larger than ever in the 1920s, as "the style factor," for a variety of reasons, became more pronounced in American business. Where style had once been associated mainly with the "clothing and personal adornment" of the wealthy, one observer noted, "style has filtered down from the upper to the lower classes," its scope had broadened to include household furnishings and automobiles, and styles had become more volatile, spreading faster and changing more rapidly.[141] Hoover himself assured bed manufacturers that simplification affected only their dimensions, not "quality or style, or anything else that is based upon ingenuity."[142] In a 1923 article describing the DSP's work in *Nation's Business*, DSP Chief Durgin stressed the limits of simplification. "[T]here is no thought of restricting individuality or curtailing art, or interfering with that initiative and invention, which is such an important part of our American capabilities," he explained. "The only object is to eliminate those useless and trivial differences which have so cluttered our producing, distributing and merchandising system, and in consequence have led to enormous wastes."[143]

The next year, Durgin's successor, Ray M. Hudson, portrayed standardization broadly as a redirection of ingenuity: "standardization compels attention to individuality in those features where there should be individuality," he maintained, "by preventing attempts at individuality in those features where individuality is superficial and useless."[144] How to assess superficiality and uselessness he did not say, but, given the DSP's favored metrics, he was surely thinking of sales data and production runs. The DSP's 1926 *Primer of Simplified Practice* likewise reassured readers:

> [Simplified practice] has nothing to do with questions of individual taste or artistic preference. It in no way restricts improvements in method or the progress of invention. It does not attempt to suppress or submerge individuality. Its object is not the creation of a rigid régime of so-called standardization where there is no regard for beauty or art. Neither does it limit the opportunity of the individual to procure those things which satisfy cultural desires.[145]

As the decade ended, reassurances – usually phrased as disavowals – continued. "[T]he simplification movement is not one which seeks to hamper the proper exercise of taste and preference on the part of the public," the 1930 *Commerce Yearbook* maintained. "Where variety has any real utility or attractiveness, neither the industries concerned nor the Department of Commerce are disposed to disregard the fact. No basis exists for the notion sometimes expressed that in the United States there is growing up a monotony of styles; the aim is solely to eliminate varieties which have no real reason for being."[146] Here, too, any "real reason for being" would presumably be reflected in sales data – "the acid test of demand," as a DSP bulletin put it.[147] On a rhetorical level, deference to the arbiters of taste and style in American business characterized simplification in peace as well as war, although what mattered most in peacetime were sales numbers that permitted mass production.

In two ways, however, Hoover's peacetime process diverged from Shaw's wartime practice, though these were differences in degree, not kind. The *voluntary nature* of the simplification process, as one would expect, was more pronounced in peacetime. The agreements reached by the War Industries Board's Conservation Division, although ostensibly voluntary, had been forged amidst the exigencies of war. In peacetime, Hoover and DSP staff stressed repeatedly, such agreements were to be entirely voluntary. "[T]he initiative of this work must necessarily come from within industry itself," the 1922 *Commerce Yearbook* emphasized, in announcing the creation of the DSP; "the division must await specific demands from individual industries before its services can be usefully extended to their problems."[148] Arch Shaw put it bluntly in the *Harvard Business Review* in 1923: the new division "orders nothing, it dictates nothing; the initiative must come from business itself."[149] Although on at least one occasion Durgin suggested that government regulation might ensue if product diversity became "a menace to the welfare of the average citizen,"[150] the DSP's publicity uniformly stressed the strictly voluntary nature of the process. "The division's part is one of cooperation only," the 1926 *Primer* insisted. "It never forces its services on any industry. When its services have been solicited, it advises and suggests, but never issues orders or makes decisions."[151] By the mid-1920s, a disclaimer to that effect appeared in the minutes of some general conferences, with variations on this phrasing: "In arriving at this unanimity of opinion, it was understood by all that the Department of Commerce, through its division of simplified practice, is not initiating this movement."[152] Articulated time and again, the division's bedrock principle, in the words of a ten-year review of its history, was that "simplified practice must always be a voluntary activity, subject neither to regulation nor enforcement."[153]

Some observers have disputed the voluntary nature of the simplification process, portraying Hoover's many conferences as operating in a top-down mode.[154] And on at least one occasion, a DSP publication seems to suggest that the division itself initiated a preliminary conference, this one to simplify taper roller bearings.[155] But some months earlier, it turns out, a prominent automobile manufacturer had asked the DSP to initiate the simplification project.[156] The official history in the taper roller bearings SPR portrayed it as a joint initiative of the DSP and the Society of Automotive Engineers.[157] As the simplified-practice program neared its 10-year anniversary, a conference of standing-committee chairmen considered whether the DSP *should* initiate projects. When he joined the division, a former DSP staff member recalled, "it was definitely stated we were to lean backward when it came to making suggestions about simplification." Should the division become more assertive? "We have rigidly adhered to the original philosophy of the movement, that we should sit back, like the bashful maiden, and wait to be proposed to and not make the proposal ourselves," DSP Chief Edwin W. Ely explained. "We have stuck to the principle of waiting to be invited, and all the time comes this pressure, 'Why don't you go out and start something?'" The discussants ultimately concluded that the DSP should continue to tread carefully, approaching trade associations but not individual firms.[158]

In practice, simplification in peacetime proceeded voluntarily, driven by the energetic efforts of DSP staff to sell it to American business. The experience of World War I had prepared fertile ground, of course, by familiarizing American business with Shaw's simplification process. With the publication of *Waste in Industry*, moreover, Hoover's personal mission to reduce waste and his enthusiasm for simplification were widely known. "Up and down the manufacturing and distributing line," *Printers' Ink* reported shortly after Hoover took office as Secretary of Commerce, "simplification is being mentioned almost as frequently as the weather."[159] Hoover expected the new division to move aggressively,[160] and it clearly did not sit back and wait to be approached. Quite to the contrary, its staff undertook a massive campaign to sell simplified practice to trade associations and whip up demand.[161] In his first year in office, Chief Durgin personally addressed 50 business associations and attended another 11 meetings. Meanwhile, his several technical or special assistants spoke before or attended the meetings of another 41 groups, bringing the total number of business groups to which the DSP reached out in its first year to more than 100.[162] Durgin also sought to enlist the business press in support of simplification, following up a speech to the Association of Business Editors with a letter to all 51 editors "asking for suggestions, editorials, and other means of propaganda furthering the simplification movement."[163] Arch Shaw reinforced this early publicity wave by sending letters to 125 of his business contacts, "expounding the gospel of Simplification."[164] Durgin and his technical assistant also placed a flurry of articles about simplification in *Scientific American* and an array of trade journals, launching a bibliography on simplification that would soon span multiple pages.[165] Emphatically voluntary in peacetime, Hoover's push for simplification was buttressed by a sweeping publicity blitz to sell simplified practice and elicit volunteers.

The DSP also differed from Shaw's Conservation Division in the *enforcement powers* it could marshal. It, too, employed social sanctions to encourage acceptance of and adherence to the recommendations – pledges, as noted earlier, as well as appeals to modernity or far-sightedness.[166] Only occasionally did the DSP, in a nod to patriotism, portray simplified practice as important to national welfare or national defense.[167] But it did not command the leverage that the War Industry Board's priorities power had given the Conservation Division. Still, it was able to wield considerable power by working closely with the Federal Specifications Board (FSB). Created in October 1921 as another pillar of Hoover's waste-elimination efforts, the FSB set parameters that products had to meet if businesses wanted to sell them to the federal government – the nation's, if not the world's, largest consumer.[168] Hoover actively enlisted state and local officials in the specifications-setting process, and federal specifications were often adopted by state and local governments as well as industrial buyers, thus shaping American markets up, down, and across the economy.[169] The FSB's first directory of specifications, which Hoover dubbed the "Buyers' Bible,"[170] encompassed 6,650 commodities and – in testimony both to enthusiasm for standardization and to the fragmentation of American standards – listed some 27,100 specifications issued by federal, state, and local officials as well as public utilities.[171] Since federal specifications generally "called for the simplified or standardized articles," Hoover later explained, "they reinforced that whole program."[172] For the Division of Simplified Practice, federal specifications thus served as a kind of soft coercion.[173] Unlike the Conservation Division, the DSP could not deny access to resources, but only those firms whose products met federal specifications – and their associated simplified practice recommendations – gained entry to federal markets.

But these were minor differences. Overall, Hoover's resurrection of simplified practice followed closely the model that Arch Wilkinson Shaw had established to extraordinary effect during the Great War. In the long run, what truly set the Division of Simplified Practice apart from the War Industries Board's Conservation Division – a difference in kind, not merely degree – was the durability of its accomplishments. While traces of the Conservation Division's work began to fade once the war ended, the DSP's promotion of simplified practice shaped American manufacturing for decades to come.

6

Diffusing Mass Production

From Arch Wilkinson Shaw's achievements during the Great War to the persistence of standard sizes today, simplified practice has traced a long arc through American history. Its elements, as this chapter shows, included impressive growth in the number of standards, expansion of the Division of Simplified Practice's mission in the late 1920s, its unlikely persistence through the Great Depression, yet another boost to simplified practice in World War II, and a sustained push to diffuse mass-production techniques both at home and abroad in the 1950s. Although the federal government's role in orchestrating "voluntary standards," as they came to be called, virtually ended in the 1970s, standard sizes and the collective agreements that underlay them proved amazingly durable. Which is why the American consumer today can comfortably buy queen-sized sheets for a queen-sized bed, letter-sized paper that fits in a letter-sized folder, and rolls of toilet paper of a width that fits in a toilet paper holder – all without thinking about it.

Initially, concrete results were slow in coming. Given the Division of Simplified Practice's complex, multi-stage process for developing simplified practice recommendations (figure 9) and the extraordinary amount of outreach that its staff were doing, this is hardly surprising. Still, in November 1922, after nine months in office, DSP Chief William A. Durgin signaled his disappointment – or perhaps anticipated Hoover's dissatisfaction – by characterizing a memo to his boss in late 1922 as "a progress report, or lack of progress report, . . . as you may decide." Only two simplified practice recommendations had been approved – No. 1 for paving bricks, which pre-dated Durgin's arrival, and No. 2, just being issued, for bedsteads, springs, and mattresses. Durgin, aided by four assistants, had established contact with manufacturers in 82 product lines or "fields," and trade-association surveys were under way to collect data on 19 products, ranging from barrels and blankets to tinfoil and warehouse forms. In another 37 fields, Durgin held out some hope that the simplification process would take hold, but 26 fields, he reported, "thus far have not been interested."[1]

Even so, word of the Commerce Department's simplified practice initiative almost immediately began to spread abroad because of its implications for competition in foreign markets. The editor of the British edition of Shaw's magazine *System*, Cecil Chisholm, brought simplification, which he lauded as "America's new industrial policy," to the attention of British business interests in an article in *The* [London] *Times Imperial and Foreign Trade and Engineering Supplement* in April 1922 (figure 15). In the same month, the British *System* also carried an article on simplification by Chisholm. These were followed by three more articles that Chisholm penned for the London *Times* supplement that year.[2] The Great War had stimulated a push for standardization not only in the U.S. but also in Europe, especially in Germany, which pursued it energetically after the war.[3] This cross-national surge of interest in standardization, centered mainly on its technical forms, had potentially widespread ramifications as competition in international markets ramped up after the war. The elimination of

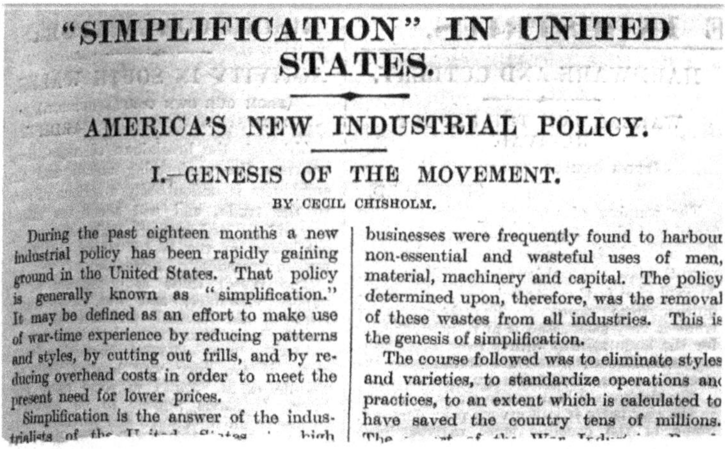

"SIMPLIFICATION" IN UNITED STATES.

AMERICA'S NEW INDUSTRIAL POLICY.

I.—GENESIS OF THE MOVEMENT.

BY CECIL CHISHOLM.

During the past eighteen months a new industrial policy has been rapidly gaining ground in the United States. That policy is generally known as "simplification." It may be defined as an effort to make use of war-time experience by reducing patterns and styles, by cutting out frills, and by reducing overhead costs in order to meet the present need for lower prices.

Simplification is the answer of the indus-

businesses were frequently found to harbour non-essential and wasteful uses of men, material, machinery and capital. The policy determined upon, therefore, was the removal of these wastes from all industries. This is the genesis of simplification.

The course followed was to eliminate styles and varieties, to standardize operations and practices, to an extent which is calculated to have saved the country tens of millions.

Figure 15. Simplification in *The* [London] *Times Supplement*: Cecil Chisholm, "'Simplification' in United States: America's New Industrial Policy: I. – Genesis of the Movement," *The* [London] *Times Imperial and Foreign Trade and Engineering Supplement*, April 29, 1922, 131.

waste in all its forms, American advocates believed, was essential if U.S. firms were to be able to compete in foreign markets after the war; Secretary Hoover regarded it to be "of profound value in maintenance of our export trade."[4] And if Britain or Germany pushed ahead with national standards faster than the U.S., their standards might become entrenched in foreign markets, shutting out American products. "[T]he day may not be far distant," an American engineer warned after attending an international standardization conference in Germany in 1922, "when American manufacturers will receive inquiries from oversea countries according to the German national standards."[5] Cecil Chisholm voiced similar concerns across the Atlantic, warning British manufacturers to take note of post-war developments in the U.S.: "wherever [simplification] enables the American maker to greatly reduce the cost of doing business as well as the cost of production per unit, it may have important effects on American export trade."[6] British manufacturers should pay careful attention, as their Swedish counterparts were doing: "It is an industrial policy of first-rate importance and one which can scarcely be ignored."[7] "One thing is certain," he warned in December 1922: "The work of the Department of Commerce is bearing practical fruit."[8]

Yet, despite what seemed like impressive achievements to outside observers, Durgin again expressed dissatisfaction with his division's results in mid-1923. Another seven SPRs – born of preliminary conferences, grounded in product surveys, approved in general conferences – were awaiting industry acceptance, and 24 new surveys of existing practice were under way.[9] Durgin, now with a staff of seven assistants, was working intensively with several large industries (e.g., lumber, farm implements, retail hardware). Meanwhile, at the suggestion of the American Marine Association, the division had created the American Marine Standards Committee (AMSC) to pursue simplification in shipbuilding, its standards published in a separate series.[10] A few months later, though Durgin lauded the AMSC's work and reported that 56 DSP-organized product surveys were now in progress, he voiced broader disappointment: "You will note that progress has been in comparatively unimportant fields," Durgin wrote to Hoover, "while we are making little advance in the great major industries to which we have given so much time." Of the 7 SPRs awaiting industry acceptance, he classified 2 as "[i]n grave difficulties." One was for paper, which would achieve the necessary 80 percent acceptance, though of paper sizes only. The other was for paint and varnish colors and containers, which did indeed fail. His comments on the prospects for certain product lines were frank: "Interminable discussion" (lumber), "Internal politics or suspicion of our motives" (automotive), "Excessive competition and high mortality" (farm implements).[11] At the end of the year, despite the fact that 10 SPRs were already "issued or at the printer," Durgin asked for Hoover's patience: "We appreciate the inadequacy of accomplishment balanced against the expenditure of funds and effort, but if you can insure continuity, we are confident Simplified Practice will ultimately take position as a major service of the Department."[12]

Despite widespread enthusiasm in some quarters for a revival of wartime conservation measures, skepticism about the Commerce Department's simplified practice initiative slowed its progress.[13] One source of resistance to the division's push for mass production came, of course, from firms whose primary competitive strategy was product diversity, the opposite of mass production. "Instances are commonplace," acknowledged the 1926 *Primer of Simplified Practice*, "of manufacturers who deliberately created widely diverse or 'odd sizes' with the expectation of securing competitive advantage."[14] Emerging from the deep 1920–1 depression, product-diversifying manufacturers were surely fearful that simplification would mean a loss of customers and force them into direct price competition with their competitors – "competition," as a machine-tool builder envisioned it, "so keen as to be destructive."[15] DSP publicity generally skirted the problem of price competition, arguing that simplification would level the playing field for small manufacturers, even as it relied on competition among them to push down consumer prices.[16] Instead, the DSP sought to allay concern by emphasizing that "united action," even in the absence of unanimity, could achieve what individual manufacturers could not and by redirecting attention from inter-firm to inter-industry competition.[17] For individual firms, however, the threat was real that simplification, if pushed too hard, would, as one businessperson worried, "'bust' small factories."[18]

Skepticism also arose from a general fear of government intervention, as Hoover and DSP officials were fully aware.[19] "The well-known expression of 'Government interference in business,'" a DSP pamphlet noted, "has been so firmly embedded in the minds of our industrial leaders that nothing short of actual proof to the contrary will open up the avenues of constructive cooperation."[20] From this perspective, simplified practice under the auspices of the Commerce Department threatened to serve as an entering wedge – or the camel's nose, as DSP Chief Hudson put it. Businesspeople feared that, "once the government gets its nose inside the business tent on the pretext of assisting the industry to set up its own self-government, then it will be but a short time until, like the proverbial camel, government is on the inside and the former occupants are out in the cold." To these members of what he dubbed "The Skeptics' Society," Hudson advised seeking assurances of the government's benign posture from groups that had already forged agreements on simplified practice recommendations.[21] Perhaps more hopefully than factually, the 1926 *Primer of Simplified Practice* maintained that early fears of simplified practice as "another form of Government interference" had "been entirely dispelled."[22]

A third, persistent obstacle was fear of antitrust prosecution.[23] The exigencies of war had justified close cooperation under government supervision during the Great War,[24] but the American antitrust tradition created legal obstacles to collective standardization in peacetime, as contemporaries well knew. Shortly after the war ended, economist Homer Hoyt stated the matter succinctly: "While standardization is not prohibited by the law, the only methods by which thoroughgoing standardization can be attained, i.e., by combination, are declared to be unlawful."[25] Post-war enthusiasm for a revision of antitrust policy was on display at the U.S. Chamber of Commerce's congress of war service committees in December 1918, and Hoover himself advocated changing antitrust law to permit trade associations to pursue his panoply of waste-elimination measures, including statistics-gathering and simplified practice.[26] But the movement made little headway.[27] At the first simplified practice conference in November 1921, Secretary Hoover offered the Commerce Department as a buffer against antitrust prosecution, but, in the prevailing legal circumstances, he did so only obliquely.[28] Just a few months later, the U.S. Supreme Court declared the statistics-gathering function of the American Hardwood Manufacturers' Association under its "open price plan" an illegal restraint of trade.[29] "Mr. Hoover and his assistants have been asking manufacturers for just the type of material which the supreme court says is illegal," *Factory*'s "International Industrial Digest" noted. "The discrepancy of having a radically different policy in each of two Government departments, is an embarrassing situation."[30] For clarification, Hoover solicited from U.S. Attorney General Harry M. Daugherty a declaration, widely publicized at the time, that as long as activities such as statistics-gathering and standardization were not used to fix prices or to limit production, they would withstand legal scrutiny.[31] In the mid-1920s, two court decisions put simplified practice on steadier legal ground, enabling the DSP's 1926 *Primer of Simplified Practice* to portray simplification under the auspices of the Commerce Department as "an avenue of cooperation which alleviates fears of misapplication and jeopardy under the anti-trust laws."[32] Still, uncertainty about the legality of collective action to reduce product variety lingered through World War II and well beyond.[33]

Nonetheless, the division's first successes – *SPR No. 1* for paving bricks and *SPR No. 2* for beds and mattresses – and its intensive promotional work with an array of industries began to yield results. By mid-1926, Chief Ray M. Hudson reported, 45 simplified practice recommendations had been published, reducing product variety by well over half in most product lines (figure 16), and another 12 recommendations were circulating for industry acceptance. The Government Printing Office's sales of SPRs were brisk, totaling some 238,000 copies by mid-1926. Altogether, from establishment of the division in early 1922 through mid-1926, DSP staff had hosted 273 conferences, addressed 289 meetings, and attended another 436.[34] By the end of the decade, the number of SPRs in effect (figure 17)

No.	Item	Reduction in varieties		Per cent reduction
		From—	To—	
1	Vitrified paving brick (fourth revision conference)	66	4	94
2	Beds, springs, and mattresses	78	4	95
3	Metal lath	125	24	81
4	Asphalt (penetrations)	88	9	87
5	Hotel chinaware	700	160	77
6	Files and rasps	1,351	496	65
7	Rough and smooth face brick	75	2	97
	Common brick	44	1	98
8	Range boilers	130	13	90
9	Woven-wire fencing	552	69	87
	Woven-wire fence packages	2,072	138	93
10	Milk bottles and caps	78	10	87
11	Bed blankets (sizes)	78	12	85
12	Hollow building tile	36	19	48
13	Structural slates for plumbing and sanitary purposes			[1] 84
14	Roofing slates, descriptive term (thicknesses and sizes)	98	48	51
15	Blackboard slates, slab heights and sizes	251	25	90
16	Lumber (first revision) [2]			
17	Forged tools	665	351	47
18	Builders hardware:			
	Items			26
	Finishes			71
19	Asbestos paper (sizes, widths, weights of rolls)	14	8	43
	Asbestos millboard (sizes, thicknesses)	10	5	50
20	Steel barrels and drums	66	24	64
21	Brass lavatory and sink traps	1,114	72	94
22	Paper	[3]	[3]	[3]
23	Plow bolts	1,500	840	44
24	Hospital beds:			
	Length	33	1	97
	Width	34	[4] 1	91
	Height	44	1	97
25	Hot-water storage tanks	120	14	88
26	Steel reinforcing bars (cross-sectional areas)	40	11	73
27	Cotton duck (widths and weights)	460	94	80
28	Sheet steel (first revision)	1,819	263	85
29	Eaves trough and conductor pipe	21	16	24
30	Terne plate (weights)	9	7	22
31	Loaded shells (first revision)	4,076	1,758	57
32	Concrete building units (length, width, and height of blocks, tile, and brick)	115	24	80
33	Cafeteria and lunch-room chinaware	668	177	73
34	Warehouse forms	[3]	15	
35	Steel lockers	65	17	74
36	Milling cutters			[1] 35
37	Commercial purchase forms	[3]	3	
38	Sand-lime brick (length, width, and height)	14	3	79
40	Hospital chinaware	700	113	84
42	Paper grocers' bags	6,280	4,700	25
44	Box board thicknesses	244	60	75
45	Grinding wheels	715,200	255,800	64
47	Cut tacks and small cut nails:			
	Sizes	428	181	58
	Packing weights	423	121	71
49	Sidewalk lights:			
	Sizes	120	6	95
	Styles	80	5	94
	Shapes	10	2	80
51	Die-head chasers (for self-opening and adjustable die heads)			75

[1] Average reduction.
[2] Standard nomenclature grades and sizes for softwood lumber.
[3] Indeterminable.
[4] 1 standard, 2 specials.
[5] Thousands.

Figure 16. Reductions in variety achieved by simplified practice recommendations: U.S. Department of Commerce, Bureau of Standards, *Annual Report of the Director of the Bureau of Standards to the Secretary of Commerce for the Fiscal Year Ended June 30, 1926*, Misc. Pub. No. 75 (Washington, DC: Government Printing Office, 1926), 37.

No.	Item
1-29.	Vitrified paving bricks (seventh edition).
2.	Beds, springs, and mattresses.
3-28.	Metal lath (second edition).
4.	Asphalt (first revision).
5.	Hotel chinaware.
6.	Files and rasps.
7.	Rough and smooth face brick; common brick.
8-29.	Range boilers and expansion tanks (second edition).
9-28.	Woven-wire fencing; woven-wire fence packages (second edition).
10.	Milk bottles and caps (first revision).
11.	Bed blankets.
12.	Hollow building tile (first revision).
13-28.	Structural slate (second edition).
14-28.	Roofing slate (second edition).
15.	Blackboard slate.
16-29.	Softwood lumber (fourth edition).
17-29.	Forged tools (third edition).
18.	Builders' hardware (first revision).
19-28.	Asbestos paper and asbestos millboard (third edition).
20-28.	Steel barrels and drums (second edition).
21.	Brass lavatory and sink traps.
22.	Paper.
23.	Plow bolts.
24.	Hospital beds.
25.	Hot-water storage tanks.
26.	Steel reinforcing bars.
27.	Cotton duck (first revision).
28-29.	Sheet steel (second edition).
29.	Eaves trough and conductor pipe.
30-28.	Roofing ternes (first revision).
31.	Loaded paper shot shells (second revision).
32.	Concrete building units.
33.	Cafeteria and restaurant chinaware.
34.	Warehouse forms.
35-28.	Steel lockers (first revision).
36.	Milling cutters.
37-28.	Invoice, purchase order, and inquiry forms (second edition).
38.	Sand-lime brick.
39.	Dining-car chinaware.
40.	Hospital chinaware.
41.	Insecticides and fungicides (package sizes).
42.	Paper grocers' bags.
43-28.	Paint and varnish brushes (first revision).
44.	Box board thicknesses.
45-29.	Grinding wheels (third edition).
46.	Tissue paper.
47-28.	Cut tacks and small cut nails (second edition).
48.	Shovels, spades, and scoops (first revision).
49.	Sidewalk, floor, and roof lights.
50.	Bank checks, notes, drafts, and similar instruments.
51-29.	Chasers for self-opening and adjustable die heads (third edition).
52.	Staple vitreous china plumbing fixtures.
53.	Steel reinforcing spirals.
54.	Sterling silver flatware.
55.	Tinware, galvanized and japanned ware.
56-28.	Carbon brushes and brush shunts (first revision).

No.	Item
57.	Wrought-iron and wrought-steel pipe, valves, and fittings.
58-28.	Classification of iron and steel scrap (first revision).
59.	Rotary-cut lumber stock for wire bound boxes.
60.	Packing of carriage, machine, and lag bolts.
61.	White glazed tile and unglazed ceramic mosaic.
62.	Metallic cartridges.
63.	Metal spools (for annealing, handling, and shipping wire).
64.	Package sizes for vegetable shortening.
65-28.	Lead pencils.
66.	Automobile brake lining.
67.	Roller bearings.
68.	Metal and fiber flash-light cases.
69.	Packaging of razor blades.
70.	Salt packages.
71-28.	Turnbuckles.
72.	Solid section steel windows.
73.	One-piece porcelain insulators.
74.	Hospital and institutional cotton textiles.
75-29.	Composition blackboard (second edition).
76.	Ash handles.
77.	Hickory handles.
78-28.	Iron and steel roofing.
79-28.	Malleable foundry refractories.
80-28.	Folding and portable wooden chairs.
81-28.	Binders' board.
82-28.	Hollow metal doors.
83-28.	Kalamein doors.
84-28.	Composition books.
85-28.	Adhesive plaster.
86-28.	Surgical gauze.
87-29.	Form dimensions for concrete ribbed floor construction.
88-29.	Floor sweeps.
89-28.	Coated abrasive products.
90-29.	Hack-saw blades (second edition).
91-29.	Glass containers for preserves, jellies, and apple butter.
92-28.	Hard fiber twines (ply and yarn goods).
93-29.	Paper shipping tags.
94.	Fire engine pumping capacities.
95-28.	Skid platforms.
96-28.	Ice cake sizes.
97.	(To be assigned.)
98-29.	Photographic paper.
99-30.	Pocket knives.
100-29.	Welded chain.
101-29.	Metal partitions for toilets and showers.
102-29.	Granite curbstone.
103-29.	Industrial truck tires.
104.	(To be assigned.)
105-29.	Wheelbarrows.
106-30.	Hospital plumbing fixtures.
107-30.	Tight cooperage and tight cooperage stock.
108-29.	Dental hypodermic needles.
109-29.	Refrigerator ice compartments.
110-29.	Soft fiber (jute) twines.
111-30.	Color for school furniture.
112-29.	Elastic shoe goring.
113-30.	Restaurant guest checks.
114-30.	No. 1 kraft sealing tape.

Figure 17. Simplified practice recommendations, 1922–30: *SPR R109–30: Refrigerator Ice Compartments* (1930), 14.

would reach more than 100, with another dozen or so in the acceptance process.[35]

The division's progress in attracting industries to its simplification process reflected, in part, its outreach strategy, which produced clusters of SPRs in related product lines. Early on, the DSP added a technical assistant specially tasked to encourage the simplification of containers.[36] A conference held in January 1923 eventually yielded at least three SPRs – No. 42 for paper grocers' bags, No. 70 for salt packages, and No. 91 for glass containers for preserves, jellies, and apple butter.[37] The following year the National Slate Association invited DSP staff to preside over the final day of its annual convention. In due course, this resulted in SPR Nos. 13–15 for structural slate (for sanitary purposes), roofing slate, and blackboard slate.[38] The DSP also added an assistant specifically for the hardware field.[39] From the 1924 annual meeting of the National Hardware Association emerged SPR Nos. 28–31 for sheet steel, eaves trough, terneplate, and loaded paper shot shells.[40] In 1926 the DSP formalized its cluster approach by creating the National Committee on Metals Utilization "for the purpose," the *Standards Yearbook 1927* noted, "of carrying the principles of simplified practice more deeply into the metals-using field."[41]

A snowball dynamic also accelerated simplification across the economy as industry approval of a simplified practice recommendation for one product line inspired simplification of competing or related product lines. The simplification of paving bricks in *SPR No. 1* was followed quickly by the simplification of a competing product, asphalt for paving purposes, and of related products, clay face and common bricks.[42] Simplification of clay bricks, in turn, inspired simplification of sand-lime bricks,[43] while the spread of simplification generally in the building trades prompted the simplification of hollow building tile and brass lavatories and sinks.[44] *SPR No. 2* for bedsteads, springs, and mattresses also spawned the simplification of related products. "The blanket manufacturers caught on to the idea," DSP Chief Hudson recounted, "and said, 'We'll follow suit, for now that we know what sizes will be staple, we can manufacture those sizes the year round, and thus cut down the losses we now take on large inventories resulting from too many different sizes.'"[45] *SPR No. 11* reduced bed blanket sizes from 78 to 12 in 1924.[46] Meanwhile, simplification of beds for the household prompted the American Hospital Association to launch an initiative to simplify hospital beds. Its survey revealed that hospital beds, as noted earlier, were available in 33 lengths, 34 widths, and 44 heights. *SPR No. 24* established a single standard length, width, and height, plus two special widths.[47] This was followed by the simplification of hospital and institutional bedding, which reduced bed sheets from 50 sizes to 4, bedspreads from 54 sizes to 2, and towels from 129 sizes to 3.[48] Successful efforts to simplify metal lath, woven-wire fencing, and other steel products inspired the simplification of steel lockers and steel reinforcing bars,[49] and simplification of steel reinforcing bars, in turn, spurred simplification of steel spiral rods for concrete reinforcement.[50] Success in simplifying loaded paper shot shells prompted the Sporting Arms and Ammunition Manufacturers' Institute to initiate the simplification of metallic cartridges.[51] A snowball dynamic also marked the simplification of tableware: the simplification of hotel chinaware in 1924 inspired the simplification of cafeteria and restaurant chinaware, which in turn spurred simplification of dining-car and hospital chinaware. By 1925, a unified "recommended" list specified "sizes, types, and capacities of chinaware for hotel, restaurant, cafeteria, hospital, dining car, and Government service."[52] Simplification begot simplification.

As the "simplification movement" gathered momentum,[53] evidence of the division's widening impact emerged in other forms. Consumer advocates such as Stuart Chase and the American Home Economics Association, as noted earlier, took up the cause, and by the mid-1920s, universities and colleges were beginning to incorporate "Simplified Practice" into their curricula. The University of Michigan's Economics Department was reported to be including simplified practice in its courses on the economics of consumption, while the Massachusetts

Institute of Technology and Boston University were planning or already offering courses on Simplified Practice. Yale University's Sheffield Scientific School was also planning to devote a session of its senior seminar to simplified practice and purchased 500 copies of simplified practice recommendations "for class work."[54] More than three dozen colleges and universities, DSP officials noted in early 1926, "are pledged to a more intensive instruction along the lines of simplification."[55]

Foreign interest also surged. Reports on the work of the Division of Simplified Practice appeared in the German and French press in the mid-1920s.[56] Cecil Chisholm, editor of the British *System*, ran another series of articles on simplification in the London *Times* trade and engineering supplement in 1925 and then published a book entitled *Simplified Practice: An Outline of a New Industrial Policy* in 1927.[57] Between mid-1925 and mid-1926, DSP Chief Hudson reported, the division hosted a stream of visitors – "[t]rade commissioners, commercial attaches, and ministers of commerce from nearly 20 foreign countries."[58] In a single month in late 1925, the DSP fielded inquiries about simplified practice from England, Germany, Holland, and Sweden.[59] By 1926 the division's pamphlet, *Simplified Practice: What It Is and What It Offers*, had been translated into Russian and French, and by 1930 into Japanese.[60] By the end of the decade, as competition in foreign markets intensified, Commerce Department standards were being translated and distributed in foreign markets, as was happening with the standards of other nations – notably Britain's throughout its empire. Meanwhile, the Commerce Department was pursuing regional agreements up and down the Western hemisphere.[61] In South America, Cecil Chisholm reported in 1925, Germans and Americans were actively competing to set local standards: "In a word, the lists are set for 'the battle of the standards' in engineering products abroad."[62]

Meanwhile, the DSP's mission expanded noticeably over the 1920s. Simplified practice recommendations initially focused squarely on manufactured products, but in the mid- to late 1920s the principle of simplification was applied, in the spirit of Arch Wilkinson Shaw, to the distribution of products as well. "Where the wartime effort had been to achieve mass production through standardization," a historian of the Bureau of Standards noted, "the postwar effort sought to achieve standardization by establishing mass production techniques . . . in every field of commerce and in the company office no less than in the shop or factory."[63] The division's first foray into distribution produced *SPR No. 34*, which reduced warehouse forms from thousands to a standard set of 15 in 1924.[64] This was followed in 1925 by *SPR No. 37*, reducing the thousands of kinds of commercial invoices, inquiry forms, and purchase orders then in use to 3 standard forms. Several trade associations had been pursuing simplification of commercial forms since 1919, and the general conference, addressed personally by Hoover, ended with a standing ovation ("rising vote of thanks") to the division "for its aid in bringing about this simplification."[65] In 1926, an agreement among banks, lithographers and printers, and users, as noted earlier, simplified bank checks and other financial instruments. In 1928, the division undertook what it portrayed as "its first major project primarily concerned with our national distribution system" – simplification of the skids (pallets) used in moving goods with a lift truck (forklift). Individual firms had long used skids of their own devising for moving goods around their property, but paper manufacturers and others had recently begun shipping products on skids, and automobile companies were insisting on receiving supplies on skids, which put a premium on inter-firm standardization.[66] Its success in simplifying skids spurred the division to turn its attention more fully to the problem of waste in distribution. At the behest of the National Retail Dry Goods Association, the division organized the simplification of the wrapping and packing of retail-store merchandise. Based on a four-month survey of department-store practice, SPR Nos. 126–9 simplified "set-up boxes," folding boxes, corrugated boxes, and notion and millinery paper bags.[67]

The division also expanded its mission as questions of product quality, perhaps inevitably, crept into simplified practice recommendations. In fact, one of the first products to be simplified – asphalt – did not have a size or shape to simplify; instead, the SPR established grades of asphalt, defined in penetration limits.[68] The 1924 lumber standards, in addition to establishing standard lumber sizes, included provisions for the grading of lumber.[69] Several other industries also incorporated grade or quality standards into their SPRs.[70] Meanwhile, federal, state, and local specifications often set standard grades, qualities, or performance benchmarks. The proliferation of specifications was on full display in the Federal Specifications Board's 1925 directory of some 27,000 federal, state, municipal, and private specifications, which included 57 specifications solely for concrete reinforcing bars.[71] Manufacturers, the division reported, "find that 'too many grades' often complicate production and distribution just as 'too many sizes' do."[72]

In the Fall of 1927, the DSP formally expanded its mandate by setting up a "commercial standards unit" to apply to specifications the core principles of simplified practice: "the elimination of unnecessary specifications and the establishment as 'commercial standards' of those most widely or generally used."[73] In other words, the Commercial Standards Unit aided industries in choosing widely used specifications to be designated collectively as nationwide standards. Firms manufacturing products to meet commercial standards were encouraged to label them as such (figure 18), and the Bureau of Standards made available a list of "willing-to-certify" manufacturers whose products complied with the standards.[74] In simplifying specifications and publicizing the manufacturers whose products met the standards, the Bureau hoped to encourage the use of specifications by smaller firms and

Figure 18. Wallpaper label to certify compliance with *CS16-29*:
U.S. Department of Commerce, *Commercial Standards Service...*
CS0-30, 15.

consumers who did not have the resources to do their own testing.[75] A new "Commercial Standards Group" in the Bureau of Standards, headed by Ray M. Hudson, now housed the Division of Simplified Practice with its new chief, Edwin W. Ely, together with the Commercial Standards Unit (renamed the Division of Trade Standards in 1929), the Division of Specifications, the American Marine Standards Committee, and the Division of Building and Housing.[76]

Despite the DSP's six years of experience in orchestrating simplified practice recommendations, the Commercial Standards Unit got off to a rocky start. Its approval process was identical to that used for simplified practice recommendations, except that a consensus in favor of a proposed standard was defined as approval by 65 rather than 80 percent of the industry by volume.[77] But, unlike the DSP's first two ventures – paving bricks, and bedsteads, springs, and mattresses – the Commercial Standards Unit's first two projects ended in failure. *Commercial Standard No. 1* was initially slated for "new billet-steel concrete reinforcement bars," a project inspired by the simplification of steel reinforcing bar sizes, but it failed to achieve the requisite acceptance threshold. So *CS1* was shifted to another product, clinical thermometers.[78] Likewise, *CS2* would initially have set quality standards for surgical gauze, inspired by the simplification of sizes of surgical gauze in *SPR No. 86*, but it too failed to gain the acceptance of manufacturers, and *CS2* was reassigned to mopsticks.[79] Also, the distinction between simplified practice recommendations and commercial standards was never absolute, since the latter were usually based on existing specifications, which sometimes included "dimensional requirements."[80] Indeed, it was a signal of continuing ambiguity that two SPRs – *No. 18, Builders' Hardware*, and *No. 52, Staple Vitreous China Plumbing Fixtures* – were merged with Commercial Standards (*CS22-30* and *CS20-30*, respectively). Both were retained in lists of SPRs but described as "now known as" (later, "included in") commercial standards.[81] Nonetheless, by 1930, alongside more than 100 simplified practice recommendations (figure 17) and 124 American Marine Standards,[82] 25 commercial standards were in effect and 2 more "in preparation" (figure 19).

As had happened during the Great War, finally, other agencies – this time both public and private – amplified the DSP's drive to push American business toward mass

CS. No.	Item	CS. No.	Item
0–30.	The commercial standards service and its value to business.	14–31.	Boys' blouses, button-on waists, shirts, and junior shirts (in preparation).
1–28.	Clinical thermometers.	15–29.	Men's pajamas.
2–30.	Mopsticks.	16–29.	Wall paper.
3–28.	Stoddard solvent.	17–30.	Diamond core drill fittings.
4–29.	Staple porcelain (all-clay) plumbing fixtures.	18–29.	Hickory golf shafts.
5–29.	Steel pipe nipples.	19–30.	Foundry patterns of wood.
6–29.	Wrought-iron pipe nipples.	20–30.	Staple vitreous china plumbing fixtures.
7–29.	Standard weight malleable iron or steel screwed unions.	21–30.	Interchangeable ground glass joints.
		22–30.	Builders' hardware (nontemplate).
8–30.	Plain and thread plug and ring gage blanks.	23–30.	Feldspar.
9–29.	Builders' template hardware.	24–30.	Standard screw threads.
10–29.	Brass pipe nipples.	25–30.	Special screw threads.
11–29.	Regain of mercerized cotton yarns.	26–30.	Aromatic red-cedar closet (lining).
12–29.	Domestic and industrial fuel oils.	27–30.	Plate-glass mirrors (in preparation).
13–30.	Dress patterns.		

Figure 19. Commercial standards, 1928–30: *CS2-30: Mopsticks* (1930), 12.

production. Specifications for federal purchases, as noted earlier, incorporated any relevant simplified practice recommendations, but the Bureau of Standards' Federal Specification Board (later, Division of Specifications) also worked directly with manufacturers to craft federal specifications that reduced product variety. During the war, for example, the Bureau of Standards had worked with the War Industries Board and manufacturers to reduce the number of battery (dry cell) sizes, and this work continued in the 1920s.[83] Specifications staff also worked on national standards for builders' hardware, which resulted in both a U.S. Government Master Specification and *SPR No. 18*,[84] while the Bureau's annual Weights and Measures Conference pushed along the simplification of milk bottles, which was complicated by a maze of state and municipal regulations.[85] The Bureau of Standards also worked directly with manufacturers to arrive at federal specifications for enameled metal kitchenware and whiteware pottery that included standard sizes.[86] And once the Commerce Department's Bureau of Foreign and Domestic Commerce (BFDC) turned its attention to domestic commerce in the mid- to late 1920s, its studies of the costs of distribution reinforced simplified practice. BFDC staff, too, an official explained, were "trying to eliminate unnecessary items – those things which are resulting in a loss rather than a profit."[87]

Meanwhile, two private associations – the Chamber of Commerce of the United States and the American Engineering Standards Committee (AESC) – were critical allies in the Division of Simplified Practice's campaign to spread "the gospel of Simplification" throughout American business. In March 1922, shortly after William Durgin arrived to head the new division, Secretary Hoover appointed an Advisory Committee whose principal purpose was to serve as the division's liaison with the Chamber and the AESC. Besides Durgin *ex officio* and the former head of wartime conservation efforts, Arch Wilkinson Shaw, the Advisory Committee consisted of

E. W. McCullough of the U.S. Chamber of Commerce and
A. A. Stevenson, chair of the AESC.[88] Even before Hoover took
office as Commerce Secretary, the Chamber had expressed
its enthusiasm for simplification, and a Chamber representative attended many early simplified practice conferences. In
its division of labor with the DSP, its role was primarily to
promote simplified practice to American business, which it did
with great energy, lending, in the words of a DPS pamphlet, "a
powerful impetus to the work."[89]

Relations between the division and the American
Engineering Standards Committee, on the other hand, were
rivalrous at times. Proposals for formation of a truly national
standards association – one that could coordinate American
standards-setting and reduce the hyper-fragmentation that
had plagued American standards since the late nineteenth
century – had circulated among engineers since 1910 but
languished until the U.S. took tentative steps toward war
mobilization. In January 1916, officials of the Naval Consulting
Board, a predecessor of the War Industries Board, met with
the presidents of five engineering societies to enlist their help
in conducting a national industrial inventory; the following month plans for a national standards organization were
suddenly revived.[90] Formally organized during the war as a
federation of the five engineering societies, the American
Engineering Standards Committee was broadened in 1919 to
include trade associations as well as representatives of the U.S.
Commerce, War, and Navy departments.[91] The AESC's goal
of unifying the United States' standards-setting community
created, as Andrew L. Russell notes, "a certain tension" with
Hoover's whirl of standards-setting activities as Secretary of
Commerce.[92] The DSP and AESC resembled each other in
their promotion of standardization as well as in their position
in the standards-setting process: neither set standards itself;
instead, both sought to facilitate nationwide agreements on
standards. The DSP provided an infrastructure for competing

firms to reach inter-firm agreements on standard products, based on commercial data. The AESC offered a mechanism for some 100, sometimes competing, standards-setting organizations to reach agreement on nationwide standards, based on technical data, which it designated "American Standards."[93] The two also shared an emphasis on collaboration and consensus, values that the AESC's long-serving secretary, Paul Agnew, may have absorbed while acting as the Bureau of Standards liaison with the War Industries Board during the war.[94] Where they differed was on the government's proper role in setting industrial standards. As early as 1919, an AESC member expressed concerns about the Bureau of Standard's recent move into "engineering standards," and, when the Commerce Department expanded its purview to encompass commercial standards in 1927, tensions with the AESC burst to the surface. During what the Bureau's historian, Rexford C. Cochrane, termed "a period of estrangement" in 1928, "the AESC formally requested Bureau withdrawal from all commercial standardization activities," it reconstituted itself as the American Standards Association, and Bureau staff no longer attended ASA meetings. "The conflict of interests was not to be entirely resolved," Cochrane concluded, "for another two decades."[95] On the broader value of simplification in American business, however, the two were united.

Meanwhile, the fourth member of the Advisory Committee – World War I conservation expert Arch Shaw – marshaled his publications to promote simplification with unalloyed enthusiasm.[96] In February 1921, a month before Hoover took office as Secretary of Commerce, *Factory*'s editor announced that the magazine would run a series of articles on "Simplification in Industry – The Next Big Step in Management."[97] In the March issue, the editor described the origins of the simplification movement in the World War I experience.[98] Thereafter, every issue of *Factory* in 1921 and 1922 carried articles on simplification, focusing on manufacturing firms' experience and often

Figure 20.   Cover of *Factory* magazine.

highlighting the topic on its cover (figure 20).[99] Meanwhile, Shaw's magazine *System* ran a parallel series of stories focusing on simplification in "trade and distribution," inaugurated by Shaw himself.[100] By mid-1923, *System* and *Factory* together had carried 38 articles on simplification. This publicity, "covering over 100 pages," DSP Chief Durgin noted in a memo to Hoover, "has been of unlimited value to the Division."[101]

A member of the DSP's Planning Committee at least into the early 1930s,[102] Shaw also provided essential support for Hoover's simplified practice project in other ways. Once the Division of Simplified Practice was up and running in 1922, as noted earlier, he sent letters promoting the division's simplified practice service to contacts at 125 companies. He helped in putting together the DSP's first pamphlet on simplified practice, which was intended for use in college courses.[103] In 1923, he published an essay in the *Harvard Business Review* that showcased the work of the division, portraying simplification not merely as the reduction of product variety but more broadly as "a philosophy of business management," an essential strategy for "mitigating the complexity present in all forms and phases of [modern] business operation."[104] As he later put it, the Division of Simplified Practice's energetic work was cultivating "a state of mind in American business" that abhorred complexity.[105] When the DSP encountered public criticism that simplified practice was encouraging overproduction and underemployment, Hoover enlisted Shaw to defend it in the pages of *System*.[106]

By the early 1930s, it seems fair to say, simplified practice was becoming embedded in American business.[107] By mid-1932, 135 simplified practice recommendations were in effect, alongside 41 commercial standards (figure 21).[108] The reductions achieved in the variety of products were striking. To be sure, they varied widely from around 90 percent in some lines (e.g., common face brick and binder's board for making books) to less than 25 percent in others (e.g., tinware and photographic paper). In a few cases, reductions defied calculation because the number of varieties before simplification – e.g., of warehouse forms or automobile brake linings – was unknown. But, overall, where numbers were available, the reductions averaged roughly two-thirds.[109]

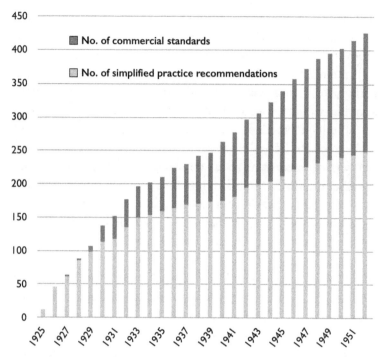

Figure 21. Simplified practice recommendations and commercial standards, 1925–52: annual reports of the Director of the (National) Bureau of Standards; annual reports of the Secretary of Commerce; (National) Bureau of Standards Letters Circular (lists of National Bureau of Standards publications); and lists of extant standards in the published simplified practice recommendations and commercial standards.

Data collected in periodic audits of industry adherence to SPRs, moreover, showed that most manufacturers in most product lines were concentrating their production on standard sizes by the end of the 1920s. Adherence rates were affected by a variety of factors, of course. While the number of products in a simplified line might remain stable, the specific products included in the simplified line might change in response to consumer demand, causing some fluctuation in adherence rates.[110] For paving bricks, the introduction of a new, popular

Degree of adherence determined by actual survey

Simplified practice recommendation No.	Commodity	Degree of adherence	Simplified practice recommendation No.	Commodity	Degree of adherence
		Per cent			*Per cent*
1	Paving brick	87.8	49	Sidewalk, floor, and roof lights	98.2
2	Bedsteads, springs, and mattresses	91.0	55	Tinware, galvanized and japanned ware	90.0
4	Asphalt	89.4			
10	Milk bottles and milk-bottle caps	79.0	62	Metallic cartridges	99.0
			63	Metal spools	43.0
11	Bed blankets	90.5	66	Automobile brake lining	78.9
			67	Roller bearings	58.0
12	Hollow building tile	89.5	68	Metal and fiber flash-light cases	93.0
13	Structural slate	63.7			
14	Roofing slate	94.5	73	One-piece porcelain insulators	91.0
15	Blackboard slate	95.6	76	Ash handles	89.0
24	Hospital beds	91.3	77	Hickory handles	80.6
			88	Floor sweeps	96.5
30	Roofing ternes	100.0	98	Photographic paper	96.6
31	Loaded paper shot shells	99.5			
43	Paint and varnish brushes	83.7		Average	86.7

Figure 22.   Adherence rates, 1930: U.S. Department of Commerce, *Standards Yearbook 1931*, 246.

size caused a temporary drop in adherence rates until the new size achieved the threshold to be designated a standard size.[111] Also, paving brick purchased for repairs had to match existing, possibly non-standard, sizes, which reduced adherence rates.[112] Consumers could prove durably resistant to standard sizes – even the U.S. Government Printing Office was still insisting in 1930 on purchasing 8½ in. by 10½ in. office paper, rather than the standard 8½ in. by 11 in. set six years earlier in *SPR No. 22*.[113] Nonetheless, measured by volume of production, the division's surveys indicated that adherence rates averaged 80 percent or more (figure 22).[114]

The broader impact of simplified practice was manifest, the Planning Committee maintained in 1931, in the fact that some 10,000 organizations and individual companies had accepted the recommendations, and federal government purchases were being "based on simplified recommendations wherever possible." The National Association of Purchasing Agents had thrown its weight behind them, and two state-level chambers of commerce had initiated simplification programs. Industry estimates put the direct savings to manufacturers at more than $250,000,000 annually.[115] "Comparison of 1930 with 1922," the *Commerce Yearbook 1930* declared, "will show how thoroughly the philosophy of simplified practice has permeated the industrial structure."[116]

But whether the imprint of simplified practice on American business would endure, once Hoover assumed the U.S. presidency in 1929, the stock market crashed, and depression set in, remained an open question. As it had in 1920–1, economic depression again spurred a scramble for the consumer's dollar that threatened to revive product diversity. The deepening depression, Secretary of Commerce Robert P. Lamont acknowledged to a conference of standing-committee chairmen in late 1930, had "created grave temptations to producers to depart from the simplified practice recommendations. In a few industries the departures have resulted in a rather general disregard of schedules."[117] E. W. McCullough of the U.S. Chamber of Commerce agreed: "Under the pressure of the times we are going through now, the sales manager is exerting pressure on the production department all the time for more variety, more individuality." And he warned of the consequences: "If we let [simplified practice] go and introduce endless variety, we will be just where we were before the war."[118] In the depths of the depression, deep budget cuts sharply limited the division's outreach. Its staff was reduced from 40 to 4, its publicity work curtailed, and travel eliminated.[119] The Bureau cut back its publications, scrapping the *Standards Yearbook* altogether and outsourcing its bulletin, the *Commercial Standards Monthly*, to the American Standards Association (ASA).[120] Responsibility for the development of building and plumbing codes was partially shifted to the ASA,[121] and, for a time, there was talk of transferring its commercial standards work as well – privatizing it, in other words.[122]

But Hoover's Division of Simplified Practice did indeed weather the Great Depression. Plans to privatize its standards work "were abandoned," a later review of the Bureau reported, "because of strong opposition from certain industry organizations utilizing standards."[123] Meanwhile, the division worked with the New Deal's short-lived National Recovery Administration to align industrial codes with or incorporate simplified practice recommendations.[124] Its staff levels gradually recovered to their pre-depression numbers.[125] The Great Depression slowed the rate of adoption of Commerce Department standards after 1932, but the overall gains between 1930 and 1939 were nonetheless impressive: the number of SPRs in effect increased by half to 173, while commercial standards tripled to 74 (figure 21).[126]

Then came another "great war" and another boost to simplified practice. The Great War had given birth to the simplification movement; Hoover's initiative had revived and driven it forward in the 1920s and 1930s; World War II enhanced and ultimately assured its place in business at home and abroad. "Total war demands simplification of American life," President Franklin D. Roosevelt declared in his 1943 budget message, calling for nationwide simplification and standardization of American production and distribution.[127] Like World War I's War Industries Board, World War II's War Production Board (WPB) included a conservation division – the Bureau of Industrial Conservation (BIC) – to which the then-chief of the DSP, Edwin W. Ely, was transferred. "Just as in the last war," a National Bureau of Standards (NBS) publication reported in 1942, "simplification is being applied as rapidly as possible."[128] The number of simplified practice recommendations effectively multiplied as orders issued by the War Production Board and the Office of Price Administration either incorporated already agreed-upon simplified practice recommendations or set out new ones.[129] Commercial standards and specifications, too, were written or rewritten to meet war needs.[130] Foreign interest in the Bureau's simplification work again surged during the war, as Canada sought its assistance in setting

up a wartime division of simplified practice and requests for
copies of simplified practice recommendations came in from
Australia, England, New Zealand, and Brazil.[131] From 1939
to 1946, the combined number of simplified practice recommendations and commercial standards in effect in the United
States grew by more than 40 percent to 352, simplified practice
recommendations increasing from 172 to 221 and commercial
standards nearly doubling from 73 to 131 (figure 21).[132]

With the end of the war and defeat of another proposal in
1945 to privatize the division's work, the Division of Simplified
Practice scaled down, yet carried its work energetically into
peacetime.[133] Its staff had reached a wartime peak of 60 but
declined to 14 by 1955, on a par with staffing levels in the
late 1920s.[134] The Bureau of Standards was optimistic – or at
least hopeful – that simplified practice would outlive the war.
"[W]hen the war is over," it declared in 1942, "the established
Simplified Practice Recommendations will tend to prevent a
recurrence of the unnecessary multiplication of variety which
occurred in many fields following the last war."[135] Indeed,
product diversity reportedly did not resurge after this war,[136]
and the numbers of simplified practice recommendations
and commercial standards continued to grow. By 1950, their
combined total reached 403 (240 simplified practice recommendations and 163 commercial standards – see figure 21).[137]

After World War II, the United States' achievements in
simplifying product lines and boosting mass production were
broadcast far and wide under the auspices of the Marshall
Plan's Productivity Program.[138] Its Anglo-American Council
on Productivity brought a cohort of British observers to tour
the U.S. in 1949 and study simplified practice – a scant century after British engineers had visited the U.S. to study the
"American system" of interchangeable-parts manufacturing
technology, the basic technology that enabled mass production.[139] The Anglo-American Council's reports, in turn,
were translated and published in 1951 by the West German

National Productivity Board as *Vereinfachung der industriellen Produktion* (*Simplification of Industrial Production*).[140] In the early 1950s, federal agencies published a series of pamphlets on "standardization, simplification, specialization" as part of the campaign to enhance industrial productivity in countries receiving Marshall Plan assistance.[141] The U.S. Bureau of Labor Statistics, meanwhile, compiled a series of reports for the agency administering the Marshall Plan, the Economic Cooperation Administration (ECA), on "productivity and factory performance" in more than 100 product lines, e.g. men's dress shirts. Sensibly, the ECA warned against "blindly" expecting "American peace-time practices" to work in the European context, since voluntary cooperation in the U.S. had been forcibly accelerated by "two great stimuli" – the "compulsory restrictions" of World Wars I and II.[142] Through 1952, Marshall Plan aid brought thousands of Europeans to the U.S. to study American production methods.[143]

As a federal government initiative to prod American manufacturers toward mass production, propelled by the exigencies of war, the Department of Commerce's simplified practice program had largely achieved Hoover's goal by the 1960s. In enabling voluntary, nationwide agreements on standard sizes, it had laid a foundation for mass production of a wide array of everyday commodities. In all, between 1922 and 1971, the Department of Commerce issued 267 simplified practice recommendations along with 274 commercial standards. In addition, the department had launched a single, unified series called "product standards" in 1965 (from 1969, "voluntary product standards") as distinctions between the two kinds of voluntary standards – size vs. quality – became increasingly untenable. At least 30 new product standards with PS numbers had been issued by 1971, bringing the total number of government-sanctioned voluntary standards to well above 500.[144]

But cumulative totals are misleading. Provisions for the

withdrawal of standards were in place by 1955,[145] and by the early 1970s large numbers of standards had been withdrawn. According to an official NBS list of "existing" voluntary standards published in 1972, only 190 remained in effect. Simplified practice recommendations had fallen sharply to 42, while commercial standards had declined to 93. The remaining 55 were in the newer PS series.[146] Even as the PS series continued to grow in the 1970s,[147] the NBS officially withdrew simplified practice recommendations and commercial standards in droves – some because they were regarded as obsolete, were unused, or were "not in the public interest," and others because alternative standards issued by private standards-setting organizations or set out in federal specifications were regarded as equivalent.[148]

Finally, amidst the economic and political turmoil of the 1970s, the Commerce Department effectively ended its half-century-long effort to encourage and support simplified practice. The increasing importance of standards as non-tariff barriers to trade in a globalizing world economy sparked rising concern that the fragmentation of voluntary standards in the U.S. would disadvantage American business in world markets, and political leaders were unwilling to centralize (and fund) standards-setting in government hands. At the same time, the Bureau was busy with new responsibilities relating to a variety of mandatory federal standards growing out of the "new social regulation" of the 1960s and 1970s.[149] In 1979, the Bureau of Standards announced that it would exit the voluntary-standards business and leave the matter to private organizations such as the American National Standards Institute (ANSI, successor to the American Standards Association).[150] Today, the Commerce Department's Voluntary Product Standards Program remains nominally in place, described on the website of the National Institute of Standards and Technology (NIST, successor to the National Bureau of Standards) in language that could have been written in the 1920s:

Producers, distributors, users, consumers, and other interested groups contribute to the establishment of Voluntary Product Standards by initiating and participating in their development. ... The use of DOC [Department of Commerce] Voluntary Product Standards is voluntary. NIST has no regulatory power in the enforcement of their provisions; however, since the standards represents [sic] a consensus of all interested groups, their provisions are likely to become established as trade customs.[151]

But only three voluntary standards remain in effect, all concerning lumber products. One of those, *PS 20-20, American Softwood Lumber Standard*, is the present-day incarnation of *SPR No. 16: Lumber*, Hoover's "Exhibit A" on behalf of government–industry cooperation, now nearly a century old.

Introduced in World War I, revived and amplified by Hoover's Commerce Department, and normalized during World War II, simplified practice – industry-wide reductions in product variety that made industry-wide mass production possible – had become embedded across the American economy by the 1950s. "[S]implified practice has become habitual in the United States," Commodity Standards Division Chief Edwin W. Ely observed in 1951, "like locking one's office door at the end of a working day, without publicity or fanfare."[152] Despite the Commerce Department's withdrawal, the habit persisted.

Afterword

The story of standard sizes requires us to think differently about the United States' status as a manufacturing powerhouse in the twentieth century. The diffusion of mass-production techniques across the American economy was not, as conventional wisdom would have it, a natural, evolutionary process of entrepreneurial emulation and learning. To be sure, the extraordinary success of the titans of mass production such as Andrew Carnegie (steel), James B. Duke (tobacco), and, above all, Henry Ford (automobile manufacturing) demonstrated the economic bounty that *could* be reaped by manufacturing a sharply restricted stable of products in massive volumes. But neither the models of large-scale production they offered, nor wartime lessons in simplification, were enough to diffuse mass-production methods throughout the economy. In many lines of business, relentless competitive pressures to offer consumers a diversity of products stymied the diffusion process. Only when the federal government stepped back in again after the war, encouraging and enabling American manufacturers to push back collectively against market forces, did mass-production techniques diffuse quickly and broadly across the economy, positioning the United States to become a global manufacturing powerhouse by the mid twentieth century.

Should we be surprised that the prominence of mass production and consumption in the mid-twentieth-century American economy, captured in the term "Fordism," can be laid at the feet of the federal government rather than entrepreneurs? Yes – but only if one gauges the government's role in the economy through a restricted conceptual lens that focuses solely on "regulation." Widen the conceptual lens, however, and regulation's counterpart, government "promotion," suddenly springs into view. Where government regulation seeks in some way to constrain business activity, government promotion does the opposite: it encourages and supports business activity. Promotion takes one of two forms. In its *constitutive* guise, government promotion provides the institutional framework that makes capitalist enterprise possible by lowering risk. It specifies property rights – both who can own property and what can be owned; it sets legal requirements for forming corporations and may limit the liability of their investors; and it enforces contracts.[1] In what one might call its *fostering* form (perhaps more familiar as Chisholm's "industrial policy"), government promotion encourages and supports particular sectors, industries, firms, or activities. This may entail direct investment in, or interest guarantees for, private enterprise; protection from foreign competition (e.g. tariffs); the offering of bounties, prizes, or research grants; and so on.[2]

In its fostering form, American promotion of enterprise has a long, unbroken history that extends back to 1789, when the second and third acts of the first U.S. Congress placed import duties on specific manufactured goods and levied tonnage taxes favoring American-owned ships.[3] It has continued without interruption through more than two centuries in an ever-changing mosaic of federal, state, and local government policies to foster American enterprise – a panoply of policies that would be tedious to enumerate here.[4] In the 1980s, state and local promotion again became more salient, as they had been in the nineteenth century, while federal policies receded from view, decentralized and "hidden."[5] But the Biden administration, with its federal subsidies for chip manufacturing and green technologies, has once again brought federal policies to foster enterprise back to the fore.[6] Like Hoover's pursuit of simplified practice, the overarching goal of fostering policies is to enhance Americans' standard of living. Notwithstanding persistent mythmaking about laissez-faire in American history, and regardless what role one thinks government *should* play in economic change, the reality is that all levels of the American government – federal, state, and local – have promoted business enterprise throughout the nation's history.

As a premier example of federal efforts to foster business enterprise, the story of standard sizes fits comfortably within – and enlarges – this rich and fulsome history. In all, at least a full century of government promotion elevated mass production to its dominant position in the American economy – a half-century of Army Ordnance Department support for nascent mass production before the Civil War,[7] plus a second half-century in which the World War I War Industries Board, Hoover's "fostering hand" in the Commerce Department, and the World War II War Production Board pushed energetically to diffuse mass-production techniques across the economy. To this, one can also add an intervening half-century of federal policies between the Civil War and the Great War that created the mass markets on which mass production was premised (think of Indian removal, land grants, transcontinental railroads, nationally chartered banks, protective tariffs). Without sustained government promotion over one and a half centuries, it seems fair to conclude, mass production would not have become so quintessentially "American" by the mid twentieth century.

The history of standard sizes in the U.S. raises, in my mind, a host of intriguing questions that I encourage others to explore.

How did individual firms negotiate, in Hartmut Berghoff's words, that "fundamental dilemma of industrial capitalism"[8] – the tension between the factory, prioritizing volume production, and the sales department's or consumer's demands for product diversity? How did simplified practice agreements affect the structure of industry – did they work to the advantage of already dominant firms, or did they, as Herbert Hoover hoped, provide a framework to support small and middling manufacturers in an age of big business? Did standard sizes actually limit consumer choice in the vaunted age of consumerism? To what extent was mass advertising used not merely to ramp up consumer demand but more specifically to quash demand for non-standard products? If collective agreements on standard sizes drove the diffusion of mass-production techniques in the 1920s, does this help to explain the puzzling surge in productivity in that decade? Did the diffusion of mass-production techniques enhance a growing mismatch between production and consumption, deepening the Great Depression? To what extent do early twentieth-century worries about "waste" resonate with present-day environmental concerns? And, finally, absent simplified practice, would the American "variety of capitalism" have more closely resembled the German or British at mid-century?

Notes

A Note on Citations

Citations to simplified practice recommendations, commercial standards, and voluntary product standards appear in shortened form in the notes. The full citation of the first simplified practice recommendation, for example, would be: U.S. Department of Commerce, *Simplified Practice Recommendation No. 1: Paving Bricks, Issued by the Bureau of Standards, August 1, 1922 (Original Draft)* (Washington, DC: Government Printing Office, 1922). In the notes, it appears as *SPR No. 1: Paving Bricks* (1922). The numbers given to commercial standards were preceded by CS and followed by the two-digit year in which they took effect. The full citation to the first commercial standard is: U.S. Department of Commerce, Bureau of Standards, *Clinical Thermometers: Commercial Standard CS1 28, Effective Date, October 1, 1928* (Washington, DC: Government Printing Office, 1928). It is cited in the notes as *CS1-28: Clinical Thermometers* (1928). Beginning in 1928, a similar numbering convention was used for simplified practice recommendations – e.g., *SPR No. 1* became *SPR R1-29* when it was revised in 1929. Voluntary product standards, a unified series introduced in 1965 with numbers beginning PS, are shortened in a similar manner. The year in parentheses in the short citations is the year of publication. As official government publications, the printed standards were sent to federal depository libraries, but they have not necessarily been retained. Fortunately, many are available online. The most complete collection, to my knowledge, is on HathiTrust (www.hathitrust.org).

To conserve space in the endnotes, periodical databases are cited by name only. The relevant URLs are:

America's Historical Newspapers, www.readex.com/products/americas-his torical-newspapers

Chronicling America: Historic American Newspapers, Library of Congress, https://chroniclingamerica.loc.gov

Gallica, Bibliothéque nationale de France, https://gallica.bnf.fr

ProQuest *Harper's Bazaar* Archive, https://about.proquest.com/en/produc ts-services/Harpers-Bazaar-Archive

ProQuest Historical Newspapers: *The New York Times*, https://pq-sta tic-content.proquest.com/collateral/media2/documents/brochure-hnp -newyorktimes.pdf

ProQuest *Vogue* Archive, https://about.proquest.com/en/products-ser vices/vogue_archive

ProQuest Women's Magazine Archive, https://about.proquest.com/en/pro ducts-services/Womens-Magazine-Archive

ProQuest *Women's Wear Daily* Archive, https://about.proquest.com/en/ products-services/www

Preface and Acknowledgments

1 Ray M. Hudson, "Organized Effort in Simplification," *Annals of the American Academy of Political and Social Science* 137, Standards in Industry (May 1928): 1.

2 Eric Boyles, "Changes in the American Surgical Industry during the Great War" (independent study paper, Department of History, University of Wisconsin–Madison, 1989); Glen Asner, "The Politics of Mass Production: Government Promotion of Standardization during the First World War" (B.A. thesis, University of Wisconsin, 1993), https:// papers.ssrn.com/abstract=3276703.

1 The Puzzle of Standard Sizes

1 "Mattress Sizes 101," www.sleepfoundation.org/mattress-sizes.

2 See, for example, *SPR No. 22: Paper* (1924), 3, which lists "stock sizes" of paper for general printing and publishing, for book publishers, and for forms and letterheads.

3 James Couzens, "What I Learned about Business from Ford," *System* 40, no. 3 (September 1921): 264.

4 In 2019, according to the U.S. Census Bureau, 401 establishments man ufactured mattresses (NAICS 337910). See County Business Patterns (*CB1900CBP*), 2019, https://data.census.gov/table/CBP2019.CB1900C BP?q=naics%20337910.

5 On collective action, the classics are Mancur Olson, *The Logic of Collective Action: Public Goods and the Theory of Groups* (Cambridge,

MA: Harvard University Press, 1965), and Claus Offe and Helmut Wiesenthal, "Two Logics of Collective Action: Theoretical Notes on Social Class and Organization Form," *Political Power and Social Theory* 1 (1980): 67–115. On capitalists, see John R. Bowman, *Capitalist Collective Action: Competition, Cooperation, and Conflict in the Coal Industry* (Cambridge, UK and New York: Cambridge University Press; Paris: Éditions de la Maison des sciences de l'homme, 1989); Luca Lanzalaco, "Business Interest Associations," in Geoffrey Jones and Jonathan Zeitlin, eds., *Oxford Handbook of Business History* (Oxford University Press, 2008), 293–315; and Kathleen Thelen, "Employer Organization and the Law: American Exceptionalism in Comparative Perspective," *Law and Contemporary Problems* 83, no. 2 (2020): 23–48. On the relationship between national political structures and the propensity and ability of firms to engage in collective action nationwide, see Colleen A. Dunlavy, *Politics and Industrialization: Early Railroads in the United States and Prussia* (Princeton University Press, 1994), 145–201. In the 1920s, the term "concerted action" (or "concert of action") was used more often than "collective action," which (according to Google's Ngram Viewer) became the dominant term only from the late 1980s.

6 Merritt Roe Smith, *Harpers Ferry Armory and the New Technology: The Challenge of Change* (Ithaca: Cornell University Press, 1977), 107.

7 National Industrial Conference Board, *Trade Associations: Their Economic Significance and Legal Status* (New York: National Industrial Conference Board, 1925), 180.

8 George G. Powers, "We Cut Factory Overhead despite Smaller Volume," *Factory* 28, no. 3 (March 1922): 276. Powers was Vice President and Treasurer of the Union Bed and Spring Company.

9 David Hemenway, *Industrywide Voluntary Product Standards* (Cambridge, MA: Ballinger Publishing Co., [1975]), 24. See also David F. Noble, *America by Design: Science, Technology, and the Rise of Corporate Capitalism* (Oxford University Press, 1977), 78–9.

10 U.S. Department of Commerce, *Simplified Practice: What It Is and What It Offers: Summary of Activities of the Division of Simplified Practice and Description of Services Offered to American Industries, Issued by the Bureau of Standards, November 26, 1924* (Washington, DC: Government Printing Office, 1924), 6.

11 *SPR No. 2: Bedsteads, Springs and Mattresses* (1922), 3–4; U.S. Department of Commerce, *Simplified Practice: What It Is* (1924), 6. The four standard sizes were reaffirmed in subsequent years with the addition of two larger sizes in the late 1950s and early 1960s because

of "the increased height and weight of the population in the United States": *SPR R2-62: Bedding Products and Components* (1962), 17.

12 U.S. Department of Commerce, Bureau of Standards, *Standards Yearbook 1931*, Misc. Pub. No. 119 (Washington, DC: U.S. Government Printing Office, 1931), 246.

13 *SPR No. 24: Hospital Beds* (1925); *SPR No. 11: Bed Blankets: Cotton, Wool, and Cotton and Wool Mixed* (1924); U.S. Department of Commerce, *Simplified Practice: What It Is* (1924), 6.

14 U.S. Bureau of Standards, The Purpose and Application of Simplified Practice, July 1, 1931, mimeograph, Washington, DC, Appendix C, which listed 121 simplified practice recommendations in effect as of June 1931 and another 17 in the process of acceptance.

15 David A. Hounshell, *From the American System to Mass Production, 1800–1932: The Development of Manufacturing Technology in the United States* (Baltimore: Johns Hopkins University Press, 1984), 217–61; Richard S. Tedlow, *New and Improved: The Story of Mass Marketing in America* (New York: Basic Books, 1990), 112–46.

16 Joshua Benjamin Freeman, *Behemoth: A History of the Factory and the Making of the Modern World* (New York: W. W. Norton, 2018), xiii.

17 Naomi Lamoreaux, *The Great Merger Movement in American Business, 1895–1904* (Cambridge University Press, 1985), 15. See also Thelen, "Employer Organization and the Law," 33. In the 1920s, the head of a New York accounting firm laid out the dichotomy in prescriptive terms – i.e., as one that firms *should* conform to, implying that too many did indeed try to straddle the two types: William R. Basset, *Taking the Guesswork out of Business* (New York: B. C. Forbes Publishing Company, 1924), 39–40; W. R. Basset, "How Far Does It Pay to Carry Simplification?" *System* 40, no. 4 (October 1921): 492, 494.

18 Alfred D. Chandler, Jr., "The Beginnings of 'Big Business' in American Industry," *Business History Review* 33, no. 1 (Spring 1959): 1–31; Alfred D. Chandler, Jr., *Strategy and Structure: Chapters in the History of the American Industrial Enterprise* (Cambridge, MA: Harvard University Press, 1962); Alfred D. Chandler, Jr., *The Visible Hand: The Managerial Revolution in American Business* (Cambridge, MA, and London: Belknap Press of Harvard University Press, 1977); Alfred D. Chandler, Jr., *Scale and Scope: The Dynamics of Industrial Capitalism* (Cambridge, MA: Harvard University Press, 1990). On the impact of Chandler's work, see Thomas McCraw, "Introduction: The Intellectual Odyssey of Alfred D. Chandler, Jr.," in *The Essential Alfred Chandler: Essays Toward a Historical Theory of Big Business* (Boston, MA: Harvard Business School Press, 1988); Richard R. John, "Elaborations, Revisions, Dissents: Alfred

D. Chandler, Jr.'s 'The Visible Hand' after Twenty Years," *Business History Review* 71, no. 2 (Summer 1997): 151–200; Steven W. Usselman, "Still Visible: Alfred D. Chandler's 'The Visible Hand,'" *Technology and Culture* 47, no. 3 (July 2006): 584–96; and "Alfred Chandler Tribute," *Enterprise and Society* 9, no. 3 (September 2009): 405–32. For an overview of the history of "big business" in the U.S., Western Europe, and Japan, see Youssef Cassis, "Big Business," in Jones and Zeitlin, eds., *Oxford Handbook of Business History*, 171–93.

19 Philip Scranton, *Endless Novelty: Specialty Production and American Industrialization, 1865–1925* (Princeton University Press, 1997), 3. The landmark studies were Philip Scranton, *Proprietary Capitalism: The Textile Manufacture at Philadelphia, 1800–1885* (Cambridge and New York: Cambridge University Press, 1983); Michael J. Piore and Charles F. Sabel, *The Second Industrial Divide: Possibilities for Prosperity* (New York: Basic Books, 1984); and Charles Sabel and Jonathan Zeitlin, "Historical Alternatives to Mass Production: Politics, Markets and Technology in Nineteenth-Century Industrialization," *Past and Present*, no. 108 (August 1985). On the subsequent development of this literature, see Charles F. Sabel and Jonathan Zeitlin, eds., *World of Possibilities: Flexibility and Mass Production in Western Industrialization* (Paris: Maison des sciences de l'homme; Cambridge, UK, and New York: Cambridge University Press, 1997); Jonathan Zeitlin, "The Historical Alternatives Approach," in Jone and Zeitlin, eds., *Oxford Handbook of Business History*, 120–40; Gerald Berk, *Louis Brandeis and the Making of Regulated Competition, 1900–1932*, Kindle ed. (Cambridge University Press, 2009); and Laura Phillips Sawyer, *American Fair Trade: Proprietary Capitalism, Corporatism, and the "New Competition," 1890–1940*, Kindle ed. (New York: Cambridge University Press, 2019). For a synthesis of studies of small business, see Mansel G. Blackford, *A History of Small Business in America*, 2nd ed. (Chapel Hill and London: University of North Carolina Press, 2003).

20 Philip Scranton, *Figured Tapestry: Production, Markets, and Power in Philadelphia Textiles, 1885–1941* (Cambridge University Press, 1989); Scranton, *Endless Novelty*.

21 Scranton, *Endless Novelty*, 21.

22 Scranton, *Endless Novelty*, 340, 348–9.

23 Though their volume focuses on the European experience (its single essay on the U.S. is by Scranton on textiles), Charles F. Sabel and Jonathan Zeitlin, "Stories, Strategies, Structures: Rethinking Historical Alternatives to Mass Production," in Sabel and Zeitlin, eds., *World of Possibilities*, offers a useful conceptual framework for moving beyond

the large/small, mass/specialty dichotomy. On American associations of specialty producers as a "third way" between large integrated firms and smaller firms acting independently, see Berk, *Louis Brandeis*; and Sawyer, *American Fair Trade*. On collective bargaining as a strategic response by specialty producers to intense competition in the United States and Germany, see Thelen, "Employer Organization and the Law," 23–48.

24 To gauge the impressive topical range of the recent literature, see Philip Scranton and Patrick Fridenson, *Reimagining Business History* (Baltimore: Johns Hopkins University Press, 2013); Jürgen Kocka and Marcel van der Linden, eds., *Capitalism: The Reemergence of a Historical Concept* (London and New York: Bloomsbury Academic, 2016); Kenneth Lipartito, "Reassembling the Economic: New Departures in Historical Materialism," *American Historical Review* 121, no. 1 (February 2016): 101–39; Walter A. Friedman, "Recent Trends in Business History Research: Capitalism, Democracy, and Innovation," *Enterprise and Society* 18, no. 4 (December 2017): 748–71; Daniel Wadhwani and Christina Lubinski, "Reinventing Entrepreneurial History," *Business History Review* 91 (Winter 2017): 768–99; Sven Beckert and Christine Desan, "Introduction," in *American Capitalism: New Histories* (New York: Columbia University Press, 2018), 1–32.

25 For a comprehensive description of types of standards, see Robert A. Brady, *Industrial Standardization* (New York: National Industrial Conference Board, Inc., 1929), 23.

26 Andrew L. Russell, *Open Standards and the Digital Age: History, Ideology, and Networks*, Kindle ed. (New York: Cambridge University Press, 2014); JoAnne Yates and Craig N. Murphy, *Engineering Rules: Global Standard Setting since 1880* (Baltimore: Johns Hopkins University Press, 2019). They also underestimate the importance of the National Bureau of Standards, both in helping to set standards, as this book shows, and in prompting engineers to organize national standardizing bodies defensively. On the latter, see, for example, Rexmond C. Cochrane, *Measures for Progress: A History of the National Bureau of Standards*, Misc. Pub. No. 275 ([Washington, DC]: U.S. Department of Commerce, National Bureau of Standards, 1966), 255, 304.

27 Yates and Murphy, *Engineering Rules*, 34, 35.

28 Ellis W. Hawley, "Herbert Hoover, the Commerce Secretariat, and the Vision of an 'Associative State,' 1921–1928," *Journal of American History* 61, no. 1 (June 1974): 125; Peri E. Arnold, "The 'Great Engineer' as Administrator: Herbert Hoover and Modern Bureaucracy," *Review of Politics* 42, no. 3 (July 1980): 342–3; Ellis Hawley, "Three Facets of

Hooverian Associationalism: Lumber, Aviation, and Movies, 1921–1930," in Thomas K. McCraw, ed., *Regulation in Perspective: Historical Essays* (Boston, MA: Division of Research, Graduate School of Business Administration, Harvard University; Cambridge, MA: Distributed by Harvard University Press, 1981), 101–4; Kendrick A. Clements, "Herbert Hoover and Conservation, 1921–1933," *American Historical Review* 89, no. 1 (February 1984): 70–3; William J. Barber, *From New Era to New Deal: Herbert Hoover, the Economists, and American Economic Policy, 1921–1933* (Cambridge and New York: Cambridge University Press, 1985), 13–14; David M. Hart, "Herbert Hoover's Last Laugh: The Enduring Significance of the 'Associative State' in the United States," *Journal of Policy History* 10, no. 4 (1998): 423; Marc Allen Eisner, *From Warfare State to Welfare State: World War I, Compensatory State-Building, and the Limits of the Modern Order* (University Park: Pennsylvania State University Press, 2000), 119–21; Regina Lee Blaszczyk, "No Place Like Home: Herbert Hoover and the American Standard of Living," in Timothy Walch, ed., *Uncommon Americans: The Lives and Legacies of Herbert and Lou Henry Hoover* (Westport, CT, and London: Praeger, 2003), 125–6; Kendrick A. Clements, *The Life of Herbert Hoover: Imperfect Visionary, 1918–1928* (New York: Palgrave Macmillan, 2010), 110–11 (cited hereafter as *Imperfect Visionary*); Glen Jeansonne, with David Luhrssen, *Herbert Hoover: A Life* (New York: New American Library, 2016), 161. On historians' changing views of Hoover, see Brian E. Birdnow, "Hoover Biographies and Hoover Revisionism," in Katherine A. S. Sibley, ed., *A Companion to Warren G. Harding, Calvin Coolidge, and Herbert Hoover* (Chichester: John Wiley & Sons, 2014), 379–96.

29 William R. Tanner, "Secretary Hoover's War on Waste, 1921–1928," in Carl I. Krog and William R. Tanner, eds., *Herbert Hoover and the Republican Era* (Lanham, MD: University Press of America, 1984), 22.

30 Chandler, *The Visible Hand*, 209, 238; Freeman, *Behemoth*, xii.

31 Hounshell, *From the American System to Mass Production*, 260–1.

32 See Robert J. Gordon, *The Rise and Fall of American Growth: The U.S. Standard of Living since the Civil War* (Princeton University Press, 2017), 557, who cites Moses Abramovitz and Paul A. David, "American Macroeconomic Growth in the Era of Knowledge-Based Progress: The Long-Run Perspective," in Stanley L. Engerman and Robert E. Gallman, eds., *Cambridge Economic History of the United States*, vol. III: *The Twentieth Century* (Cambridge, UK, and New York: Cambridge University Press, 2000), 48, who in turn cite Hounshell. See also Freeman, *Behemoth*, 144 (citing Hounshell). In an earlier, influential study,

economic historian Nathan Rosenberg also portrayed the diffusion of Ford's techniques in the 1920s implicitly as a learning process: Nathan Rosenberg, *Technology and American Economic Growth* (Armonk, NY: Sharpe, 1972), 112–13. See, more recently, David Mowery and Nathan Rosenberg, "Twentieth-Century Technological Change," in Engerman and Gallman, eds., *Cambridge Economic History of the United States*, vol. III, 834–35. See also Jonathan Levy, *Ages of American Capitalism: A History of the United States*, Kindle ed. (New York: Random House, 2021), 326.

33 David E. Nye, *America's Assembly Line* (Cambridge, MA: MIT Press, 2013), 53.

34 M. D. Cooper, "Simplification in the Lamp Industry," *Electrical World* 82, no. 12 (1923): 630. Cooper was in the Engineering Department of General Electric's National Lamp Works.

35 Arthur A. Bright, Jr., *The Electric-Lamp Industry: Technological Change and Economic Development from 1800 to 1947* (New York: Macmillan Company, 1949), 202–3.

36 U.S. Department of Commerce and Labor, Bureau of Standards, *Standard Specifications for the Purchase of Carbon-Filament Incandescent Lamps, Bureau Circular No. 13* (Washington, DC: Bureau of Standards, May 1, 1907), 3, available at https://hdl.handle.net/2027/uiug.3011210692 0736; U.S. Department of Commerce, Bureau of Standards, *Standards Yearbook 1927*, Misc. Pub. No. 77 (Washington, DC: Government Printing Office, 1927), 3; Cochrane, *Measures for Progress*, 112. The specifications were periodically revised in formal or informal conferences and then were adopted by the new Federal Specifications Board in 1922: Cochrane, *Measures for Progress*, 112n118; U.S. Department of Commerce, *United States Government Specifications for Large Tungsten Filament Incandescent Electric Lamps, Circular of the Bureau of Standards, No. 13 [10th Edition Issued February 7, 1923]: Federal Specifications Board, Standard Specification No. 23* ([Washington, DC]: [Government Printing Office], 1923), 1, available at https://hdl.handle .net/2027/uiug.30112106920728.

37 U.S. Department of Commerce, *Standards Yearbook 1927*, 3.

38 Ray M. Hudson, "The New Conservation – II," *Scientific American* 128, no. 1 (January 1923): 28 (editor's note in text box).

39 On economic actors and strategic reflection, see Sabel and Zeitlin, "Stories, Strategies, Structures," 1–33.

40 Cecil Chisholm, "Simplification in British Industry: I. – Progress at Home and Abroad," *The Times Imperial and Foreign Trade and Engineering Supplement* (London), August 8, 1925, 513. See also U.S. Department

of Commerce, Division of Simplified Practice, "Supplement: British Interest in Simplified Practice," *Monthly News Bulletin*, no. 8 (November 15, 1925): 3.

41 On varieties of capitalism, the foundational study is Peter A. Hall and David W. Soskice, eds., *Varieties of Capitalism: The Institutional Foundations of Comparative Advantage* (New York: Oxford University Press, 2001), which has spawned an enormous literature. Among many possible points of entry, see Colleen A. Dunlavy and Thomas Welskopp, "Myths and Peculiarities: Comparing U.S. and German Capitalism," *German Historical Institute Bulletin*, no. 41 (Fall 2007): 33–64; Bob Hancké, ed., *Debating Varieties of Capitalism: A Reader* (Oxford University Press, 2009); "'Varieties of Capitalism' Roundtable," *Business History Review* 84, no. 4 (Winter 2010) ; "Business–Government Relations and National Economic Models," *Business History* 63, no. 8 (2021). On Fordism, see Stefan Link, *Forging Global Fordism: Nazi Germany, Soviet Russia, and the Contest over the Industrial Order*, Kindle ed. (Princeton and Oxford: Princeton University Press, 2020), esp. the section "What Was Fordism?" in the Introduction.

2 "A Profusion of Styles" on the Eve of the Great War

1 The "product diversity" described here is different from product "diversification." Following Chandler, the strategy of diversification, increasingly popular in the 1920s, entailed adding new product lines that were technologically related to existing product lines or could be handled by the existing sales organization. See Chandler, *The Visible Hand*, 473–6. "Product diversity" also differs from the marketing strategy of "product differentiation" when that strategy is defined solely in terms of marketing (e.g., branding). See Peter R. Dickson and James L. Ginter, "Market Segmentation, Product Differentiation, and Marketing Strategy," *Journal of Marketing* 51, no. 2 (April 1987): 1–10. On product differentiation as a unilateral competitive strategy, see also Bowman, *Capitalist Collective Action*, 34. As used here, "product diversity" means that styles and sizes proliferated *within* product lines and that commodities were modified *physically* to differentiate them from competitors' products – in other words, a form of product differentiation that necessitated alterations in the manufacturing process. For example, when manufacturers of sterling silver flatware agreed to limit new patterns of flatware collectively, they defined a "new pattern" as one "requiring for its manufacture a set of front dies or the use of tools which change the character of an already existing pattern": *SPR No. 54: Sterling Silver Flatware* (1926), 2–3.

2 Benedict Crowell and Robert Forrest Wilson, *The Giant Hand: Our Mobilization and Control of Industry and Natural Resources, 1917–1918* (New Haven: Yale University Press, 1921), 66.

3 Stella Stewart, *Consumer Goods (Other than Food): Government Controls in 1918*, U.S. Department of Labor, Bureau of Labor Statistics, Historical Studies of Wartime Problems No. 40 (April 1942), 5–6, 7, 9. Stewart's study was part of a comprehensive set of mimeographed reports on World War I policies produced during World War II by the U.S. Department of Labor's Bureau of Labor Statistics, many concerning conservation. See Historical Studies of Wartime Problems Nos. 1–54, available at https://catalog.hathitrust.org/Record/102565939.

4 E.g., "News of the Industry: Conservation Schedule for Electric Heating Appliances," *Electrical World* 72, no. 14 (October 5, 1918): 660.

5 S. H. Ditchett, "Effect of Advertising of Limitation of Styles and Sizes: The Advertisable Possibilities of a Simplified Product," *Printers' Ink* 105, no. 5 (October 31, 1918): 81. A single bed manufacturer was reported to have "carried 901 designs" on the eve of the Great War: William A. Durgin, "Alice in Modernland: The Sixth of a Series on Distribution," *Nation's Business* 11, no. 6 (June 1923): 13.

6 *Second Annual Report of the Council of National Defense for the Fiscal Year Ended June 30, 1918*, House Doc. No. 1440, 65th Cong., 3d sess. (Washington, DC: Government Printing Office, 1918), 199 (cited hereafter as *Second Annual Report of the CND*); *SPR No. 6: Files and Rasps* (1924), 7; Stella Stewart, *Industrial Conservation: Evolution of Policies and Procedures, 1917–1918*, U.S. Department of Labor, Bureau of Labor Statistics, Historical Studies of Wartime Problems No. 24 (November 1941), 34, 36; James A. McDevitt, *Condition and Regulation of the Shoe Industry, 1914–1918*, U.S. Department of Labor, Bureau of Labor Statistics, Historical Studies of Wartime Problems No. 7 (May 1941), 18.

7 George B. Heckel, *The Paint Industry: Reminiscences and Comments* (St. Louis: American Paint Journal Company, 1931), 590.

8 Herbert Hoover, as interviewed by Theodore M. Knappen, "Making Profits by Cutting Waste," *Magazine of Wall Street* 30, no. 1 (May 13, 1922): 9.

9 "A Message from Herbert Hoover: To the International Milk Dealers Association through William A. Durgin," *The Milk Dealer* 12, no. 2 (November 1922): 84.

10 U.S. War Industries Board, *An Outline of the Board's Origin, Functions, and Organization, Compiled as of November 10, 1918* (Washington, DC: Government Printing Office, 1918), 40.

11 "Eliminating Color as a Selling Point: Desire to Narrow Range of Retail

Stocks Is Reason for Fewer Colors," *Printers' Ink* 104, no. 12 (September 19, 1918): 72. See also *Waste in Industry: By the Committee on Elimination of Waste in Industry of the Federated American Engineering Societies* (Washington, DC: Federated American Engineering Societies, 1921), 396: "Extravagances of distribution"; Bernard Baruch, *American Industry in the War: A Report of the War Industries Board* (Washington, DC: Government Printing Office, 1921), 235: "extravagant use of cloth."

12 *Second Annual Report of the CND*, 196. See also *SPR No. 6: Files and Rasps* (1924), 7: "excessive varieties" of files and rasps in World War I.

13 *SPR No. 23: Plow Bolts* (1925), 6. See also U.S. Department of Commerce, Division of Simplified Practice, "Our Standards or Theirs?" *Monthly News Bulletin*, no. 6 (September 15, 1925): 1: "weed out the superfluous."

14 "Standardizing Flags," *Duluth News Tribune* (Duluth, MN), November 17, 1922, 6 (America's Historical Newspapers). See also U.S. Department of Commerce, *Tenth Annual Report of the Secretary of Commerce* (Washington, DC: Government Printing Office, 1922), 138: "freak varieties"; C. W. Giller, "How Fewer Varieties Changed Losses into Profits," *Factory* 29, no. 6 (December 1922): 666: "freak [sales] forms and books."

15 "Fixing Standard of U.S. Flags: Commerce Branch Seeks to Regulate Sizes to Ten in Number," *Kalamazoo Gazette* (Kalamazoo, MI), November 24, 1922, 19 (America's Historical Newspapers); "Hoover's Aid Declares Simplified Practice in Lumber Business Would Save a Billion Dollars in a Year," *Aberdeen Daily News* (Aberdeen, SD), August 12, 1922, 3 (quotation) (America's Historical Newspapers).

16 Melvin T. Copeland, "Standardization of Products: I. As a National Economy," *Bulletin of the Taylor Society* 6, no. 2 (April 1921): 57. During the war, Copeland served as secretary of the Council of National Defense's Commercial Economy Board and as executive secretary of the War Industries Board's Conservation Division: *Second Annual Report of the CND*, 257, 261. For details on the two agencies, see chapter 3.

17 Ernest T. Trigg, "Industries in Readjustment," *Annals of the American Academy of Political and Social Science* 82, Industries in Readjustment (March 1919): 4.

18 "Standardization of Tires Brings Order out of Chaos," *Printers' Ink* 104, no. 1 (July 4, 1918): 92.

19 Heckel, *The Paint Industry*, 590.

20 "Models Drastically Reduced and Marketability Greatly Improved," *Printers' Ink* 104, no. 11 (September 12, 1918): 77.

21 "Curtailments in Railway Tools: Suggestion Made to War Industrial

Board by Manufacturers Eliminates Many Styles and Sizes," *Electric Railway Journal* 52, no. 19 (November 9, 1918): 863.

22 "Initial Steps Taken to Standardize Sizes of Beds and Bedding," *The Furniture Index* 42, no. 3 (July 1922): 146.

23 "Millman," "Why Not Simplification in Steel Sheets?" *Iron Age* 113, no. 12 (March 20, 1924): 874, 876.

24 Bruce Sinclair, "At the Turn of a Screw: William Sellers, the Franklin Institute, and a Standard American Thread," *Technology and Culture* 10, no. 1 (January 1969): 31.

25 *Progress Report of the National Screw Thread Commission (Authorized by Congress, July 18, 1918, H. R. 10852) As Approved June 19, 1920*, Misc. Pub. No. 42 (Washington, DC: Government Printing Office, January 4, 1921), 86; Cochrane, *Measures for Progress*, 201. The commission was abolished by President Franklin D. Roosevelt on cost-cutting grounds in 1933: Franklin D. Roosevelt, Section 13 – National Screw Thread Commission, June 10, 1933, Executive Order 6166: Organization of Executive Agencies, available at https://en.wikisource.org/wiki/Executive_Order_6166; U.S. Department of Commerce, *Twenty-First Annual Report of the Secretary of Commerce* (Washington, DC: Government Printing Office, 1933), viii. It was revived in 1939–40 as the Interdepartmental Screw Thread Commission: U.S. Department of Commerce, *Twenty-Eighth Annual Report of the Secretary of Commerce* (Washington, DC: Government Printing Office, 1940), xxv.

26 George V. Thompson, "Intercompany Technical Standardization in the Early American Automobile Industry," *Journal of Economic History* 14, no. 1 (Winter 1954): 10–12. On transportation, see also Steven W. Usselman, *Regulating Railroad Innovation: Business, Technology, and Politics in America, 1840–1920* (Cambridge and New York: Cambridge University Press, 2002), 231–9, 359–71; Dunlavy, *Politics and Industrialization*, 144–201, 245–53; and Bruce E. Seely, "Engineers and Government–Business Cooperation: Highway Standards and the Bureau of Public Roads, 1900–1940," *Business History Review* 58, no. 1 (Spring 1984): 51–77.

27 Scranton, *Endless Novelty*, 300.

28 Ernest T. Trigg, "We Increased Volume When We Cut Our Line 60%," *System* 42, no. 4 (October 1922): 489 (quotation); Heckel, *The Paint Industry*, 115–16.

29 Heckel, *The Paint Industry*, 393, 405–11.

30 "Initial Steps Taken," 146.

31 Asner, "The Politics of Mass Production," 32–8. U.S. Department of Commerce, Bureau of Corporations, *Farm-Machinery Trade*

Associations (Washington, DC: Government Printing Office, March 15, 1915) offers a detailed history of prewar associations in the agricultural implement sector. I am indebted to Dr. Asner for this reference.

32 John W. Blodgett and W. M. Ritter, *High Lights of a Decade of Achievement of the National Lumber Manufacturers Association* ([Columbus, OH]: [Hann & Adair Printing Co.], [1929]), 46–7; William G. Robbins, "Voluntary Cooperation vs. Regulatory Paternalism: The Lumber Trade in the 1920s," *Business History Review* 56, no. 3 (Autumn 1982): 371–2.

33 *SPR No. 1: Paving Bricks* (1925), 7; Sterling R. March, "Evidence Study No. 38 of the Structural Clay Products Industry (Preliminary Draft)" (National Recovery Administration, Division of Review, September 1935), 28; Paul Willard Garrett, with Isador Lubin and Stella Stewart, *Government Control over Prices*, W. I. B. Price Bulletin No. 3 (Washington, DC: Government Printing Office, 1920), 333.

34 Homer Hoyt, "Industrial Combination and the Standardization of Production," *Journal of Political Economy* 27, no. 2 (February 1919): 95. See also Homer Hoyt, "Standardization and Its Relation to Industrial Concentration," *Annals of the American Academy of Political and Social Science* 82, Industries in Readjustment (March 1919): 272–3. Hoyt was with the War Trade Board when these articles were published.

35 Hoyt, "Industrial Combination," 97.

36 Jonathan Barron Baskin and Paul J. Miranti, Jr., *A History of Corporate Finance* (Cambridge University Press, 1997), 194.

37 Scranton, *Endless Novelty*, 340.

38 *SPR No. 19: Asbestos Paper and Asbestos Millboard* (1924), 4.

39 Scranton, *Figured Tapestry*, 9–10. See also Berk, *Louis Brandeis*, 58.

40 Susan Strasser, *Satisfaction Guaranteed: The Making of the American Mass Market* (1989; repr. ed., Washington, DC: Smithsonian Institution Press, 1995), 136. On product diversification, see note 1 in this chapter.

41 Copeland, "Standardization of Products: I," 57.

42 Leverett S. Lyon, *Hand-to-Mouth Buying: A Study in the Organization, Planning, and Stabilization of Trade* (Washington, DC: Brookings Institution, 1929), 427, 429–30, 442. See also Melvin T. Copeland, "Marketing," in *Recent Economic Changes in the United States*, vol. I (New York: McGraw-Hill Book Company, 1929), 343, who dates the term to 1872. A professor of marketing, however, placed the origins of the practice in the 1890s and saw it ("Buy little and buy often") as a merchandising technique that wholesalers deployed to fend off direct selling by manufacturers: Paul H. Nystrom, Discussion, in William

O. Jelleme, "Hand to Mouth Buying: An Appraisal of Current Buying Practice," *Bulletin of the Taylor Society* 12, no. 1 (February 1927): 299.

43 Lyon, *Hand-to-Mouth Buying*, vii; Copeland, "Marketing," 343; Scranton, *Figured Tapestry*, 329–47.

44 "'Hand to Mouth' Buying Not a Sign of Hard Times," *Magazine of Wall Street*, June 1914, 108. On the influence of "fashion and style" on hand-to-mouth buying, see Lyon, *Hand-to-Mouth Buying*, 453–8; on transportation and communication technologies, see George A. Gade and Robert Morris Associates, *Hand-to-Mouth Buying and the Inventory Situation* (Lansdowne, PA: Robert Morris Associates, 1929). See also Charles P. White, "Hand-to-Mouth Buying," *Annals of the American Academy of Political and Social Science* 139, no. 1, Stabilization of Commodity Prices (September 1928): 136–45. A ribbon manufacturer advocated the practice as integral to "scientific store-keeping": Brice P. Disque, "Making Hand-to-Mouth Buying Profitable," *System* 46, no. 4 (October 1924): 415–20, 454, 456, 458.

45 See Lyon, *Hand-to-Mouth Buying*, 407; Gade and Robert Morris Associates, *Hand-to-Mouth Buying*, 15. On the "inventory burden" or "stock burden" that hand-to-mouth buying shifted from wholesalers and retailers to manufacturers, see Richard A. Feiss, Discussion, in Jelleme, "Hand to Mouth Buying," 300; Scranton, *Figured Tapestry*, 338–47; and Philip Scranton, "'Have a Heart for the Manufacturers!': Production, Distribution, and the Decline of American Textile Manufacturing," in Sabel and Zeitlin, eds., *World of Possibilities*, 337–8. See also the chapters on "Stock Burden" in Lyon, *Hand-to-Mouth Buying*, 221–76. On what might be termed a shift in the "style burden" to manufacturers, see Sanford E. Thompson, Discussion, in Jelleme, "Hand to Mouth Buying," 302; and Fred E. Clark, "An Analysis of the Causes and Results of Hand-to-Mouth Buying," *Harvard Business Review* 6, no. 4 (July 1928): 396. On "hand-to-mouth inventories" in Detroit auto manufacturing in the World War I era, see Michael Schwartz and Andrew Fish, "Just-in-Time Inventories in Old Detroit," *Business History* 40, no. 3 (1998): 48–71. Although the concept of "lean production" is associated with the Toyota Motor Co. in the 1950s, its origins extend back to the U.S. in the 1920s. Kiichiro Toyoda, "notorious [for his] aversion to waste," pioneered his "just in time" production system in the 1930s, after touring American manufacturing facilities in the 1920s: Jeffrey R. Bernstein, "Toyoda Automatic Looms and Toyota Automobiles," in Thomas K. McCraw, ed., *Creating Modern Capitalism: How Entrepreneurs, Companies, and Countries Triumphed in Three Industrial Revolutions*

(Cambridge, MA, and London: Harvard University Press, 1997), 407, 426–7; James P. Womack, Daniel T. Jones, and Daniel Roos, *The Story of Lean Production – Toyota's Secret Weapon in the Global Car Wars that Is Revolutionizing World Industry*, Kindle ed. [1990; New York: Free Press, 2007], 46–68.

46 Dunlavy and Welskopp, "Myths and Peculiarities," 48–9. See also W. F. Gephart, "Grading and Standardization in Marketing Foods," *Annals of the American Academy of Political and Social Science* 82, Industries in Readjustment (March 1919): 265.

47 See, for example, U.S. Congress, House of Representatives, Committee on Coinage, Weights, and Measures, *Hearings on H.R. 5956 to Fix the Size of Baskets or Other Open Containers for Small Fruits or Berries, before the Committee on Coinage, Weights, and Measures*, 62nd Cong., 1st sess., May 9, 1911, and *To Establish Standard Barrel for Fruits, Vegetables, and Other Dry Commodities and to Establish a Standard Box for Apples: Hearings before the Committee on Coinage, Weights, and Measures*, 63rd Cong., 2nd sess., May 26–27, 1914. The legal basis for these initiatives was not Congress's Constitutional power to regulate interstate commerce, which would have limited their scope, but its power to standardize weights and measures nationwide.

48 U.S. Department of Commerce, Bureau of Standards, *State and National Laws Concerning Weights and Measures of the United States*, 2nd ed., rev. by William Parry (Washington, DC: Government Printing Office, 1912), vii–viii.

49 U.S. Department of Commerce, Bureau of Standards, *Federal and State Laws Relating to Weights and Measures*, 3rd ed., Misc. Pub. No. 20 (Washington, DC: Government Printing Office, August 1926).

50 Gephart, "Grading and Standardization," 265. See also U.S. Department of Commerce, Bureau of Standards, *Annual Report of the Director of the Bureau of Standards to the Secretary of Commerce for the Fiscal Year Ended June 30, 1922*, Misc. Pub. No. 50 (Washington, DC: Government Printing Office, 1922), 249.

51 Earl E. Whitehorne, "Practical Economies the Keynote," *Electrical World* 81, no. 1 (January 6, 1923): 40.

52 Hoyt, "Industrial Combination," 95.

53 American Society for Testing Materials, ed., *Proceedings of the Twenty-Second Annual Meeting, Held at Atlantic City, New Jersey, June 24–27, 1919*, vol. XIX, Part 1, Committee Reports, Tentative Standards (Philadelphia: American Society for Testing Materials, 1919), 83.

54 "Millman," "Why Not Simplification in Steel Sheets?" 876.

55 Regina Lee Blaszczyk, *The Color Revolution* (Cambridge, MA, and Washington, DC: MIT Press in association with Lemelson Center, Smithsonian Institution, 2012), 117.

56 J. George Frederick, *Book of Business Standards* (New York: Nicholas L. Brown, 1925), 112.

57 Crowell and Wilson, *The Giant Hand*, 66. For a fascinating account of the diversity of wagon gauges and wheels before World War I and the constraints on consumer choice imposed by the existing ruts in unsurfaced roads, see E. E. Parsonage, "What Simplification Saves Us," *System* 40, no. 6 (December 1921): 709–10.

58 Baruch, *American Industry in the War*, 67.

59 Copeland, "Standardization of Products: I," 57.

60 On competing conceptions of competition in this era, see Sawyer, *American Fair Trade*. My focus is on competition in domestic markets, but foreign competition could also induce product variety. For example, even though American woolen manufacturers used "double-width" looms, they also made narrow-width fabrics because their competitors, English and Scottish manufacturers of fine woolens, did so: Arch Wilkinson Shaw, *Enlarging the War Effort through Simplification* (Chicago: [Arch W. Shaw], February 1943), 4.

61 Chamber of Commerce of the United States of America, Domestic Distribution Department, *A Commercial Tower of Babel: "Piling Variety upon Variety"* (Washington, DC: Chamber of Commerce of the U.S., 1923), 2, 3.

62 Whitehorne, "Practical Economies the Keynote," 40.

63 "Standardization of Tires Brings Order out of Chaos," 92.

64 Hoyt, "Industrial Combination," 96.

65 J. Donald Edwards, *Paint and Varnish: Conservation of Finished Product and Control of Raw Materials, 1917–1918*, U.S. Department of Labor, Bureau of Labor Statistics, Historical Studies of Wartime Problems No. 34 (March 1942), 42. See also Waldon Fawcett, "Paper Conservation Put up to Commercial Printers and Allied Trade Interests," *The Inland Printer* 61, no. 2 (May 1918): 200.

66 Copeland, "Standardization of Products: I," 57.

67 Walter J. Matherly, "Financial Economies of Simplified Industrial Practice," *The Annalist* 20, no. 509 (October 16, 1922): 383.

68 E. W. McCullough, "The Relation of the Chamber of Commerce of the United States of America to the Growth of the Simplification Program in American Industry," *Annals of the American Academy of Political and Social Science* 137, Standards in Industry (May 1928): 9.

69 Lester G. Herbert, "After the War Co-operation: Business Gained Many

Advantages during the War through Co-operation – What the Trade Must Do to Retain These Gains," *Paint, Oil and Drug Review* 67, no. 1 (January 1, 1919): 14.

70 Couzens, "What I Learned," 263–4; Allan Nevins and Frank Ernest Hill, *Ford: The Times, the Man, the Company* (New York: Charles Scribner's Sons, 1954), 387–414, 452. Ford offered four versions of the Model T (runabout, touring car, town car, and delivery), all built on the same chassis: Nevins and Hill, *Ford*, 452.

71 Benjamin P. Chass, "Inefficiency and Waste in American Industry," *Industrial Management* 70, no. 4 (October 1925): 240–1.

72 Whitehorne, "Practical Economies the Keynote," 39. For an expression of this concern by an electrical wiring device manufacturer, see "Manufacturing and Markets: Sentiment for Simplification Spreading," *Electrical World* 81, no. 24 (June 16, 1923): 1438.

73 Heckel, *The Paint Industry*, 590.

74 "Models Drastically Reduced," 78.

75 Durgin, "Alice in Modernland," 13.

76 On salesmen and jobbers in this era, see Glenn Porter and Harold C. Livesay, *Merchants and Manufacturers: Studies in the Changing Structure of Nineteenth-Century Marketing* (Baltimore and London: Johns Hopkins University Press, 1971); Strasser, *Satisfaction Guaranteed*, 58–88; Walter A. Friedman, *Birth of a Salesman: The Transformation of Selling in America* (Cambridge, MA: Harvard University Press, 2004). As the following comments suggest, salesmen or sales departments seem to have had considerable discretion in taking orders for customized products.

77 Leon I. Thomas, "Simplification in Industry, II: The Source of This Movement in War-Time Conservation," *Factory* 26, no. 6 (March 15, 1921): 754.

78 Copeland, "Standardization of Products: I," 57.

79 A. M. Maddock, "How Simplification Removed Production Difficulties: Ninth Article in the Simplification in Industry Series," *Factory* 27, no. 5 (November 1921): 612.

80 Trigg, "We Increased Volume," 427.

81 "The Trend toward Simplification: A Review of the Simplification of Industry in War Times and Its Present Status," *Printers' Ink* 119, no. 5 (May 4, 1922): 42. See also Arthur McClure, with James G. Lamb, Secretary, Scott Paper Company, Chester, PA, "Two Thousand Brands Reduced to Three," *Printers' Ink* 118, no. 5 (February 2, 1922): 123–4, 127–8; Strasser, *Satisfaction Guaranteed*, 58–9.

82 Baruch, *American Industry in the War*, 69.

83 "The Trend toward Simplification," 41. See also Hemenway, *Industrywide Voluntary Product Standards*, 21–2.

84 Hounshell, *From the American System to Mass Production*, 217–61; Karel Williams, Colin Haslam, and John Williams, "Ford versus 'Fordism': The Beginning of Mass Production?" *Work, Employment & Society* 6, no. 4 (December 1992): 517–55; Nye, *America's Assembly Line*, 41–65.

85 Jennifer Karns Alexander, *The Mantra of Efficiency: From Waterwheel to Social Control* (Baltimore: Johns Hopkins University Press, 2008), 76–100. On the concepts of waste and efficiency, see also Samuel P. Hays, *Conservation and the Gospel of Efficiency: The Progressive Conservation Movement, 1890–1920* (Cambridge, MA: Harvard University Press, 1959); Samuel Haber, *Efficiency and Uplift: Scientific Management in the Progressive Era, 1890–1920* (University of Chicago Press, 1964); Cecelia Tichi, *Shifting Gears: Technology, Literature, Culture in Modernist America*, Kindle ed. (Chapel Hill and London: University of North Carolina Press, 1987), ch. 2; and John M. Jordan, *Machine-Age Ideology: Social Engineeering and American Liberalism, 1911–1939* (Chapel Hill: North Carolina University Press, 1994), 33–67.

86 Cochrane, *Measures for Progress*; Noble, *America by Design*, 69–83; Russell, *Open Standards*; Yates and Murphy, *Engineering Rules*.

87 Morris Llewellyn Cooke, *Academic and Industrial Efficiency: A Report to the Carnegie Foundation for the Advancement of Teaching*, Bulletin No. 5 (New York: [Carnegie Foundation for the Advancement of Teaching], 1910). A review in the *New York Evening Post* and a facetious report "to the trustees of the Buncombe Fund" in the *New York Sun* were reprinted in *Science*: "Quotations: Academic and Industrial Efficiency," *Science* 32, no. 835 (December 30, 1910): 953–5.

88 Alexander, *The Mantra of Efficiency*, 78–9.

89 Alexander, *The Mantra of Efficiency*, 79 (original italics).

90 "Sales Rise as Different Models Are Merged into One Line," *Printers' Ink* (September 7, 1916): 28.

91 Henry Ford, "'If My Business Were Small,'" *System* 43, no. 6 (June 1923): 792. The article, ghost-written by Samuel Crowther, came with an endorsement by the retailer Edward A. Filene.

92 Hoyt, "Standardization," 271–2.

93 U.S. Department of Commerce, Bureau of Standards, *Annual Report of the Director of the Bureau of Standards to the Secretary of Commerce for the Fiscal Year Ended June 30, 1921*, Misc. Pub. No. 47 (Washington, DC: Government Printing Office, 1921), 23. See also U.S. Department

of Commerce, *Annual Report of the Director of the Bureau of Standards
... 1922*, 7.

94 National Industrial Conference Board, *Trade Associations*, 182.

95 Noble, *America by Design*, 69.

96 Grosvenor B. Clarkson, *Industrial America in the World War: The
Strategy behind the Line, 1917–1918*, rev. ed. (Boston and New York:
Houghton Mifflin Company, 1924), 454, quoted in Cochrane, *Measures
for Progress*, 179n149.

3 Suppressing Product Diversity in the Great War

1 On the complex politics of mobilizing the American economy in World
War I and the post-war consequences, see Paul A. C. Koistinen, "The
'Military-Industrial Complex' in Historical Perspective: World War
I," *Business History Review* 41, no. 4 (Winter 1967): 378–403; Robert
D. Cuff, *The War Industries Board: Business–Government Relations
during World War I* (Baltimore: Johns Hopkins University Press, 1973);
David M. Kennedy, *Over Here: The First World War and American
Society* (Oxford University Press, 1982), 93–143; Eisner, *From Warfare
State to Welfare State*; and Hugh Rockoff, *America's Economic Way of
War: War and the US Economy from the Spanish–American War to the
Persian Gulf War* (Cambridge University Press, 2012), 99–154.

2 See Cuff, *The War Industries Board*, 16–30, on Howard E. Coffin,
president of the Society of Automotive Engineers, and Hollis Godfrey,
president of the Drexel Institute (now Drexel University).

3 *First Annual Report of the Council of National Defense ... for the Fiscal
Year Ended June 30, 1917*, Senate Doc. No. 156, 65th Cong., 2nd sess.
(Washington, DC: Government Printing Office, 1918), 37 (hereafter
cited as *First Annual Report of the CND*); *Second Annual Report of
the CND*, 193; Baruch, *American Industry in the War*, 58–60; Bernard
M. Baruch, *American Industry in the War: A Report of the War
Industries Board (March 1921)*, ed. Richard H. Hippelheuser (New
York: Prentice-Hall, Inc., 1941), 71n–72n; Stella Stewart, "Industrial
Conservation in the First World War," *Monthly Labor Review* 54, no.
1 (January 1942): 17, 28–9; Cuff, *The War Industries Board*, 133–4,
202–3.

4 On the evolution of these World War I agencies, see the sources cited
in note 1 above; Asner, "The Politics of Mass Production," 12–27;
and contemporary sources such as U.S. War Industries Board, *An
Outline of the Board's Origin*, and Baruch, *American Industry in the
War*, 17–29. The Council of National Defense, although established
in 1916, was not fully operational until March 1917; it was com-

posed of six cabinet secretaries and aided by an advisory commission staffed by leading businessmen. The CND created the War Industries Board in July 1917; in March 1918, as the mobilization nearly collapsed, President Woodrow Wilson made it an independent agency, headed by Bernard Baruch and reporting directly to the president. On Baruch, see Cuff, *The War Industries Board*; Jordan A. Schwarz, *The Speculator: Bernard M. Baruch in Washington, 1917–1965* (Chapel Hill: University of North Carolina Press, 1981); and James Grant, *Bernard Baruch: The Adventures of a Wall Street Legend*, Kindle ed. (1983; Edinburg, VA: Axios Press, 2012).

5 "Standardization of Products: Discussion," *Bulletin of the Taylor Society* 6, no. 2 (April 1921): 65 (emphasis added). See also *Second Annual Report of the CND*, 193; Baruch, *American Industry in the War*, 58–60; Clarkson, *Industrial America*, 209; Stewart, *Industrial Conservation*, 8; Shaw, *Enlarging the War Effort*, 11. In many industries, however, output was "curtailed" during the war – that is, restricted to a certain percentage of prewar output – usually in exchange for access to economic resources: Cuff, *The War Industries Board*, 203–4. On the curtailment of civilian automobile production, see Irving Bernstein, *Curtailment of Automobile Production in World War I*, U.S. Department of Labor, Bureau of Labor Statistics, Historical Studies of Wartime Problems No. 23 (November 1941); Cuff, *The War Industries Board*, 204–19. The most severely curtailed industry was non-war-related construction, which, in the last months of the war, could only be undertaken with a permit: Baruch, *American Industry in the War*, 57, 363–7. For a comprehensive list of curtailed industries, see Stewart, *Industrial Conservation*, Appendix III.

6 Crowell and Wilson, *The Giant Hand*, 57.

7 Clarkson, *Industrial America*, 209, 218–19; Baruch, *American Industry in the War* (1941 ed.), 71n–72n (Editor's Note); Shaw, *Enlarging the War Effort*, 11.

8 Clarkson, *Industrial America*, 211–12, 228. On Shaw's relationship with WIB chairman Bernard Baruch, see Baruch, *American Industry in the War* (1941 ed.), 62 (Editor's Note).

9 Friedman, *Birth of a Salesman*, 159. On Shaw's career, see also Melvin T. Copeland, "Arch W. Shaw," *Journal of Marketing* 22, no. 3 (1958): 313–15; Robert Cuff, "Edwin F. Gay, Arch W. Shaw, and the Uses of History in Early Graduate Business Education," *Journal of Management History* 2, no. 3 (1996): 9–25; and Morgen Witzel, "Shaw, Arch Wilkinson," in Morgen Witzel, ed., *Encyclopedia of History of American Management* (London: Bloomsbury Publishing Plc, 2005),

465–6. Shaw also published a British edition of *System* and introduced a third U.S. magazine, *System on the Farm*, just as the Commercial Economy Board was being created. See A. W. Shaw, "Announcement," *System on the Farm* 1, no. 1 (1917): 2.

10   William Leach, *Land of Desire: Merchants, Power, and the Rise of a New American Culture* (New York: Pantheon Books, 1993), 161–3; Cuff, "Edwin F. Gay." See also Arthur E. Swanson, "Notes: The Harvard Bureau of Business Research," *Journal of Political Economy* 22, no. 9 (November 1914): 896–900; Herbert Heaton, *A Scholar in Action: Edwin F. Gay* (Cambridge, MA: Harvard University Press, 1952), 78.

11   A. W. Shaw, "Some Problems in Market Distribution," *Quarterly Journal of Economics* 26, no. 4 (August 1912): 703–65; Dickson and Ginter, "Market Segmentation," 2; Strasser, *Satisfaction Guaranteed*, 80; Friedman, *Birth of a Salesman*, 162–5. Shaw's article appeared in book form in 1915; the following year, he published a textbook based on his Harvard lecture materials: Arch Wilkinson Shaw, *Some Problems in Market Distribution* (Cambridge, MA: Harvard University Press, 1915); Arch Wilkinson Shaw, *An Approach to Business Problems* (Cambridge, MA: Harvard University Press, 1916).

12   Shaw, "Some Problems in Market Distribution," 705–6.

13   Swanson, "Notes," 900; "Expenses in Operating Retail Grocery Stores," *Bulletin of the Bureau of Business Research*, no. 5 (1915): 5; Leach, *Land of Desire*, 163. The first ten numbers of the *Bulletin of the Bureau of Business Research*, published from 1913 to 1918, dealt with the retailing and wholesaling of shoes and groceries.

14   A. W. Shaw, "To Checkmate Europe's War-Begotten Efficiency: A Plan by Which the Department of Commerce Would Assist American Business to Attain Full Stature at Home and Overseas," *Nation's Business* 5, no. 2 (February 1917): 10.

15   Clarkson, *Industrial America*, 211.

16   Shaw, "To Checkmate Europe's War-Begotten Efficiency," 10–12 (quotation, 12). Shaw's comments endorsed a proposal by the U.S. Chamber of Commerce to enhance the functions of the Commerce Department.

17   "Expects War to Bring Widespread Business Activity" and "Two Members Are Added to Defense Economy Board," *Official U.S. Bulletin* 1, no. 3 (May 12, 1917): 5.

18   Cuff, "Edwin F. Gay"; Leach, *Land of Desire*, 162. See also Heaton, *A Scholar in Action*. Shaw also recruited George Rublee, a former member of the Federal Trade Commission; Henry S. Dennison, treasurer of a Massachusetts manufacturing firm; and Wallace D. Simmons,

president of a St. Louis hardware company: "Two Members Are Added," 5.

19 "Two Members Are Added," 5; Clarkson, *Industrial America*, 213; Franklin H. Martin, *Digest of the Proceedings of the Council of National Defense during the World War*, Senate Doc. No. 193, 73rd Cong., 2nd sess. (Washington, DC: Government Printing Office, 1934), 114.

20 On wartime wheat policies, see Garrett, *Government Control over Prices*, 45–6, 59–78; and Stella Stewart, *Controls of Wheat, Flour and Bread in World War I, 1917–1919*, U.S. Department of Labor, Bureau of Labor Statistics, Historical Studies of Wartime Problems No. 47 (November 1940).

21 Guy Alchon, *The Invisible Hand of Planning: Capitalism, Social Science, and the State in the 1920s* (Princeton University Press, 1985); Strasser, *Satisfaction Guaranteed*, 146–61; Friedman, *Birth of a Salesman*, 151–89; and Walter A. Friedman, *Fortune Tellers: The Story of America's First Economic Forecasters* (Princeton and Oxford: Princeton University Press, 2014). On price data in particular, see Eli Cook, *The Pricing of Progress: Economic Indicators and the Capitalization of American Life* (Cambridge, MA: Harvard University Press, 2017), 233–54.

22 *First Annual Report of the CND*, 38; Stewart, *Controls of Wheat, Flour and Bread*, 39–40. The board sent surveys to "some 500 bakers in all parts of the country": "Federal Economy Board Studies Bakers' Problems," *Official U.S. Bulletin* 1, no. 3 (May 12, 1917): 2. See also "Commercial Economy Board of Council of National Defense and Its Work," *The Sunday Star* (Washington, DC), September 16, 1917, Part 4, 1 (Chronicling America: Historic American Newspapers); and "War Burdens Made Easier by the Commercial Economy Board," *Burlington Weekly Free Press* (Burlington, VT), January 3, 1918, 10 (Chronicling America: Historic American Newspapers).

23 "War Burdens Made Easier," *Burlington Weekly Free Press*, 10. See also "Economy in Bakers' Bread Sought by Defense Board," *Official U.S. Bulletin* 1, no. 24 (June 7, 1917): 3; and *First Annual Report of the CND*, 38.

24 "Economy in Bakers' Bread Sought by Defense Board," 3; "Bread Economy Campaign Steps Urged upon State Defense Councils by National Body," *Official U.S. Bulletin* 1, no. 41 (June 27, 1917): 8; *First Annual Report of the CND*, 38; Baruch, *American Industry in the War*, 62; Stewart, *Controls of Wheat, Flour and Bread*, 39–40.

25 "Commercial Economy Board Shows Progress in Savings," *Official U.S.*

Bulletin 1, no. 80 (August 13, 1917): 5; *First Annual Report of the CND*, 38; Stewart, *Controls of Wheat, Flour and Bread*, 39–40.

26 For examples of broader publicity, see "Commercial Economy Board of Council of National Defense," 1; "War Burdens Made Easier by the Commercial Economy Board," *Daily Ardmoreite* (Ardmore, OK), September 24, 1917, 5 (Chronicling America: Historic American Newspapers); "War Burdens Made Easier," *Burlington Weekly Free Press*, 10.

27 "Federal Economy Board Studies Bakers' Problems," 2; "Economy in Bakers' Bread Sought by Defense Board," 3; "Bakers Given More Time," *Official U.S. Bulletin* 1, no. 34 (June 19, 1917): 3; "Bread Economy Campaign Steps," 8; "Bread Saving Campaign," *Official U.S. Bulletin* 1, no. 46 (July 3, 1917): 4; "Commercial Economy Board Shows Progress," 5.

28 "Plea to Women to Back Bakers in No-Return Bread Plan Is Made by Miss Ida M. Tarbell," *Official U.S. Bulletin* 1, no. 38 (June 23, 1917): 3; Ida M. Tarbell, "Women Can Help to Win War by Helping to Save Bread," *Arizona Republican* (Phoenix, AZ), June 24, 1917, 5 (Chronicling America: Historic American Newspapers); *First Annual Report of the CND*, 99.

29 See, for example, a newspaper advertisement placed by the Oklahoma City Master Bakers: "War on Waste! Local Bakers Co-operate," *Oklahoma City Times* (Oklahoma City), July 16, 1917, 5 (Chronicling America: Historic American Newspapers).

30 *Second Annual Report of the CND*, 194. The savings were reported as 600,000 barrels, and a barrel typically contained 196 lb of flour: "Allow Barrel Weight Increase," *Packages* 19, no. 1 (January 1916): 55. In September 1917, the wheat conservation program was handed over to the U.S. Food Administration, headed by Herbert Hoover, by then internationally known for his relief efforts in Belgium: *Second Annual Report of the CND*, 194; George H. Nash, *The Life of Herbert Hoover: Master of Emergencies, 1917–1918* (New York and London: W. W. Norton and Co., 1996); Jeansonne, *Herbert Hoover: A Life*, 94–117.

31 Studies of consumers and consumption are largely silent on the World War I conservation measures. See, e.g., Susan Porter Benson, *Counter Cultures: Saleswomen, Managers, and Customers in American Department Stores, 1890–1940* (Urbana and Chicago: University of Illinois Press, 1986); Leach, *Land of Desire*; Strasser, *Satisfaction Guaranteed*; Tracey Deutsch, *Building a Housewife's Paradise: Gender, Politics, and American Grocery Stores in the Twentieth Century* (Chapel Hill: University of North Carolina Press, 2010).

32 *First Annual Report of the CND*, 39.

33 *First Annual Report of the CND*, 39; Henry S. Dennison, quoted in "National Garment Retailers' Association Arranges Meeting at Waldorf-Astoria, November 27, to Discuss the Conservation of Wool," *American Cloak and Suit Review* 14, no. 6 (December 1917): 143.

34 "Stores Urged to Eliminate Unnecessary Service as War Measure by Economy Board," *Official U.S. Bulletin* 1, no. 44 (June 30, 1917): 2; "Merchants Willing to Stop Unnecessary Store Service," *Official U.S. Bulletin* 1, no. 52 (July 11, 1917): 1; "Commercial Economy Board of Council of National Defense," 1; "National Garment Retailers' Association Arranges Meeting," 142, 143; *First Annual Report of the CND*, 39–40; Baruch, *American Industry in the War*, 62; George Soule, *Prosperity Decade: From War to Depression: 1917–1929* (New York: Rinehart & Company, 1947). On pre-World War I returned-goods policies, which were linked to liberal credit policies and free or COD deliveries, see Leach, *Land of Desire*, 123, 127.

35 "Revolution in Delivery System," *Illinois Retail Merchants' Journal* 16, no. 2 (May 1918): 13. See also "Modernizing Delivery Service," *Illinois Retail Merchants' Journal* 16, no. 1 (April 1918): 7. The changes do not appear to have persisted beyond the war, however; by 1929 returned goods were estimated to total 15 percent of gross sales in major U.S. cities: Leach, *Land of Desire*, 301–2.

36 Baruch, *American Industry in the War*, 62–3.

37 Baruch, *American Industry in the War*, 61.

38 "To the Shopping Public," advertisement, *Washington Herald* (Washington, DC), January 6, 1918, 11 (Chronicling America: Historic American Newspapers).

39 "Urgent Plea to Women to Aid Merchants in Reducing Deliveries before the Draft," *Official U.S. Bulletin* 1, no. 73 (August 4, 1917): 4.

40 Bernard M. Baruch, "Just What Is Wartime Thrift? The Question All Women Are Asking Authoritatively Answered for Them," *Ladies' Home Journal* (September 1918): 29 (ProQuest Women's Magazine Archive).

41 "Advertising and the Wool Shortage," *Printers' Ink* 51, no. 10 (December 6, 1917): 137.

42 "'Carry Your Own' Campaign On," *Official U.S. Bulletin* 1, no. 49 (July 7, 1917): 13; "National Garment Retailers' Association Arranges Meeting," 142; Baruch, "Just What Is Wartime Thrift?" 29; Baruch, *American Industry in the War*, 62. Clarkson, *Industrial America*, 216, referred to it as a "buy-and-carry" policy.

43 *Second Annual Report of the CND*, 23.

44 Baruch, *American Industry in the War*, 61, 63.

45 Clarkson, *Industrial America*, 217.

46 Shaw, *An Approach to Business Problems*, 253. The first sentence quoted here also appeared in his 1912 article: Shaw, "Some Problems in Market Distribution," 720. Shaw used the term "product differentiation" to encompass both differentiation via marketing and "product diversity" as I use the term – requiring changes in the manufacturing process. See Shaw, "Some Problems in Market Distribution," 710; Shaw, *An Approach to Business Problems*, 244–54; and chapter 2, note 1 above.

47 Crowell and Wilson, *The Giant Hand*, 66. Shaw's war experience evidently changed his view of product diversity. "Quite properly, in its pioneer stage," he wrote in 1923, "each commodity runs the gamut of various types and patterns, shapes and sizes, in finding those best suited to its purpose and market. After these are established, however, useless differentiations tend to persist. ... Once the pioneer stage in the production of any variety or type of a commodity is past, it should be subjected to a scrutinizing survey, rather than to wait on the slow processes of natural elimination": A. W. Shaw, "Simplification: A Philosophy of Business Management," *Harvard Business Review* 1, no. 4 (July 1923): 427.

48 Quoted in Thomas, "Simplification in Industry, II," 716.

49 On the importance of the assembly line, see Hounshell, *From the American System to Mass Production*, esp. 237–56; Williams, Haslam, and Williams, "Ford versus 'Fordism,'" 517–55. In introducing the assembly line, Hounshell maintains, "the Ford production engineers wrought *true* mass production" (237, emphasis added), a claim that Williams et al. dispute.

50 H. W. Allingham, "Mass Production," *The Electrician* 84, no. 18 (April 30, 1920): 478.

51 "Standardization of Products: Discussion," 65.

52 Shaw, *Enlarging the War Effort*, 6–7. See also Clarkson, *Industrial America*, 219. For a post-World War I analysis of the economics of "simplified manufacturing," see Matherly, "Financial Economies of Simplified Industrial Practice," 382, 384. On the impact of the reduction in metal bed styles on manufacturers and dealers, see Charles W. Wood, *The Great Change: New America as Seen by Leaders in American Government, Industry and Education Who Are Remaking Our Civilization* (New York: Boni and Liveright, 1918), 60–2.

53 Garrett, *Government Control over Prices*, 231. See also Clarkson, *Industrial America*, 219.

54 Garrett, *Government Control over Prices*, 231–2. See also Baruch, *American Industry in the War*, 65–9; Crowell and Wilson, *The Giant Hand*, 67–70; and Stewart, *Industrial Conservation*, Appendix I, Restricted Industries: Regulations of Conservation Division.

55 Wood, *The Great Change*, 63.

56 Crowell and Wilson, *The Giant Hand*, 69.

57 For descriptions of the Conservation Division's process, see Wood, *The Great Change*, 58–9; *Second Annual Report of the CND*, 194; Baruch, *American Industry in the War*, 63; Crowell and Wilson, *The Giant Hand*, 66–7. Shaw suggested early on that his methods were inspired by "the experience of British merchants": "Expects War to Bring Widespread Business Activity," 5.

58 Asner, "The Politics of Mass Production," 48–56, 59–77. For suggested product reductions that railway tool manufacturers submitted to the War Industries Board, see "Curtailments in Railway Tools," 862–3.

59 Crowell and Wilson, *The Giant Hand*, 67. See also Wood, *The Great Change*, 58–9.

60 Frederic L. Paxson, "The American War Government, 1917–1918," *American Historical Review* 26, no. 1 (October 1920): 72. For the furniture schedule, see "Complete Conservation Schedule for Manufacturers of Furniture Issued by War Industries Board," *Official U.S. Bulletin* 2, no. 449 (October 29, 1918): 18–19; "Conservation Schedule of the Furniture Industry," *Good Furniture Magazine* 11, no. 5 (November 1918): 210–12. Restrictions on paper stock (mainly weights and colors) were reprinted in "War Industries Board Issues Regulations Governing Manufacture of Paper," *Typothetae Bulletin* 13, no. 2 (August 1918): 13–15. The limitations on paint and varnish manufacturers were reported in "Number of Paint Shades and Sizes of Containers Reduced," *Official U.S. Bulletin* 2, no. 213 (January 21, 1918): 8; and "Government Fixes Shades," *Paint, Oil and Drug Review* 65, no. 5 (January 30, 1918): 3. On wartime restrictions on colors (other than in house paint), see "Eliminating Color as a Selling Point," 71–2. On color standardization in World War I, see Blaszczyk, *The Color Revolution*, 71–113. The Textile Color Card Association and its Standard Color Card of America were both products of World War I: ibid., 78.

61 Baruch, *American Industry in the War*, 63.

62 Cuff, *The War Industries Board*, 274; Eisner, *From Warfare State to Welfare State*. On the relationship between wars and the growth of civic associations, see Theda Skocpol et al., "Patriotic Partnerships:

Why Great Wars Nourished American Civic Voluntarism," in Ira
Katznelson and Martin Shefter, eds., *Shaped by War and Trade:
International Influences on American Political Development* (Princeton
University Press, 2002), 134–80.

63 Chandler, *The Visible Hand*, 316–17. On trade associations in this era,
see L. E. Warford and Richard A. May, under the direction of Julius
Klein, *Trade Association Activities*, U.S. Department of Commerce,
Elimination of Waste Series (Washington, DC: Government Printing
Office, 1923); Louis Galambos, *Competition and Cooperation: The
Emergence of a National Trade Association* (Baltimore: Johns Hopkins
University Press, 1966) (the pioneering work in business history);
Berk, *Louis Brandeis*; Sawyer, *American Fair Trade*; and Thelen,
"Employer Organization and the Law."

64 U.S. Department of Commerce and Labor, Bureau of Foreign and
Domestic Commerce, *Commercial and Agricultural Organizations of
the United States*, Misc. Series No. 8 (Washington, DC: Government
Printing Office, 1913), 3 (quotation), 4–10.

65 "Notes," *Bulletin of the National Association of Credit Men* 12, no. 5
(1912): 300; N. I. Stone, "Notes: The Chamber of Commerce of the
United States of America," *American Economic Review* 2, no. 3 (1912):
776; Richard Hume Werking, "Bureaucrats, Businessmen, and Foreign
Trade: The Origins of the United States Chamber of Commerce,"
Business History Review 52, no. 3 (Autumn 1978): 321–41.

66 On the war service committees and their predecessors (coopera-
tive committees), see *Second Annual Report of the CND*, 79–81;
Baruch, *American Industry in the War*, 21–3, 103–284; Koistinen,
"The 'Military-Industrial Complex,'" 386, 391–4; and Cuff, *The War
Industries Board*, 68–85, 148–90. For descriptions of individual war
service committees, see "Paint Conservation: War Service Committee
Agree on Practical Matters with United States Government . . .",
Paint, Oil and Drug Review 65, no. 4 (January 23, 1918): 12–16;
and "Cooperating with the Government," *Bulletin of the National
Association of Wool Manufacturers* 47, no. 3 (July 1918): 281–95.

67 Koistinen, "The 'Military-Industrial Complex,'" 380. The Chamber had
lobbied strongly for creation of the CND: *Second Annual Report of the
CND*, 79.

68 Baruch, *American Industry in the War*, 23–4. In Baruch's words, trade
associations were "industries organized so as to act as units": Baruch,
American Industry in the War, 63.

69 Paxson, "The American War Government," 68. Paxson put the number
of war service committees formed during the war at "nearly five hun-

dred." Another source put it at "more than 300": McCullough, "The Relation of the Chamber of Commerce," 9.

70 Baruch, *American Industry in the War*, 103, 108.

71 Quoted in Scranton, *Figured Tapestry*, 285. The war conditions did not preclude foreign competition entirely, however. On the continued competition between British and American woolen mills, see "Editorial and Industrial Miscellany: Conserving the Wool Supply: An Obligation on Foreign as well as on American Manufacturers," *Bulletin of the National Association of Wool Manufacturers* 47 (October 1917): 323–5.

72 "Expects War to Bring Widespread Business Activity," 5. After the war, Shaw apparently no longer saw intra-industry competition as an obstacle to industry-wide reductions in product variety. Now he envisioned – unrealistically, history suggests – "an evolutionary process" that began within the firm, then extended across an industry, and finally encompassed "associated groups of industries": "Standardization of Products: Discussion," 65.

73 Baruch, *American Industry in the War*, 63–5. See also Garrett, *Government Control over Prices*, 332–3.

74 Baruch, *American Industry in the War*, 63. See also "Fashion: Woollen [*sic*] Costumes that Save Wool," *Vogue*, February 1, 1918, 46 (ProQuest *Vogue* Archive); John Allen Murphy, "Can You Be Patriotic without Adulterating Your Brand? The Wool Situation and the Changes in Merchandising that It Is Causing," *Printers' Ink* 102, no. 10 (March 7, 1918): 105–6, 109–10.

75 *Second Annual Report of the CND*, 194. See also *First Annual Report of the CND*, 38.

76 Baruch, *American Industry in the War*, 65. See, for example, a description of the pledge that printers were asked to accept in "Conservation Campaign," *Typothetae Bulletin* 13, no. 3 (September 1918): 24. The pledges to be signed by metal bed and spring manufacturers and dealers and by farm implement manufacturers were reprinted in Baruch, *American Industry in the War*, 373–4, 376.

77 Cuff, *The War Industries Board*, 141–7.

78 Quoted in Cuff, *The War Industries Board*, 191. As a contemporary observer put it, "There was no iron fist at work, at least not in sight": Wood, *The Great Change*, 60.

79 On the evolution of the priorities administration, see Cuff, *The War Industries Board*, 191–219. See also Wood, *The Great Change*, 68–80. For an example of an Industry Priority Certification, see Stewart, *Industrial Conservation*, Appendix IV. In his two case studies (of

left-handed plows and buggies), Asner concludes that the priorities power to deny access to resources was more persuasive for smaller manufacturers than the "appeal to increased efficiency and reduced production costs": Asner, "The Politics of Mass Production," 77.

80 Baruch, *American Industry in the War*, 63. See also Paxson, "The American War Government," 72.

81 Baruch, *American Industry in the War*, 65 (quotation), 127.See also "National Garment Retailers' Association Arranges Meeting," 142; Paxson, "The American War Government," 72; McDevitt, *Condition and Regulation of the Shoe Industry*, 1–18; Asner, "The Politics of Mass Production," 25–6.

82 Copeland, "Standardization of Products: I," 55; Clarkson, *Industrial America*, 220; Shaw, *Enlarging the War Effort*, 8; Cochrane, *Measures for Progress*, 177. For details on specific wartime restrictions by commodity, see U.S. War Industries Board, *An Outline of the Board's Origin*, 39–42; and Stewart, *Consumer Goods (Other than Food)*.

83 Clarkson, *Industrial America*, 210. On Clarkson, see "G. B. Clarkson Dies; Defense Advocate," *New York Times*, January 24, 1937, 46 (ProQuest Historical Newspapers: *The New York Times*); and Cuff, *The War Industries Board*, 20–1, 39–40.

Conservation restrictions extended well beyond product variety. For a compilation of wartime regulations, see Stewart, *Consumer Goods (Other than Food)*. See also *Second Annual Report of the CND*; U.S. War Industries Board, *An Outline of the Board's Origin*, 40–2; Baruch, *American Industry in the War*, 65–8; Copeland, "Standardization of Products: I," 56–7; Crowell and Wilson, *The Giant Hand*, 68–9; Ray M. Hudson, "Simplification and Standardization," in L. P. Alford, ed., *Management's Handbook: By a Staff Specialist* (New York: Ronald Press Company, 1924), 992–4; Stewart, *Industrial Conservation*; and commodity-specific reports in the series Historical Studies of Wartime Problems published during World War II (see chapter 2, note 3).

84 U.S. Food Administration, *The Standard Loaf: Conclusions Based on Investigation of Federal Trade Commission and Report of Bakery Section – Licensing of Bakeries Pursuant to the Presidents' Proclamation*, Bulletin No. 11 (Washington, DC: Government Printing Office, December 1917). It also mandated weight labels, encouraged the wrapping of bread loaves, and required use of alternative grains such as rye, whole wheat, and graham, changes that persisted long after the war: Stewart, *Controls of Wheat, Flour and Bread*, 48. On the U.S. Food Administration, see also Garrett, *Government Control over Prices*, 40–150, 568–639; Nash, *The Life of Herbert Hoover: Master of*

Emergencies, 1917–1918; Meg Jacobs, *Pocketbook Politics: Economic Citizenship in Twentieth-Century America* (Princeton University Press, 2005), 56–64. On the Food Administration's multifaceted use of publicity, see Tanfer Emin Tunc, "Less Sugar, More Warships: Food as American Propaganda in the First World War," *War in History* 19, no. 2 (April 2012): 193–216; Jeansonne, *Herbert Hoover: A Life*, 114–15.

85 *Second Annual Report of the CND*, 103.

86 Quoted in Asner, "The Politics of Mass Production," 32.

87 Garrett, *Government Control over Prices*, 333. On product diversity and control of prices, see also Arthur Robert Burns, *The Decline of Competition: A Study of the Evolution of American Industry* (New York and London: McGraw-Hill Book Company, 1936), 69n62.

88 In revealing a diversity of accounting practices, the war experience – when companies had to open their books to government agencies – also proved eye-opening: Leonard Etherington, "Shoe Business Permanently Strengthened by War's Restrictions," *Printers' Ink* 105, no. 10 (December 5, 1918): 138; Guilliam Clamer, "Standardization: Annual Address by the President," in American Society for Testing Materials, ed., *Proceedings of the Twenty-Second Annual Meeting, Held at Atlantic City, New Jersey, June 24–27, 1919*, vol. XIX, Part 1, Committee Reports, Tentative Standards, 86. Studies that place uniform cost accounting in the broader context of "regulated competition" in the 1920s include Gerald Berk and Marc Schneiberg, "Varieties in Capitalism, Varieties of Association: Collaborative Learning in American Industry, 1900–1925," *Politics and Society* 33, no. 1 (March 2005): 46–87; Berk, *Louis Brandeis*; and Sawyer, *American Fair Trade*.

89 U.S. Department of Commerce, Bureau of Standards, *War Work of the Bureau of Standards*, Misc. Pub. No. 46 (Washington, DC: Government Printing Office, 1921), 99. On electrical manufacturers' "enthusiasm" for product standardization during the war, see "Electrical Manufacturers Plan to Continue Beneficial Co-operation," *Electrical Review* 74, no. 4 (January 25, 1919): 149.

90 See, for example, Soule, *Prosperity Decade*, 17; and Kennedy, *Over Here*, 140.

91 This table, differently formatted, first appeared in Shaw's magazine *Factory* in August 1922: "Steps in Simplification," *Factory*, 29, no. 2 (August 1922): 146. The version from *Industrial Management* in January 1923 is included here because it lends itself better to reproduction.

92 Fruit containers were standardized by Congressional legislation before the war, and the paving-brick reductions were effected after the war.

On the latter, see pp. 78–80 below. The reductions in sizes and styles of farm implements given in the table are identical to those described elsewhere "as developed under war conditions" by a national trade association and the WIB's Conservation Division: Ernest L. Priest, *A Primer of Simplified Practice, Issued by the Bureau of Standards, November 1, 1926* (Washington, DC: Government Printing Office, 1926), 6.

93 On negotiations between farm-implements interests and conservation officials, see Asner, "The Politics of Mass Production."

94 Examples of media reports on reductions include "Germans Change Opinion of Yanks ... Purchasers Now Find Fewer Varieties from Which to Choose, Because of Conservation," *Cresco Plain Dealer* (Cresco, IA), August 23, 1918, 2 (Chronicling America: Historic American Newspapers); Ditchett, "Effect of Advertising of Limitation of Styles and Sizes," 81; Wood, *The Great Change*, 55–67; "Order out of Chaos by Standardization," *Literary Digest* 62, no. 7 (Whole No. 1530) (August 16, 1919): 77, 79, 82, 84.

95 Baruch, *American Industry in the War*, 254.

96 Baruch, *American Industry in the War*, 253; Stewart, *Industrial Conservation*, 33; McDevitt, *Condition and Regulation of the Shoe Industry*, 18. On the WIB's negotiations with the shoe industry, largely over prices, see Cuff, *The War Industries Board*, 234–40. Shaw and Gay would have had intimate knowledge of shoe retailing, which, as noted earlier in this chapter, was the subject of the Harvard Bureau of Business Research's first research project.

97 Stewart, *Industrial Conservation*, 36; "The Trend toward Simplification," 42.

98 Baruch, *American Industry in the War*, 67.

99 *SPR No. 6: Files and Rasps* (1924), 7.

100 "Standardizing Paints and Containers in War-Time," *Scientific American*, February 16, 1918, 160; Edwards, *Paint and Varnish*, 3–4. It should be noted that ready-mixed paints at this time were colored in the factory; in-store mixing of colors was not introduced until after World War II: Kathleen McDermott and Davis Dyer, *America's Paint Company: A History of Sherwin–Williams* (Cleveland: The Sherwin–Williams Company, 1991), 65. One company reported having offered ready-mixed house paint in 108 colors in 1908: Trigg, "We Increased Volume," 425. Most large ready-mixed paint manufacturers, according to a CEB survey, offered between 48 and 64 house paint colors: Edwards, *Paint and Varnish*, 37. Around 1915, The Sherwin–Williams Company, for example, offered its best exterior paint in 52 colors,

while Sears, Roebuck and Co. and Montgomery Ward and Co. offered their best in 48 and 42 colors, respectively: The Sherwin–Williams Company, Combined Price List and Color Charts Sept. 1915, The Sherwin–Williams Company Center of Excellence, Cleveland, OH, 7; Sears, Roebuck and Co., *Seroco Paints* (Chicago: Sears, Roebuck and Co., [1915]), 3; Montgomery Ward, *Paint* (Chicago: The Company, [1915–16]), 13. The limit of 32 colors, excluding black and white, was proposed by the paint war service committee. When the Conservation Division then surveyed the committee members' dealers, it discovered that the majority preferred a maximum of 12 colors. However, the war service committee members, all from major paint companies, persuaded the division that companies distributing paints nationally needed 32 colors to satisfy demand that varied regionally: "W. H. Phillips Feels Confident of the Future," *Painters Magazine and Paint and Wall Paper Dealer* 46, no. 2 (February 1919): 11. Restrictions were also set on the number of colors or grades of other products, such as enamels, floor paints, and roof and barn paint, as well as on raw materials.

101 Clarkson, *Industrial America*, 221.

102 Baruch, *American Industry in the War*, 68.

103 "Order out of Chaos by Standardization," 77.

104 Edwards, *Paint and Varnish*, 3–4. On civilian painting during the war, see Ernest T. Trigg, "The Paint Trade and the War," *Paint, Oil and Drug Review* 67, no. 6 (February 5, 1919): 6.

105 General Trade Sales Department Manager, The Sherwin–Williams Company, Bulletin No. 44, February 20, 1919, Subject: Reinstatement of Dropped Packages, 1919, The Sherwin–Williams Company Center of Excellence, Cleveland, OH. See also U.S. Department of Commerce, Bureau of Standards, *Limitation of Variety Recommendation No. 1: Paints and Varnishes, Issued by the Bureau of Standards, Original Draft; September 1, 1924* (Washington, DC: Government Printing Office, 1924), 6, which describes the wartime restrictions as having been "put into definite operation."

106 "How Industry Is Demobilizing," *Business Digest and Investment Weekly* 22, no. 11 (December 10, 1918): 377. See also *Second Annual Report of the CND*, 198, which estimated the time between the preparation of manufacturers' samples and retail sales at eight to nine months in the shoe and clothing trades.

107 E.g., Mary Louise Roberts, *Civilization without Sexes: Reconstructing Gender in Postwar France, 1917–1927* (University of Chicago Press, 1994), 63–87; Mary Lynn Stewart, *Dressing Modern Frenchwomen:*

Marketing Haute Couture, 1919–1939 (Baltimore: Johns Hopkins University Press, 2008), 73–4; Rhonda K. Garelick, *Mademoiselle: Coco Chanel and the Pulse of History*, Kindle ed. (New York: Random House, 2014), ch. 3; Maude Bass-Krueger, Hayley Edwards-Dujardin, and Sophie Kurkdjian, eds., *Fashion, Society and the First World War: International Perspectives* (London: Bloomsbury Publishing, 2021). While some historians of fashion do mention, in general terms, wool conservation measures during World War I, most fail to recognize the extent to which those government restrictions shaped women's fashions. Exceptions include Susan Voso Lab, "'War' Drobe and World War I," in *Dress in American Culture*, ed. Patricia Cunningham and Susan Voso Lab (Bowling Green State University Popular Press, 1993), 200–19; and Nina Edwards, *Dressed for War: Uniform, Civilian Clothing and Trappings, 1914 to 1918* (London and New York: I. B. Tauris, 2015), 77–9. A war-induced shortage of dyes also shaped American fashion, especially in the years 1915–17: Jacqueline Field, "Dyes, Chemistry and Clothing," *Dress* 28, no. 1 (2001): 77–91.

108 "Commercial Economy Board of Council of National Defense," 1; *First Annual Report of the CND*, 38–41; Shaw, *Enlarging the War Effort*, 3. On the WIB's broader wool conservation effort, which included control of the wool clip (raw wool), see Albert W. Elliott, "The Wool Control in the United States during the World War," *Bulletin of the National Association of Wool Manufacturers* 54, no. 4 (October 1924): 454–72; J. Donald Edwards, *The Effect upon the Civilian Market of the Wartime Control of Wool and Wool Products*, U.S. Department of Labor, Bureau of Labor Statistics, Historical Studies of Wartime Problems No. 3 (April 1941), 10, 12–13; and Thomas J. Mayock, *The Government and Wool, 1917–20*, Agricultural History Series No. 6 ([Washington, DC]: U.S. Dept. of Agriculture, August 1943). Wool conservation was also intended to free up shipping cargo space, since two-thirds of raw wool was imported at that time.

109 "Official Proceedings: Conference on Simplified Practice in Industry: Meeting of Officials of the Federal Government with Chairmen of Standing Committees in Charge of Recommendations for Simplified Practice, Washington, DC, November 24 and 25, 1930, Complete Stenographic Record," *Supplement to The United States Daily* 5, no. 241, Section II (December 13, 1930): 3.

110 "National Garment Retailers' Association Arranges Meeting," 140–1. For a summary of the events recounted here, see Shaw, *Enlarging the War Effort*, 3–5.

111 Fredric J. Haskin, "Styles and the Wool Market," *The Omaha Bee* (Omaha, NE), July 10, 1917, 6 (Chronicling America: Historic American Newspapers); "Commercial Economy Board of Council of National Defense," 1; "National Garment Retailers' Association Arranges Meeting," 140–1; *First Annual Report of the CND*, 40–1. Details on the protracted negotiations, which also involved wool imports and exports, and on trade resistance through October 1917 are recounted in Winthrop L. Marvin, "The Wool Manufacture in the War," *Bulletin of the National Association of Wool Manufacturers* 47, no. 4 (October 1917): 287–99. On the technical difficulties of using wool substitutes and ongoing competition from British woolen mills, see "Editorial and Industrial Miscellany: Conserving the Wool Supply," 323–5. The reduction in fabric sample sizes was estimated to have saved 3 to 4 million yards of cloth: U.S. War Industries Board, *An Outline of the Board's Origin*, 40.

112 Victor S. Clark, *History of Manufactures in the United States*, vol. III: *1893–1928* (New York: McGraw-Hill for the Carnegie Institution of Washington, 1929), 344.

113 *First Annual Report of the CND*, 41.

114 "National Garment Retailers' Association Arranges Meeting," 141.

115 "What You Can Do to Help: Here Are the Ways You Can Do It and Still Be Well Dressed," *Ladies' Home Journal* (September 1918), 32 (ProQuest Women's Magazine Archive). On the prewar influence of Parisian fashion in the U.S., see Marlis Schweitzer, "American Fashions for American Women: The Rise and Fall of Fashion Nationalism," in Regina Lee Blaszczyk, ed., *Producing Fashion: Commerce, Culture, and Consumers* (Philadelphia: University of Pennsylvania Press, 2008), 130–49.

116 "Nouvelles syndicales: la réduction du métrage des robes," *Les Élégances Parisiennes* (October 1917): 288 (Gallica, Bibliothèque nationale de France); "National Garment Retailers' Association Arranges Meeting," 140; *Second Annual Report of the CND*, 197; Ditchett, "Effect of Advertising of Limitation of Styles and Sizes," 81; Clarkson, *Industrial America*, 220–1; Martin, *Digest of the Proceedings of the Council of National Defense*, 520; Shaw, *Enlarging the War Effort*, 5; Heaton, *A Scholar in Action*, 99–100; Maude Bass-Krueger, "The Crisis of 1917: 'National Fashion' and American Textile Restrictions," in Maude Bass-Krueger and Sophie Kurkdjian, eds., *French Fashion, Women and the First World War* (New York: Bard Graduate Center, 2019), 447. On French competition for the American market during the period of U.S. neutrality, see Mary Lynn Stewart, "Wartime Marketing of Parisian

Haute Couture in the United States, 1914–17," in Bass-Krueger et al., eds., *Fashion, Society and the First World War*, 17–28.

117 "What You Can Do to Help," 32.

118 "Conservative Lines and Simplicity Still Dominate Fall Fashion Plans," *Dry Goods Guide* 42, no. 1 (July 1918): 37.

119 A detailed account of the November 1917 conference appeared in "National Garment Retailers' Association Arranges Meeting," 139–45, which included excerpts from speeches. Briefer reports on the conference also appeared in "Wool Manufactures – Wool Conservation," *Textile World Journal* 53, no. 22 (December 1, 1917): 65, 67; "Advertising and the Wool Shortage," 137; and "Plans for Conservation of Wool in Women's Wear Trades to Have Far Reaching Effect," *Women's Wear Daily* 15, no. 125 (November 28, 1917): 1 (ProQuest *Women's Wear Daily* Archive).

120 "National Garment Retailers' Association Arranges Meeting," 143.

121 "National Garment Retailers' Association Arranges Meeting," 140; "Advertising and the Wool Shortage," 137.

122 The resolution was reprinted in "National Garment Retailers' Association Arranges Meeting," 145, which is the source of quotations in this paragraph. It was also reprinted in "Wool Manufactures – Wool Conservation," 67; and "The Wool Conservation Recommendations," *Women's Wear Daily* 15, no. 125 (November 28, 1917): 1 (ProQuest *Women's Wear Daily* Archive). Similar restrictions were placed on women's clothing during World War II: "Material for Dresses Limited by WPB Order: 'Basic Silhouette' Restricts Nonfunctional Details," *Victory Bulletin: Official Weekly Publication of the Office of War Information* 4, no. 21 (May 26, 1943): 365; Frank L. Walton, *Thread of Victory: The Conversion and Conservation of Textiles, Clothing and Leather for the World's Biggest War Program* (New York: Fairchild Publishing Co., 1945), 76–86.

123 On the merchandising challenges of selling fabrics that were not "pure" wool, see Murphy, "Can You Be Patriotic?" 105–6, 109–10.

124 "National Garment Retailers' Association Arranges Meeting," 142.

125 "Fashion: Woollen [*sic*] Costumes that Save Wool," 47. See also "Les Dernières Créations de la mode: la silhouette de 1917–1918," *Les Élégances Parisiennes* (October 1917): 277 (Gallica, Bibliothèque nationale de France). On allegations that some French couturiers resisted the restrictions, see "French Creators Must Recognize Wool Saving Idea," *Women's Wear Daily* 15, no. 131 (December 6, 1917): 1.

126 "Trade Mass Meeting to Advocate Slender Lines as Wool Saving

Move," *Women's Wear Daily* 15, no. 118 (November 20, 1917): 1 (ProQuest *Women's Wear Daily* Archive).

127 The WIB's priorities power did not become effective until mid-1918 (see p. 40), but a manufacturing member of the CEB warned the attendees at the November 1917 garment-trades meeting that, if voluntary cooperation were not forthcoming, "we are at war, ladies and gentlemen, and the strength will be given": "National Garment Retailers' Association Arranges Meeting," 142.

128 "Fashion: Woollen [*sic*] Costumes that Save Wool," 47.

129 "Trade Mass Meeting," 2.

130 "National Garment Retailers' Association Arranges Meeting," 140.

131 Charlotte Perkins Gilman, "Concerning Clothes," *Independent* 94, no. 3629 (June 22, 1918): 478.

132 "Advertising and the Wool Shortage," 137.

133 "National Garment Retailers' Association Arranges Meeting," 144; *Second Annual Report of the CND*, 198. An early hint of the November proposals appeared in a newspaper report on New York holiday fashions that mentioned "the slim silhouette" and "a rumor to the effect that it will be good style, when the Spring days have come, to wear no wool at all": "Simplicity in Yuletide Fashions: Tight Skirts and Plain Hats . . .", *New York Times*, December 9, 1917, 80 (ProQuest Historical Newspapers: *The New York Times*).

134 Shaw, *Enlarging the War Effort*, 5.

135 Sophie Kurkdjian, "The Emergence of French *Vogue*: French Identity and Visual Culture in the Fashion Press, 1920–40," *International Journal of Fashion Studies* 6, no. 1 (April 2019): 66. For other examples, see "Fashion: Woollen [*sic*] Costumes that Save Wool," 46–7; Mrs. A. Sherman Hitchcock, "Dame Fashion Bows to Decree of Conservation," *Automobile Journal*, February 25, 1918, 44–5; "Seen in the Shops," *Vogue*, March 1, 1918, 66–7 (ProQuest *Vogue* Archive); [Anna] van Campen Stewart, "Paris Says, 'Tighter Bodice, Scanter Skirt'; 'More of Silk and Less of Wool,' Says War," *Harper's Bazaar* (March 1918), 48–55, 104 (ProQuest *Harper's Bazaar* Archive); Helen Koues, "Fashions: French Openings Continue the Straight Silhouette . . .", *Good Housekeeping* (April 1918), 68 (ProQuest Women's Magazine Archive); "Fashion: Novel Details Characterize the Models of 1918," *Vogue*, September 15, 1918, 27–9, 102 (ProQuest *Vogue* Archive); "What You Can Do to Help," 32; [Anna] van Campen Stewart, "Paris Openings Decree the Slim Silhouette with Many Changes in Details," *Harper's Bazaar* (October 1918), 49–53, 64–9 (ProQuest *Harper's Bazaar* Archive). A women's coat and suit manufacturer hit all the

essential points of the conservation program in an advertisement aimed at local "Leaders of Fashion": The H. Black Co., "A War-Time Message to the Leaders of Fashion," *Ladies' Home Journal* (advertisement) (September 1918), 61 (ProQuest Women's Magazine Archive). By November 1918, the restrictions on clothing design had become fodder for jokes: Fred W. Gage, "War Problems and the Printing Business," *Typothetae Bulletin* 13, Convention Number, no. 5 (November 1918): 168; Wood, *The Great Change*, 55–6.

136 "Fashion: Save Wool and Serve the Soldier," *Vogue*, January 15, 1918, 48 (ProQuest *Vogue* Archive).

137 "Fashion: Every Bit of Wool that Your Suit Denies Itself Goes to Keep a Soldier's Shoulders Warm . . .," *Vogue*, January 15, 1918, 32 (ProQuest *Vogue* Archive).

138 "Announcements: This Is the Forecast of Spring Fashions Number of Vogue," *Vogue*, February 1, 1918, 25 (ProQuest *Vogue* Archive).

139 "Fashion: Cheruit's Top-Coats Grow Shorter as the List of Government Uses for Wool Grows Longer," *Vogue*, February 1, 1918, 48 (ProQuest *Vogue* Archive).

140 "The Importance of Being Correctly Corseted," *Vogue*, February 1, 1918, 63 (ProQuest *Vogue* Archive).

141 "Seen in the Shops [Feb. 15, 1918]," 66.

142 Schweitzer, "American Fashions for American Women," 132. See also Linda Hall, "Fashion and Style in the Twenties: The Change," *Historian* 34, no. 3 (Summer 1972): 485–6; and Valerie Steele, *Paris Fashion: A Cultural History*, [3rd] ed. (New York: Bloomsbury USA, 2017), 193.

143 Mrs. Ralston, "What Paris Says Will Be Correct," *Ladies' Home Journal*, September 15, 1910, 3 (ProQuest Women's Magazine Archive); Alice Long, "What I See on Fifth Avenue," *Ladies' Home Journal* (September 1912), 83 (ProQuest Women's Magazine Archive); "The Slim Silhouette in Spite of Draperies," *Harper's Bazaar* (February 1913), 98–9 (ProQuest *Harper's Bazaar* Archive).

144 Helen Koues, "Fashions: after Six O'Clock," *Good Housekeeping* (October 1916), 65 (ProQuest Women's Magazine Archive).

145 "Paris Couturiers Promise America Gorgeous Gowns," *Women's Wear Daily* 14, no. 148 (June 26, 1917): 3 (ProQuest *Women's Wear Daily* Archive).

146 A. S., "Fashion: A Forecast of the Spring Mode," *Vogue*, February 1, 1917, 30–1 (ProQuest *Vogue* Archive).

147 Ralph Breed, "As Paris Sees the Fall Fashions," *Harper's Bazaar* (September 1917), 64, 65, 67 (ProQuest *Harper's Bazaar* Archive).

148 "Fashion: Combining the Silhouettes of Yesterday and To-Day," *Vogue*, November 1, 1915 (ProQuest *Vogue* Archive).

149 "Paris Displays Forecast Next Season's Modes," *Women's Wear Daily*, January 13, 1917, 1 (ProQuest *Women's Wear Daily* Archive).

150 Lucy Adlington, *Great War Fashion: Tales from the History Wardrobe* (Stroud, Glos.: The History Press, 2013), 40. According to Herbert Heaton's biography of economic historian Edwin F. Gay, who contacted the French ambassador on behalf of the CEB, Parisian *couturiers* had used 5½ meters of cloth in 1916 and 8 meters in 1915. "Gay's friends," Heaton notes, "jestingly held him responsible for the increased immodesty of feminine apparel": Heaton, *A Scholar in Action*, 100.

151 Sophie Kurkdjian, "Jeanne Paquin, Jeanne Lanvin, Jenny, and Gabrielle Chanel, 1914–18," in Bass-Krueger and Kurkdjian, eds., *French Fashion, Women and the First World War*, 340; Bass-Krueger, "The Crisis of 1917," 447.

152 Kurkdjian, "Jeanne Paquin, Jeanne Lanvin, Jenny, and Gabrielle Chanel, 1914–18," 304; Stewart, "Wartime Marketing," 21.

153 Stewart, "Wartime Marketing," 21. To fend off incipient competition from American designers, French houses also sent models to the Panama–Pacific International Exposition in San Francisco in 1915: Stewart, "Wartime Marketing," 20–1. On French fashion associations during the war, see Kurkdjian, "Restructuring French Couture, 1914–1918," in Bass-Krueger and Kurkdjian, eds., *French Fashion, Women and the First World War*, 373–413.

154 Clarkson, *Industrial America*, 220. See also Shaw, *Enlarging the War Effort*, 5.

155 Helen Koues, "Winter War-Time Fashions," *Good Housekeeping* (December 1918), 64 (ProQuest Women's Magazine Archive). See also "Fashion: The Simplicity of Mastery," *Vogue*, February 1, 1921, 30–1 (ProQuest *Vogue* Archive); "Paris Determines the Winter Mode," *Harper's Bazaar* (October 1921), 41 (ProQuest *Harper's Bazaar* Archive).

156 Clarkson, *Industrial America*, 220–1.

157 "Fashion: The Simplicity of Mastery," 31. *Vogue* used the term to describe Coco Chanel's dresses as emblematic of a larger trend. See also "Gabrielle Chanel Whose Designs Are as Youthful and Chic as Herself," *Vogue*, May 15, 1923, 41 (ProQuest *Vogue* Archive).

158 "The Debut of the Winter Mode," *Vogue*, October 1, 1926, 69 (ProQuest *Vogue* Archive); Nancy J. Troy, *Couture Culture: A Study in Modern Art and Fashion* (Cambridge, MA: MIT Press, 2003), 316–17; Mary

E. Davis, *Classic Chic: Music, Fashion, and Modernism* (Berkeley: University of California Press, 2006), 164–5. On Chanel and mass production, see also Jessica Burstein, *Cold Modernism: Literature, Fashion, Art* (University Park: Pennsylvania State University Press, 2012), 131–3. Given Chanel's growing prominence in French couture during the war, her social connections, and the resonance between her designs and the Conservation Division's slim silhouette, she may well have been a party to the French designers' agreement with American conservation officials: A. S., "Fashion: Paris Lifts Ever so Little the Ban on Gaiety," *Vogue* 48, no. 10 (November 15, 1916): 41–3 (ProQuest *Vogue* Archive); Davis, *Classic Chic*, 161–3; Garelick, *Mademoiselle*, ch. 3. In any case, she would surely have welcomed the wartime initiative to promote the silhouette with which her designs were already closely associated.

On business difficulties faced by fabric and garment manufacturers in the 1920s because of changes in fashion, see Copeland, "Marketing," 326–7; Hall, "Fashion and Style in the Twenties: The Change," 490–6. On the related fashion of bobbed hair in the 1920s, see Mary Louise Roberts, "Samson and Delilah Revisited: The Politics of Women's Fashion in 1920s France," *American Historical Review* 98, no. 3 (June 1993): 657–84.

159 Winifred Aldrich, "The Impact of Fashion on the Cutting Practices for the Woman's Tailored Jacket 1800–1927," *Textile History* 34, no. 2 (2003): 134–70.

160 Leon I. Thomas, "Simplification in Industry," *Factory* 26, no. 4 (February 15, 1921): 451.

161 "Permanent Government Organization to Standardize American Industries Is Advocated by Chairman Baruch," *Official U.S. Bulletin* 2, no. 464 (November 15, 1918): 3.

162 Clarkson, *Industrial America*, 225.

4 Product Diversity Resurgent, 1918–1921

1 Cuff, *The War Industries Board*, 246n219.

2 "Permanent Government Organization," 3.

3 Baruch, *American Industry in the War*, 69.

4 Wood, *The Great Change*, 62, 64.

5 Thomas, "Simplification in Industry," 451–3 (quotation, 451); "The Establishment of Simplification," Editorial, *System* 43, no. 5 (May 1923): 581. See also Shaw, "Simplification," 417–27.

6 On Dennison, see Alchon, *The Invisible Hand of Planning*, 16–17. After the WIB was reconfigured in 1918, Dennison sat on both sides of

the table, serving in its Division of Planning and Statistics, which was chaired by Edwin F. Gay, and on the Stationery war service committee: Baruch, *American Industry in the War*, 292, 408.

7 "National Garment Retailers' Association Arranges Meeting," 143.

8 Scranton, *Figured Tapestry*, 319.

9 Thomas, "Simplification in Industry, II," 716 (textbox).

10 Trigg, "Industries in Readjustment," 4. See also Heckel, *The Paint Industry*, 596.

11 Clamer, "Standardization," 83.

12 "Manufacturers May Retain Some War Restrictions," *Printers' Ink* 105, no. 9 (November 28, 1918): 89.

13 "Manufacturers May Retain Some War Restrictions," 89.

14 "Reconstruction: Reconstruction Congress of American Industries at Atlantic City," *Monthly Labor Review* 8, no. 1 (January 1919): 40, 42 (quotation). The Chamber's monthly publication, *Nation's Business*, devoted its January 1919 issue to the congress. See also Sawyer, *American Fair Trade*, 146.

15 Hoyt, "Standardization," 274.

16 "Standardization of Products: Discussion," 65.

17 Thomas, "Simplification in Industry, II," 718, 752.

18 "How Industry Is Demobilizing," 375–8; Cuff, *The War Industries Board*, 241–64.

19 "Manufacturers May Retain Some War Restrictions," 89. Also quoted in "How Industry Is Demobilizing," 377.

20 "Additional Activities of War Industries Board Taken Over by Commerce Department," *Commerce Reports*, no. 5 (January 7, 1919): 81–2; William C. Redfield, *With Congress and Cabinet* (Garden City, NY: Doubleday, Page & Company, 1924), 218; Robert F. Himmelberg, "The War Industries Board and the Antitrust Question in November 1918," *Journal of American History* 52, no. 1 (June 1965): 70–1; Robert F. Himmelberg, "Business, Antitrust Policy, and the Industrial Board of the Department of Commerce, 1919," *Business History Review* 42, no. 1 (Spring 1968): 4–5.

21 "Electrical Manufacturers Plan to Continue Beneficial Co-operation," 149.

22 U.S. Department of Commerce, *Annual Report of the Secretary of Commerce 1919* (Washington, DC: Government Printing Office, 1919), 70; Redfield, *With Congress and Cabinet*, 216 (quotation), 218.

23 "Manufacturers May Retain Some War Restrictions," 89–90. See also "How Industry Is Demobilizing," 377.

24 U.S. Department of Commerce and Labor, *Commercial and Agricultural*

Organizations of the United States, 4–10; U.S. Department of Commerce, Bureau of Foreign and Domestic Commerce, *Commercial and Industrial Organizations of the United States, Revised to November 1, 1919,* Misc. Series No. 99 (Washington, DC: Government Printing Office, 1920), 5–16 (interstate, national, and international; excluding engineering, foreign, and some miscellaneous associations). Trade association executives formed their own professional association in 1919: Berk, *Louis Brandeis,* 167.

25 Hudson, "Organized Effort in Simplification," 1; Clark, *History of Manufactures,* vol. III, 327; Lyon, *Hand-to-Mouth Buying,* 10; Wilson F. Payne, *Business Behavior, 1919–1922: An Account of Post-war Inflation and Depression,* Studies in Business Administration (University of Chicago Press, 1942), 209; Soule, *Prosperity Decade,* 101; Lawrence B. Glickman, *Buying Power: A History of Consumer Activism in America* (University of Chicago Press, 2009), 203. On present-day anti-consumerism, see Kim Humphery, *Excess: Anti-consumerism in the West* (Cambridge, UK, and Malden, MA: Polity, 2010).

26 Daniel Kuehn, "A Note on America's 1920–21 Depression as an Argument for Austerity," *Cambridge Journal of Economics* 36, no. 1 (2012): 155–60; James Grant, *The Forgotten Depression: 1921 – The Crash that Cured Itself* (New York: Simon & Schuster, 2015), esp. 67–72. Wholesale prices fell by 37 percent from 1920 to 1921. On the plight of individual industries (leather and shoes, cotton, wool, silk, steel and steel-consuming industries, and iron, coal, and coke), see Payne, *Business Behavior.*

27 Lyon, *Hand-to-Mouth Buying,* 10.

28 Williams Haynes, "Better Ethical Standards for Business: The Purpose of the Commercial Standards Council," *Annals of the American Academy of Political and Social Science* 101, The Ethics of the Professions and of Business (May 1922): 221–3. See also Butler D. Shaffer, "In Restraint of Trade: Trade Associations and the Emergence of 'Self Regulation,'" *Southwestern University Law Review* 20, no. 3 (1991): 289–348. On the broader history of "fair trade," see Sawyer, *American Fair Trade.*

29 Sawyer, *American Fair Trade,* 150.

30 For comments to this effect, see "W. H. Phillips," 11; Copeland, "Standardization of Products: I," 58; and Maddock, "How Simplification Removed Production Difficulties," 613. Phillips was president of the New York paint manufacturing firm Devoe and Raynolds; Copeland was director of Harvard's Bureau of Business Research and a former CND official; Maddock was president of the sanitary ceramic ware

manufacturer Thomas Maddock's Sons Company in Trenton, NJ. See also Hudson, "Simplification and Standardization," 994–5.

31 Herbert, "After the War Co-operation," 14.

32 "Reconstruction: Reconstruction Congress," 42, 46–8. On post-war business lobbying for a relaxation of restrictions on collective action among competitors, see Himmelberg, "The War Industries Board," 59–74; Himmelberg, "Business, Antitrust Policy, and the Industrial Board," 1–23.

33 Hoyt, "Standardization," 275. As head of the U.S. Food Administration, Hoover had obtained "a ruling from the Attorney General" that exempted the trade associations' war service committees from antitrust prosecution "so long as our 'War Committees' were carrying out our wishes": Herbert Hoover, *The Memoirs of Herbert Hoover*, vol. I: *Years of Adventure, 1874–1920* (New York: MacMillan Company, 1951), 246–7. See also Ellis W. Hawley, "Herbert Hoover and the Sherman Act, 1921–1933: An Early Phase of a Continuing Issue," *Iowa Law Review* 74, no. 5 (July 1989): 1068. The exemption would have lapsed, of course, when the WIB was dissolved.

34 "How Industry Is Demobilizing," 377. See also Copeland, "Standardization of Products: I," 57.

35 "A Message from Herbert Hoover," 80.

36 Etherington, "Shoe Business Permanently Strengthened," 134 (quotation), 136, 138.

37 Copeland, "Standardization of Products: I," 57.

38 Trigg, "We Increased Volume," 486. Former president of the Philadelphia Chamber of Commerce, Trigg wrote this article as vice president and general manager of the Philadelphia paint manufacturing firm John Lucas and Company.

39 Sears, Roebuck and Co., [*Catalog*] (Chicago, Fall and Winter, 1926–7), 994; Montgomery Ward and Co., *Fall and Winter Catalogue No. 105* (Chicago, 1926–7), 559; The Sherwin–Williams Company, *Sherwin–Williams Products: Price List No. 69 Effective August 7, 1929*, The Sherwin–Williams Center of Excellence, Cleveland, OH, 9.

40 Trigg, "We Increased Volume," 489. See also Quarterly Report of Activities of the Division of Simplified Practice, April 1, 1924, 7, in RG 40, Department of Commerce, General Correspondence, 1923–1927, File 67009/80, National Archives II (hereafter cited as RG 40, File 67009/80); U.S. Department of Commerce, *Limitation of Variety Recommendation No. 1*, 6.

41 Steven Klepper and Kenneth L. Simons, "The Making of an Oligopoly: Firm Survival and Technological Change in the Evolution of the U.S.

Tire Industry," *Journal of Political Economy* 108, no. 4 (August 2000): 733.

42 "Tire Making and Size Simplification," *Society of Automotive Engineers Journal* 22, no. 1 (January 1928): 136.

43 "Tire Making and Size Simplification," 136.

44 Thompson, "Intercompany Technical Standardization," 1–20.

45 U.S. Department of Commerce, Division of Simplified Practice, *Monthly News Bulletin*, no. 24 (March 15, 1927): 5; U.S. Department of Commerce, Bureau of Standards, "Tire Simplified Practice Recommendation," *Technical News Bulletin*, no. 130 (February 1928): 25–6; H. M. Crane, "Simplification of Tire Sizes," *Society of Automotive Engineers Journal* 22, no. 2 (February 1928): 227–8. On military concerns about the proliferation of tire sizes, see U.S. Department of Commerce, Bureau of Standards, "Army Men Report Too Many Tire Sizes," *Technical News Bulletin*, no. 131 (March 1928): 41.

46 "The Trend toward Simplification," 41.

47 Thomas, "Simplification in Industry, II," 752. See also "The Trend toward Simplification," 42.

48 Report of the Planning Committee of the Division of Simplified Practice, Bureau of Standards, to the Secretary of Commerce ... 1921 to 1931, 3, in RG 40, File 67009/80 (hereafter cited as Report of the Planning Committee [1931]).

49 U.S. Department of Commerce, *Limitation of Variety Recommendation No. 1*, 6; *SPR No. 57: Wrought-Iron and Wrought-Steel Pipe Valves and Fittings* (1927), 7.

50 "Hoover Works Out Plans to Save Billions Now Wasted in Business," *Jackson Citizen Patriot* (Jackson, MI), August 17, 1922, 2 (America's Historical Newspapers) (quoting William A. Durgin). For similar assessments of the immediate post-war years, see Hudson, "Organized Effort in Simplification," 1; E. Pendleton Herring, *Public Administration and the Public Interest* (New York and London: McGraw-Hill Book Company, Inc., 1936), 322; Charles A. Pearce, *Trade Association Survey*, U.S. Temporary National Economic Committee Investigation of the Concentration of Economic Power, Monograph No. 18 (Washington, DC: Government Printing Office, 1941), 310; and Cochrane, *Measures for Progress*, 179.

51 *SPR No. 18: Builders' Hardware* (1925), 1.

52 *SPR No. 26: Steel Reinforcing Bars* (1925), 5.

53 *SPR No. 45: Grinding Wheels* (1926), 19.

54 *SPR R6-40: Files and Rasps* (1940), 5.

55 "The Trend toward Simplification," 42.

56 Ewan Clague, "Index of Productivity of Labor in the Steel, Automobile, Shoe, and Paper Industries," *Monthly Labor Review* 23, no. 1 (July 1926): 14–15.

57 Roy W. Johnson, "How Advertising Affects Standardization," *Printers' Ink* 115, no. 11 (June 16, 1921): 81.

58 U.S. Department of Commerce, Bureau of Standards, *Simplified Practice: What It Is and What It Offers (1928 Edition): Summary of Activities of the Division of Simplified Practice and Description of Services Offered to American Industries* (Washington, DC: Government Printing Office, 1929), 28–50.

59 On the FAES, Hoover, and *Waste in Industry*, see Haber, *Efficiency and Uplift*, 155–9; Alchon, *The Invisible Hand of Planning*, 63–7; Edwin T. Layton, *The Revolt of the Engineers: Social Responsibility and the American Engineering Profession* (1971; Baltimore: Johns Hopkins University Press, 1986), 179–95; and Clements, *Imperfect Visionary*, 44–7.

60 Herbert Hoover, "Industrial Waste," *Bulletin of the Taylor Society* 6, no. 2 (April 1921): 77. See also L. W. Wallace, "Industrial Waste," *Annals of the American Academy of Political and Social Science* 97, no. 186, The Revival of American Business (September 1921): 36–42; Donald R. Stabile, "Research Note: Herbert Hoover, the FAES, and the AF of L," *Technology and Culture* 27, no. 4 (October 1986): 822. On the standard of living as a political issue in the early twentieth century, see Jacobs, *Pocketbook Politics*, 38–52.

61 *Waste in Industry*, ix, 8. The six industries were the building trades, men's clothing manufacturing, shoe manufacturing, printing, the metal trades, and textile manufacturing. Initial plans were to include the pulp and paper industry and automobile tire manufacturing, but both were dropped, the former "for lack of time and funds" and the latter "due to a failure to secure co-operation in the industry itself": *Waste in Industry*, v.

62 Hoover, "Industrial Waste," 78–9.

63 *Waste in Industry*, 9. For contemporary discussions of the report, see Edward A. Filene, *The Way Out: A Forecast of Coming Changes in American Business and Industry* (Garden City, NY: Doubleday, Page and Company, 1924), 110–25; and Stuart Chase, in conjunction with the Labor Bureau, Inc., *The Tragedy of Waste* (New York: The Macmillan Company, 1925), 149–59. On Hoover's disappointment with the labor provisions of an industrial conference report and his discussions with Samuel Gompers of the American Federation of Labor just before he proposed the FAES waste study, see Clements, *Imperfect Visionary*, 40–5.

5 Hoover's "Fostering Hand": Simplified Practice in Peacetime

1 On Hoover's career, see George H. Nash et al., *The Life of Herbert Hoover*, 6 vols. (New York: W. W. Norton and Palgrave Macmillan, 1983–2010); and Jeansonne, *Herbert Hoover: A Life*.

2 Jeansonne, *Herbert Hoover: A Life*, 83.

3 Herbert Hoover, "Some Notes on Industrial Readjustment," *Saturday Evening Post*, December 27, 1919, 3–4, 145–6; Herbert Hoover, *American Individualism* (Garden City and New York: Doubleday, Page & Company, 1922). On Hoover's social philosophy and his assessment of the problems facing the U.S. after the war, see Clements, *Imperfect Visionary*, 41–3, 195–207. "Reconstruction" was the more commonly used term, but Wilsonians, partly in deference to Southerners, preferred the term "readjustment": Schwarz, *The Speculator*, 105.

4 Hoover, *American Individualism*, 4, 18.

5 Clements, *Imperfect Visionary*, 41. On the cost of living as a political issue from the turn of the twentieth century through the 1920s, see Jacobs, *Pocketbook Politics*, 15–92.

6 Hoover, "Some Notes on Industrial Readjustment," 4; Clements, *Imperfect Visionary*, 229. On "new era" economic thought and policies in the 1920s, see Barber, *From New Era to New Deal*, 1–64.

7 On the extraordinary scope of Hoover's initiatives while Secretary of Commerce, see Hawley, "Herbert Hoover, the Commerce Secretariat," 116–40; Joan Hoff Wilson, *Herbert Hoover, Forgotten Progressive* (Boston: Little, Brown, 1975), 79–121; Clements, *Imperfect Visionary*; Jeansonne, *Herbert Hoover: A Life*, 152–85. Studies that help to situate Hoover's push to reduce product diversity in its broader context include Noble, *America by Design*, 69–83; Barber, *From New Era to New Deal*, 1–64; Kendrick A. Clements, "Agent of Change: Herbert Hoover as Secretary of Commerce," in Walch, ed., *Uncommon Americans*, 93–105.

8 Quoted in Jordan, *Machine-Age Ideology*, 118.

9 Quoted in Clements, *Imperfect Visionary*, 42.

10 U.S. Department of Commerce, *Tenth Annual Report of the Secretary of Commerce*, 2.

11 On Hoover's reorganization of the Commerce Department, see Hawley, "Herbert Hoover, the Commerce Secretariat," 120–39; Eisner, *From Warfare State to Welfare State*, 114–21; Clements, *Imperfect Visionary*, 109–13.

12 See above, p. 58. Secretary Redfield also sought, but ultimately failed, to bring into the Commerce Department the WIB's price-fixing activities. On the Industrial Board, see Himmelberg, "Business, Antitrust

Policy, and the Industrial Board," 1–23; Schwarz, *The Speculator*, 208–11.

13 Waldon Fawcett, "Helpful Data a Sales Manager Is Able to Get from Washington," *Sales Management* 4, no. 12 (September 1922): 468. On Hoover's relations with Congress in the 1920s, see Clements, *Imperfect Visionary*.

14 Jeansonne, *Herbert Hoover: A Life*, 160.

15 Clements, *Imperfect Visionary*, 110.

16 Clements, *Imperfect Visionary*, 44.

17 Clarkson, *Industrial America*, 215.

18 "F. M. Feiker Vice-President of McGraw-Hill Company," *Electrical World* 75, no. 2 (January 10, 1920): 90; "Frederick Feiker, Hoover Aide, Dead," *New York Times*, January 15, 1967, 84 (ProQuest Historical Newspapers: *The New York Times*); Tanner, "Secretary Hoover's War on Waste," 5–6; Clements, *Imperfect Visionary*, 110.

19 On Shaw's post-war support, see below, pp. 121–3.

20 U.S. Department of Commerce, *Ninth Annual Report of the Secretary of Commerce 1921* (Washington, DC: Government Printing Office, 1921), 6.

21 Eisner, *From Warfare State to Welfare State*, 115–21. According to a biographer, WIB chair Bernard Baruch later expressed annoyance that "Hoover's skillful self-promotion" obscured the World War I origins of the Commerce Department's waste-elimination programs: Schwarz, *The Speculator*, 226.

22 Clements, *Imperfect Visionary*, 111. Though he does not link the Bureau's commodity divisions to the WIB's commodity sections, Clements refers to them with the World War I term. They were called "commodity divisions" in the Secretary's annual reports.

23 U.S. Department of Commerce, *Tenth Annual Report of the Secretary of Commerce*, 96–8; Herring, *Public Administration*; Hawley, "Herbert Hoover, the Commerce Secretariat," 123; Eisner, *From Warfare State to Welfare State*, 116–19. In the mid-1920s, the bureau began to strengthen its services for "domestic commerce," which became a prominent concern by the end of the decade: U.S. Department of Commerce, *Thirteenth Annual Report of the Secretary of Commerce* (Washington, DC: Government Printing Office, 1925), 25–6; U.S. Department of Commerce, *Seventeenth Annual Report of the Secretary of Commerce* (Washington, DC: Government Printing Office, 1929), 106, 108–13. See also "Official Proceedings: Conference on Simplified Practice," 4.

24 Clarkson, *Industrial America*, 486.

25 Its establishment was dated variously to October 1921, December
    1921, and January 1922. See, respectively, Gustavus A. Weber, *The
    Bureau of Standards: Its History, Activities, and Organization*, Service
    Monographs of the U.S. Government No. 35 (Baltimore: Johns Hopkins
    University Press, 1925), 172; U.S. Department of Commerce, *Simplified
    Practice: What It Is* (1924), 3; U.S. Department of Commerce, *Tenth
    Annual Report of the Secretary of Commerce*, 138. A number of histo-
    ries, particularly of Hoover or standardization, mention the Division
    of Simplified Practice but only in passing. The most detailed secondary
    source is Tanner, "Secretary Hoover's War on Waste." See also, for an
    economist's perspective, Hemenway, *Industrywide Voluntary Product
    Standards*, 8–9, 21–32, on "standards for uniformity."
26 U.S. Department of Commerce, *Annual Report of the Director of the
    Bureau of Standards . . . 1922*, 265–6. A virtually identical statement
    was included in U.S. Department of Commerce, *Simplified Practice:
    What It Is* (1924), 24. In the early years, DSP publicity frequently
    drew an explicit link between the wartime simplification initiative
    and the work of the Division of Simplified Practice. See, for example,
    F. M. Feiker, "The Trend of 'Simplification': How the Movement Is
    Growing, and What the Paving Brick Action Signifies," *Factory* 28,
    no. 2 (February 1922): 156; U.S. Department of Commerce, *Simplified
    Practice: What It Is* (1924), 1; Priest, *A Primer of Simplified Practice*, 6.
    On the WIB's Conservation Division as "the model" for the Division of
    Simplified Practice, see Cochrane, *Measures for Progress*, 233; Eisner,
    From Warfare State to Welfare State, 119.
27 Brady, *Industrial Standardization*, 27–9; Herring, *Public
    Administration*, 323; John Perry, *The Story of Standards* (New York:
    Funk & Wagnalls, 1955), 133.
28 U.S. Department of Commerce, *Simplified Practice: What It Is* (1924),
    ii.
29 Herbert Hoover, "Industrial Standardization," in Edward Eyre Hunt,
    ed., *Scientific Management since Taylor: A Collection of Authoritative
    Papers* (New York: McGraw-Hill, 1924), 193.
30 Edward Eyre Hunt, "Introduction," in Hunt, ed., *Scientific Management
    since Taylor*, xiii. At Hoover's behest, Hunt had organized the FAES
    committee on industrial waste. He served as a Hoover aide and
    publicist in the Department of Commerce and as secretary of the
    Committee on Recent Economic Changes, which Hoover chaired
    (with Arch Shaw serving as acting chair when Hoover could not
    attend): "Foreword," in *Recent Economic Changes in the United States*,
    vol. I (New York: McGraw-Hill Book Company, Inc., 1929), v; Layton,

The Revolt of the Engineers, 194; Jordan, *Machine-Age Ideology*, 79; Stephen Ponder, *Managing the Press: Origins of the Media Presidency, 1897–1933* (New York: St. Martin's Press, 1998), 131.

31 Rexford G. Tugwell, "America's War-Time Socialism," *The Nation* 124, no. 3222 (April 6, 1927): 367.

32 "William A. Durgin Leaves Company Temporarily for Government Service in Washington," *The Edison Round Table Weekly* 6, no. 16 (1921), 1, 3; "Company Employees' Organizations: Mr. Durgin Loaned to Government," *National Electric Light Association Bulletin* 9, no. 2 (February 1922): 123 (quotations); William A. Durgin, *Electricity: Its History and Development* (Chicago: A. C. McClurg & Co., 1912); Arnold, "The 'Great Engineer' as Administrator," 346. See also U.S. Department of Commerce, Division of Simplified Practice, *Monthly News Bulletin*, no. 5 (August 15, 1925): 2, which described Durgin as having been "borrowed" from Commonwealth Edison.

33 Tanner, "Secretary Hoover's War on Waste," 6.

34 See also "A Message from Herbert Hoover," 78, 80, 82, 84, 86; and American Society for Testing Materials, ed., *Proceedings of the Twenty-Sixth Annual Meeting, Held at Atlantic City, New Jersey, June 26–29, 1923*, vol. 23, part 1 (Philadelphia: American Society for Testing Materials, 1923), 18.

35 Ray M. Hudson, "How to Determine Cost of Living in an Industrial Community," *Industrial Management* 56, no. 3 (September 1918); *Bulletin of the Taylor Society* 6, no. 1 (February 1921): [i]; "Standardization of Products: Discussion," 71.

36 "Tire Making and Size Simplification," 136.

37 U.S. Department of Commerce, Division of Simplified Practice, *Monthly News Bulletin*, no. 31 (October 15, 1927): 2; U.S. Civil Service Commission, comp., *Official Register of the United States 1957* (Washington, DC: Government Printing Office, 1957), 514; James F. Schooley, *Responding to National Needs: The National Bureau of Standards Becomes the National Institute of Standards and Technology, 1969–1993*, Special Publication 955 (Washington, DC: U.S. Dept. of Commerce, Technology Administration, National Institute of Standards and Technology, 2000), 940, 943, 946.

38 Durgin, "Alice in Modernland," 14. See also William A. Durgin, "Standardization Planned by Sec. Hoover Explained," *San Jose Mercury Herald*, December 6, 1922, 3 (America's Historical Newspapers).

39 "A Message From Herbert Hoover," 80.

40 E.g., "Plan Simpler Dress Styles to Save the Wool Supply," *Official U.S. Bulletin* 1, no. 20 (June 2, 1917): 2; "Cut in Farm Tool Output Planned

as War Measure," *Official U.S. Bulletin* 2, no. 300 (May 3, 1918): 3; Marion Weller, "The Clothing Situation," *Journal of Home Economics* 10, no. 9 (September 1918): 403.

41 "A Fundamental Step in Management," *Factory* 26, no. 4 (February 15, 1921): 428; "The Establishment of Simplification," 581; Leon I. Thomas, "The Beginning of the Simplification Movement," *Factory* 30, no. 6 (June 1923): 688; Francis L. Impey, "A British Test of Simplification," *System* 48, no. 4 (October 1925): 431 (footnote in text box).

42 Hudson, "Simplification and Standardization," 990–1.

43 "Current Editorial Comment: Sidelights on Standardization," *Industrial Management* 65, no. 1 (January 1923): 33–4; Ray M. Hudson, "Group Simplification Gains Momentum," *Factory* 35, no. 2 (August 1925): 193–6, 286.

44 U.S. Bureau of Standards, The Purpose and Application of Simplified Practice, 2; U.S. Department of Commerce, National Bureau of Standards, Simplified Practice: Its Purpose and Application, December 2, 1935, Letter Circular LC-456, 1–2; U.S. Department of Commerce, National Bureau of Standards, Simplified Practice: Its Purpose and Application, April 15, 1940, Letter Circular LC-590 (Supersedes LC-456), 3.

45 Feiker, "The Trend of 'Simplification,'" 156. Feiker's article included a lengthy excerpt from Hoover's address to the conference; a briefer excerpt appeared in *SPR No. 1: Paving Bricks* (1922), 5–6. See also Tanner, "Secretary Hoover's War on Waste," 5.

46 Quoted in Hoover, "Making Profits by Cutting Waste," 10.

47 Feiker, "The Trend of 'Simplification,'" 156.

48 See, for example, U.S. Department of Commerce, *Annual Report of the Director of the Bureau of Standards . . . 1922*, 266; "Current Editorial Comment: Sidelights on Standardization," 33; Ray M. Hudson, "Simplification – The New Fundamental in Business: Significance of Standardization to Railways as Largest Consumers and Transporters of Materials," *Railway Review* 72, no. 23 (June 9, 1923): 962; Hudson, "Simplification and Standardization," 995; U.S. Department of Commerce, *Simplified Practice: What It Is* (1924), 3; William J. Quinn, Jr., "Standardization and Waste Elimination," *Annals of the American Academy of Political and Social Science* 137, Standards in Industry (May 1928): 220; W. E. Braithwaite, "Glass Containers Simplified," *Commercial Standards Monthly* 6, no. 6 (December 1929): 162; Alice L. Edwards, *Product Standards and Labeling for Consumers* (New York: Ronald Press Company, 1940), 57.

49 Priest, *A Primer of Simplified Practice*, 32.

50 "Germans Change Opinion of Yanks," 2.

51 Early summaries of benefits appeared in Shaw's publications in 1921: Thomas, "Simplification in Industry, II," 717; Parsonage, "What Simplification Saves Us," 756–7.

52 For a detailed description of the impact of simplification on paper manufacturing and distribution, for example, see George A. Galliver, "How We 'Applied' Simplification," *System* 40, no. 3 (September 1921): 265–8, 313–14, 316, 320, 322; George A. Galliver, "12 Savings We Have Made: Eighth Article in the 'Simplification in Industry' Series," *Factory* 27, no. 4 (October 1921): 463–6.

53 E.g., *SPR R2-62: Bedding Products and Components* (1962), [24]. For a more detailed enumeration of benefits, see U.S. Department of Commerce, *Simplified Practice: What It Is* (1924), 20–2 (reprinted from a U.S. Chamber of Commerce bulletin); and Hudson, "Simplification and Standardization," 998–1000. Advocates of simplification referred to inventories as "frozen investment" or "frozen capital": *SPR No. 51: Die Head Chasers (For Self-Opening and Adjustable Die Heads)* (1926), 8; *SPR No. 53: Steel Spiral Rods (For Concrete Reinforcement)* (1926), 4; *SPR No. 63: Metal Spools (For Annealing, Handling, and Shipping Wire)* (1928), 3.

54 "Models Drastically Reduced," 77–8, 81–2.

55 "Official Proceedings: Conference on Simplified Practice," 3.

56 Johnson, "How Advertising Affects Standardization," 81.

57 *SPR No. 1: Paving Bricks* (1922), 5; Feiker, "The Trend of 'Simplification,'" 156–8. For other evidence of the department's early activities related to simplification, see "Steps in Simplification," *Factory* 28, no. 6 (June 1922): 657; and "Steps in Simplification," *Factory* 29, no. 1 (July 1922): 37.

58 U.S. Department of Commerce, *Standards Yearbook 1931*, 246.

59 This description of the paving-brick conference is based on *SPR No. 1: Paving Bricks* (1922), 5–9; Feiker, "The Trend of 'Simplification,'" 156–8; and Report of the Planning Committee (1931), 4–6.

60 Chamber of Commerce of the United States of America, *A Commercial Tower of Babel*; Durgin, "Alice in Modernland," 14; Stuart Chase and F. J. Schlink, *Your Money's Worth: A Study in the Waste of the Consumer's Dollar* (New York: Macmillan Company, 1927), 223.

61 Between 1925 and 1940, the standard sizes fluctuated between four and six. In addition to the published revisions of the simplified practice recommendations, see E. L. Beller, "Economic Effect of Simplification in the Paving Brick Industry," *Annals of the American Academy of Political and Social Science* 139, no. 1, Stabilization of Commodity

Prices (September 1928): 71–2, and a summary of the 1922–35 revision conferences in *SPR R1-36: Vitrified Paving Brick* (1936), 3–9.

62 For an example of an acceptance circular, see U.S. Department of Commerce, Bureau of Standards, *Elimination of Waste: Paper* (Washington, DC: Government Printing Office, March 10, 1924), available at the Library of Congress. A generic acceptance form was illustrated in U.S. Department of Commerce, *Simplified Practice: What It Is* (1924), 4. Some of the printed simplified practice recommendations that were circulated for acceptance have survived with the acceptance form at the end of the pamphlet.

63 For descriptions of the process in subsequent years, see U.S. Department of Commerce, *Simplified Practice: What It Is* (1924), 3–4; U.S. Department of Commerce, *Simplified Practice: What It Is* (1928), 2–5; U.S. Department of Commerce, Simplified Practice: Its Purpose and Application [LC-456], 3–4; U.S. Department of Commerce, Simplified Practice: Its Purpose and Application [LC-590], 9; Economic Cooperation Administration, Technical Assistance Division, Special Project Branch, *Increasing Productivity thru Simplification, Standardization, Specialization* (Washington, DC, March 1, 1951), 23–6; Donald R. Mackay, "The Development and Use of National Voluntary Standards," *Food Drug Cosmetic Law Journal* 24, no. 11 (November 1969): 552–4; "Title 15 – Commerce and Foreign Trade, Subtitle A, Part 10 – Procedures for the Development of Voluntary Product Standards," *Federal Register* 35, no. 104 (May 28, 1970): 8349–53.

64 Herring, *Public Administration*, 322.

65 This description is based, in part, on the published simplified practice recommendations. They included not only the recommendation itself but also a brief history of the process, conference minutes, and lists of attendees and of the entities (trade associations, firms, government agencies) that had accepted the recommendation. It is also based on general descriptions of the process in Hudson, "Group Simplification Gains Momentum," 196; U.S. Department of Commerce, Simplified Practice: Its Purpose and Application [LC-456], 3–7; U.S. Department of Commerce, Simplified Practice: Its Purpose and Application [LC-590], 4–9; Edwards, *Product Standards*, 57–9; Economic Cooperation Administration, *Increasing Productivity*, 23–6; Tanner, "Secretary Hoover's War on Waste," 6–7; Eisner, *From Warfare State to Welfare State*, 120; and Clements, *Imperfect Visionary*, 254–5.

66 Calculations based on U.S. Department of Commerce, *Commercial and Industrial Organizations of the United States, Revised to November*

1, 1919; and U.S. Department of Commerce, Bureau of Foreign and Domestic Commerce, *Commercial and Industrial Organizations of the U.S.*, 8th ed., Domestic Commerce Series No. 5 (Washington, DC: Government Printing Office, September 1931) (interstate, national, and international; excluding professional, foreign, and some miscellaneous associations).

67 *SPR No. 50: Bank Checks, Notes, Drafts and Similar Instruments* (1926), 4–5. The arrangement of information on bank checks and other financial forms was also cleared with the Federal Reserve Board.

68 There is now a vast literature on "associationalism." Among newer contributions, see William J. Novak, "The American Law of Association: The Legal–Political Construction of Civil Society," *Studies in American Political Development* 15, no. 2 (Fall 2001): 163–88; Skocpol et al., "Patriotic Partnerships"; Berk and Schneiberg, "Varieties *in* Capitalism, Varieties *of* Association"; Brian Balogh, *The Associational State: American Governance in the Twentieth Century* (Philadelphia: University of Pennsylvania Press, 2015); Sawyer, *American Fair Trade*; and Thelen, "Employer Organization and the Law."

69 Glickman, *Buying Power*, esp. 201–5.

70 Chase, *The Tragedy of Waste*, 167–74; Chase and Schlink, *Your Money's Worth: A Study in the Waste of the Consumer's Dollar*, 168–96; F. J. Schlink and Robert A. Brady, "Standards and Specifications from the Standpoint of the Ultimate Consumer," *Annals of the American Academy of Political and Social Science* 137, Standards in Industry (May 1928): 231–9. On Chase and Schlink's *Your Money's Worth*, see Charles McGovern, *Sold American: Consumption and Citizenship, 1890–1945* (Chapel Hill: University of North Carolina Press, 2006), 163–85; Glickman, *Buying Power*, 194–205.

71 For a hard-hitting critique of the Bureau of Standards' treatment of retail or "ultimate" consumers, see Robert A. Brady, "How Government Standards Affect the Ultimate Consumer," *Annals of the American Academy of Political and Social Science* 137, Standards in Industry (May 1928): 247–52. See also Julia Mottier Frank, "Standardization and Simplification in the Textile Industry" (M.A. thesis, Home Economics Course, University of Wisconsin–Madison, 1929), 120, http://digital .library.wisc.edu/1793/52993; Herring, *Public Administration*, 327.

72 Edwards, *Product Standards*, 60.

73 On the American Home Economics Association and standardization in the 1920s, see Carolyn M. Goldstein, *Creating Consumers: Home Economists in Twentieth-Century America* (Chapel Hill: University of North Carolina Press, 2012), 112–33. The General Federation of

Women's Clubs was also reported in 1925 to be "conducting a study of Simplified Practice, and the elimination of waste through standardization": U.S. Department of Commerce, Division of Simplified Practice, *Monthly News Bulletin*, no. 9 (December 15, 1925): 3.

74 *SPR No. 11: Bed Blankets: Cotton, Wool, and Cotton and Wool Mixed* (1924), 3, 7; "Standardization of Blankets," Editorial, *Journal of Home Economics* 16, no. 4 (April 1924): 197 (quotation).

75 P. G. Agnew, "Work of the American Engineering Standards Committee," *Annals of the American Academy of Political and Social Science* 137, Standards in Industry (May 1928): 15–16; Edwards, *Product Standards*, 94–6; P. G. Agnew, "Twenty-Five Years – the American Standards Association: 2. Development of the ASA," *Industrial Standardization* 14, no. 12 (December 1943): 327; McGovern, *Sold American*, 167.

76 "Standardization of Blankets," 197–8; *SPR No. 11: Bed Blankets: Cotton, Wool, and Cotton and Wool Mixed* (1924), 3, 7; *SPR No. 35: Steel Lockers (Single and Double Tier)* (1925), 8; *SPR No. 54: Sterling Silver Flatware* (1926), 5, 7; *SPR No. 55: Tinware, Galvanized and Japanned Ware* (1926), 9, 11; *SPR R96-28: Ice Cake Sizes* (1929), 9, 11–12. The AHEA's representative at the general conference to simplify sterling silver flatware was Dr. Louise Stanley of Department of Agriculture's Bureau of Home Economics, established in 1923. The Bureau of Home Economics was also represented at the conference to simplify ice cakes. On the Bureau, see Goldstein, *Creating Consumers*.

77 Katharine Blunt, "President's Address, Eighteenth Annual Meeting American Home Economics Association," *Journal of Home Economics* 17, no. 10 (October 1925): 541; U.S. Department of Commerce, Division of Simplified Practice, *Monthly News Bulletin*, no. 7 (October 15, 1925): 2 (quotation). See also "Editorial: Thrift through Simplified Practice," *Journal of Home Economics* 18, no. 1 (January 1926): 30; R. M. Hudson and E. L. Priest, "Saving through Simplified Practice," *Journal of Home Economics* 18, no. 1 (January 1926): 6–12; "Editorial: Sheets, Standardization, and Home Economics," *Journal of Home Economics* 19, no. 8 (August 1927): 452–3; Alice L. Edwards, "Standardization in the Household," *Annals of the American Academy of Political and Social Science* 137, Standards in Industry (May 1928): 213–19. In the late 1930s, the National Retail Dry Goods Association joined forces with women's organizations to create the National Consumer–Retailer Relations Council as a forum for cooperation on the standardization of consumer goods: Pearce, *Trade Association Survey*, 312.

78 Edwards, *Product Standards*, 60.

79 Hoover, "Some Notes on Industrial Readjustment," 145; *Report of*

the President's Conference on Unemployment (Washington, DC: Government Printing Office, 1921), 7–14.

80 See *Waste in Industry*, Part III, General Reports, 263–390.

81 U.S. Department of Commerce, Division of Simplified Practice, *Monthly News Bulletin*, no. 4 (July 15, 1925): 2. See also Priest, *A Primer of Simplified Practice*, 37–8.

82 William Green, "The Effect on Labor of the New Standardization Programs of American Industry," *Annals of the American Academy of Political and Social Science* 137, Standards in Industry (May 1928): 43–6.

83 Priest, *A Primer of Simplified Practice*, 45.

84 Economic Cooperation Administration, *Increasing Productivity*, 35–6. This section did not appear in any published SPR that I have seen.

85 Ray M. Hudson, as head of the DSP, proposed in 1925 that collaboration be widened to include, among others, the National Consumers League and the American Federation of Labor, but nothing seems to have come of the idea: Tanner, "Secretary Hoover's War on Waste," 15.

86 U.S. Department of Commerce, *Simplified Practice: What It Is* (1924), 3. See also "A Message from Herbert Hoover," 84; *SPR No. 24: Hospital Beds* (1925), 4.

87 Priest, *A Primer of Simplified Practice*, 13.

88 Hudson, "Group Simplification Gains Momentum," 195. See also Hudson, "The New Conservation – II," 28; Priest, *A Primer of Simplified Practice*, 13; U.S. Department of Commerce, Bureau of Standards, "The New Viewpoint in Business, by Ray M. Hudson, Assistant Director, Commercial Standards," *Monthly News Bulletin of Commercial Standards Group*, no. 32 (November 15, 1927), para. 1; U.S. Department of Commerce, Bureau of Standards, "Keeping Step with Style through Simplification," *Technical News Bulletin*, no. 129 (January 1928): 7; U.S. Department of Commerce, Simplified Practice: Its Purpose and Application [LC-590], 4. The DSP's 80–20 axiom appears to have been truly empirical.

89 *SPR No. 11: Bed Blankets: Cotton, Wool, and Cotton and Wool Mixed* (1924), 6–7.

90 John R. Bangs, Jr., in collaboration with C. D. Hart, *Factory Management* (New York: Alexander Hamilton Institute, 1930), 234 (original italics). See also Julius H. Barnes, based on an interview by Roy Dickinson, "Standardization as a Creator of New Advertising," *Printers' Ink Monthly* 6, no. 3 (March 1923): 100. Barnes was President of the Chamber of Commerce of the United States.

91 U.S. Department of Commerce, *Simplified Practice: What It Is* (1924),

3; U.S. Bureau of Standards, *The Purpose and Application of Simplified Practice*, 7. For an example of the way such data was presented to a general conference, see the illustration "Tabulation of Actual Shipments of Vitrified Paving Brick, 1914–1921," with eliminated varieties lined out, in Feiker, "The Trend of 'Simplification,'" 157.

92 *SPR No. 42: Paper Grocers' Bags* (1926), 6, 10–11. On the use of insignia to identify simplified products, see Priest, *A Primer of Simplified Practice*, 38–40; U.S. Department of Commerce, Bureau of Standards, Division of Simplified Practice, *Report on Identification of Simplified Lines in Trade Literature* (Washington, DC, December 15, 1932).

93 *SPR 99-30: Pocket Knives* (1929), 1, 3.

94 *SPR No. 45: Grinding Wheels* (1926), 19, 21.

95 See, for example, *SPR No. 1: Paving Bricks* (1922), 9; *SPR No. 10: Milk and Cream Bottles and Bottle Caps* (1924), 2; *SPR No. 25: Hot Water Storage Tanks* (1925), 7; *SPR No. 60: Packing of Carriage, Machine, and Lag Bolts* (1927), 16.

96 *SPR No. 10: Milk and Cream Bottles and Bottle Caps* (1924), 2–3. It also approved the elimination altogether of the quarter-pint size (previously available in 10 varieties). The industry pushed closer to full simplification in 1927, when varieties (heights) were reduced to 2 for quart bottles and 1 each for pint and half-pint bottles: *SPR No. 10: Milk and Cream Bottles and Bottle Caps* (1927), 5.

97 *SPR No. 22: Paper* (1924), 6. For insights into the troubles that non-standard paper sizes created for manufacturers of paper-folding machinery and printing presses, see James S. Gilbert, "How Simplification Profited Us, Our Workers, and an Entire Industry," *Factory* 28, no. 1 (January 1922): 36–7.

98 Emphasis added. For exceptions, see *SPR No. 22: Paper* (1924), 6; *SPR No. 32: Concrete Building Units (Block, Tile, and Brick)* (1925), 6; *SPR No. 50: Bank Checks, Notes, Drafts and Similar Instruments* (1926), 4–5.

99 Priest, *A Primer of Simplified Practice*, 13, 16; *SPR No. 48: Shovels, Spades and Scoops* (1926), 5; U.S. Bureau of Standards, *The Purpose and Application of Simplified Practice*, 7. The threshold to acceptance was lowered in 1970: Mackay, "The Development and Use of National Voluntary Standards," 553–4; "Title 15 – Commerce and Foreign Trade, Subtitle A, Part 10 – Procedures for the Development of Voluntary Product Standards," 8351.

100 "Official Proceedings: Conference on Simplified Practice," 11, 12.

101 Even in later years (1935–54), the American paint business was intensely competitive: Chandler, *Scale and Scope*, 152–3. According

to newspaper surveys in the late 1940s, local brands of paint were more popular in many markets than national brands were: *Ten Market Comparison of Consumer Preferences: A Digest of Product Popularity, Brand Positions and Preference Percentages Tabulated for 110 Classifications in 10 Representative Markets* ([Milwaukee]: Journal Co., 1947), 42–3; *Thirteen Market Comparison of Consumer Preferences: A Digest of Product Use and Brand Preference for 137 Classifications in 13 Important Markets* ([Milwaukee]: Journal Co., 1948), 114–17.

102   U.S. Department of Commerce, *Limitation of Variety Recommendation No. 1; SPR R144-32: Paints, Varnishes and Containers* (1933); Heckel, *The Paint Industry*, 594–600.

103   U.S. Department of Commerce, Bureau of Standards, *Annual Report of the Director of the Bureau of Standards to the Secretary of Commerce for the Fiscal Year Ended June 30, 1925*, Misc. Pub. No. 69 (Washington, DC: Government Printing Office, 1925), 23; *SPR No. 48: Shovels, Spades and Scoops* (1926), 5. Polished finishes on hand tools had been eliminated during World War I: John M. Williams, "Simplification in Industry, III: What Simplification Accomplished for Us," *Factory* 26, no. 8 (April 15, 1921): 953.

104   See SPR nos. 64–5 in *SPR R3-28: Metal Lath* (1928), 10, and *SPR R2-32: Bedsteads, Springs, and Mattresses* (1933), 11.

105   On the difficulties of garment sizing, see S. P. Ashdown, ed., *Sizing in Clothing: Developing Effective Sizing Systems for Ready-to-Wear Clothing* (Cambridge, UK, and Boca Raton, FL: Woodhead Publishing Limited and CRC Press, 2007).

106   Except as noted otherwise, this description is based on *SPR No. 16: Lumber* (1924), 17–30; and L. W. Smith and L. W. Wood, *History of Yard Lumber Size Standards*, Forest Products Laboratory, Forest Service, U.S. Department of Agriculture (Madison, WI, September 1964), 5–13. The latter is helpful on freight rates, regional interests, and the technical difficulties of standardizing a non-manufactured product. See also Hawley, "Three Facets of Hooverian Associationalism," 101–8; Robbins, "Voluntary Cooperation vs. Regulatory Paternalism," 358–79; and, on trade associations in the lumber industry, *Report of the Federal Trade Commission on Lumber Manufacturers' Trade Associations* (Washington, DC: Government Printing Office, 1922). Another complex case, involving the Federal Specifications Board, concerned builders' hardware for dwellings: *SPR No. 18: Builders' Hardware* (1925), 1.

107   O. H. Cheney, *The New Competition in the Lumber Industry*, [Speech]

before the Twenty-Fifth Annual Convention of the National Lumber Manufacturers Association, April 28, 1927, Chicago, Illinois (Chicago and Washington: National Lumber Manufacturers Association, n.d.). See also Wilson Compton, *The Organization of the Lumber Industry, with Special Reference to the Influences Determining the Prices of Lumber in the United States* (Chicago: American Lumberman, 1916), 126–9; Wilson Compton, *Is the "Future" of Lumber Ahead or Behind?*, [Speech] before the National Lumber Trade Extension Conference, February 15, 1926, Chicago, Illinois (Chicago and Washington: National Lumber Manufacturers Association, n.d.); U.S. Department of Commerce, Division of Simplified Practice, "Meeting 'The New Competition' with Simplified Practice, by Ray M. Hudson, Chief, Division of Simplified Practice," *Monthly News Bulletin*, no. 16 (July 15, 1926): 1. The "new competition," defined here as inter-industry (rather than inter-firm) competition, encouraged, as a defensive maneuver, the "new competition" that Sawyer explores (i.e., cooperative or "regulated competition" among firms in the same industry): Sawyer, *American Fair Trade*.

108 Blaszczyk, "No Place Like Home," 113–35. On the Commerce Department's Division of Building and Housing, created by Hoover, see also Cochrane, *Measures for Progress*, 249–53; Clements, *Imperfect Visionary*, 222–3, 255–6. On the tug of war between Hoover and Secretary of Agriculture Henry C. Wallace over lumber standardization, see Clements, *Imperfect Visionary*, 287–9.

109 Smith and Wood, *History of Yard Lumber Size Standards*, 5–13.

110 *SPR No. 16: Lumber* (1924), 19.

111 *SPR No. 16: Lumber* (1924), 4–5. For 2-inch boards, the SPR also set two standard thicknesses, which differed by ⅛ in.

112 Blodgett and Ritter, *High Lights*, 5, 48–9. See also Smith and Wood, *History of Yard Lumber Size Standards*, 13; Hawley, "Three Facets of Hooverian Associationalism," 108; Robbins, "Voluntary Cooperation vs. Regulatory Paternalism," 377.

113 *SPR 16-53: Lumber: American Lumber Standards for Softwood Lumber* (1953), 11; and *PS 20-70: American Softwood Lumber Standard* (1970), 6. The most recent softwood lumber standard (2020) is available on the website of the Voluntary Product Standards Program, National Institute of Standards and Technology www.nist.gov/standardsgov/voluntary-product-standards-program.

114 "Initial Steps Taken," 147.

115 R. M. Hudson, Chief, Division of Simplified Practice, to Secretary Hoover, January 21, 1927, in RG 40, File 67009/80. For lists of available

standards, see U.S. Department of Commerce, *Simplified Practice: What It Is* (1928), 54; Bureau of Standards, Division of Simplified Practice, List of Publications, Letter Circular 345, October 1932, in RG 40, File 67009/80; U.S. Department of Commerce, National Bureau of Standards, List of Simplified Practice Recommendations: Revised to October 15, 1940, October 15, 1940, Letter Circular LC-612 (Supersedes LC-594); U.S. Department of Commerce, National Bureau of Standards, Simplified Practice Recommendations: Alphabetical List Revised to February 1, 1950, Letter Circular LC979 (Supersedes LC958), February 1, 1950; U.S. Department of Commerce, National Bureau of Standards, *List of Voluntary Product Standards, Commercial Standards, and Simplified Practice Recommendations,* NBS List of Publications 53, Revised September 1972 ([Washington, DC], September 1972). By the mid-1960s, the relevant industry covered the cost of the initial printing of recommendations: Mansfield Lonie, "Voluntary Product Standards: What They Mean to the Consumer," *Journal of Home Economics* 58, no. 1 (January 1966): 23.

116 Johnson, "How Advertising Affects Standardization," 88.

117 E.g., *SPR No. 11: Bed Blankets: Cotton, Wool, and Cotton and Wool Mixed* (1924), 5.

118 *SPR No. 1: Paving Bricks* (1924), 6. Beginning in 1927, the SPRs included a generic section on the standing committee's organization and duties: *SPR No. 60: Packing of Carriage, Machine, and Lag Bolts* (1927), 15–16.

119 Priest, *A Primer of Simplified Practice,* 17–18.

120 *Waste in Industry,* 104.

121 Ralph R. Patch, "Lower Prices, Doubled Volume – through Simplification," *System* 46, no. 1 (July 1924): 33–4.

122 Patch, "Lower Prices, Doubled Volume," 33. The testimonials that appeared in *System* and *Factory* are rife with fascinating details on the pros and cons of simplification from the firm's perspective. For a sampling, see "Industry's Own Opinions," *Factory* 35, no. 4 (October 1924): 538–9.

123 Harvey S. Firestone, "Why We Invested $7,000,000 in 'Simplification,'" *Factory* 27, no. 6 (December 1921): 739.

124 Schlink and Brady, "Standards and Specifications," 232.

125 1924 General Electric catalog, quoted in Agenda for Meeting of the Planning Committee of the Division of Simplified Practice . . . [to be held] December 16, 1932, 4, in RG 40, File 67009/80.

126 J. F. Tinsley, Vice President and General Manager, Crompton and Knowles Loom Works, quoted in "Industry's Own Opinions," 538.

127 Howard Coonley, "Simplification in Industry, VII: We Reduced Our Line from 17,000 to 610 Items," *Factory* [27], no. 3 (September 1921): 319.

128 Williams, "Simplification in Industry, III," 952–3.

129 Galliver, "How We 'Applied' Simplification," 313–14; *Waste in Industry*, 187. On the company's experience with simplification, see also Galliver, "12 Savings We Have Made," 463–6.

130 McClure, "Two Thousand Brands Reduced to Three," 123–4, 127–8.

131 See the generic acceptance form in U.S. Department of Commerce, *Simplified Practice: What It Is* (1924), 4. Priest, *A Primer of Simplified Practice*, 16, referred to this as a pledge.

132 *SPR No. 50: Bank Checks, Notes, Drafts and Similar Instruments* (1926), 5.

133 Hudson, "Simplification and Standardization," 1034.

134 U.S. Department of Commerce, Division of Simplified Practice, "Extra Dividends," *Monthly News Bulletin*, no. 9 (December 15, 1925): 1. See also U.S. Department of Commerce, *Simplified Practice: What It Is* (1928), v, 57.

135 Priest, *A Primer of Simplified Practice*, 17.

136 Schlink and Brady, "Standards and Specifications," 232–3.

137 McGraw-Hill Company, Inc., "What Is Simplification?" advertisement, *Printers' Ink* 123, no. 3 (April 19, 1923): 74 (emphasis omitted).

138 Advertising expenditures, boosted during the war by a favorable tax status, are estimated to have increased from $82 million in 1914 to $1.4 billion in 1919 and to $3.0 billion in 1929: Roland Marchand, *Advertising the American Dream: Making Way for Modernity, 1920–1940* (Berkeley: University of California Press, 1985), 6. On the history of advertising from 1870 to 1920, see Pamela Walker Laird, *Advertising Progress: American Business and the Rise of Consumer Marketing* (Baltimore: Johns Hopkins University Press, 1998); during World War I, Daniel Pope, "The Advertising Industry and World War I," *Public Historian* 2, no. 3 (Spring 1980): 4–25; and in the 1920s, Copeland, "Marketing," 402–21; Marchand, *Advertising the American Dream*; and McGovern, *Sold American*, 21–131.

139 Barnes, "Standardization as a Creator of New Advertising," 23 (comments by the interviewer).

140 Barnes, "Standardization as a Creator of New Advertising," 103 (comments by the interviewer).

141 Charles P. White, "Shall We Control Demand or Follow It?" *Annals of the American Academy of Political and Social Science* 139, no. 1, Stabilization of Commodity Prices (September 1928): 126–7.

142 *SPR No. 2: Bedsteads, Springs and Mattresses* (1922), 5. See also Hoover, "Industrial Standardization," 192.

143 Durgin, "Alice in Modernland," 14.

144 Hudson, "Simplification and Standardization," 1032.

145 Priest, *A Primer of Simplified Practice*, 1, 3. The *Primer* returned to the question of style or individuality several more times. See pp. 19, 42, 45–6.

146 U.S. Department of Commerce, Bureau of Foreign and Domestic Commerce, *Commerce Yearbook 1930 (Eighth Number)*, vol. I: *United States* (Washington, DC: Government Printing Office, 1930), 46.

147 U.S. Department of Commerce, Division of Simplified Practice, "Editor's Note," *Monthly News Bulletin*, no. 1 (April 15, 1925): 1.

148 U.S. Department of Commerce, *Commerce Yearbook 1922 (Including Early Part of 1923)* (Washington, DC: Government Printing Office, 1923), 44.

149 Shaw, "Simplification," 425. Identical language appeared in U.S. Department of Commerce, *Simplified Practice: What It Is* (1924), 24, and "Divisions of the Commercial Standards Group," *Commercial Standards Monthly* 6, no. 1 (July 1929): [i].

150 "A Message from Herbert Hoover," 82.

151 Priest, *A Primer of Simplified Practice*, 32. See also Herbert Hoover, "'No Imposition of Government in Business,'" *Factory* 35, no. 4 (October 1925): 536; U.S. Department of Commerce, *Simplified Practice: What It Is* (1928), 2.

152 *SPR No. 9: Woven-Wire Fencing* (1923), 6. For other examples, see *SPR No. 11: Bed Blankets: Cotton, Wool, and Cotton and Wool Mixed* (1924), 6; *SPR No. 15: Blackboard Slate* (1925), 6; *SPR No. 35: Steel Lockers (Single and Double Tier)* (1925), 7–8.

153 Report of the Planning Committee (1931), 4.

154 Herring, *Public Administration*, vii, 300; Tanner, "Secretary Hoover's War on Waste," 28n16.

155 U.S. Department of Commerce, Bureau of Standards, "Reduction in Variety of Taper Roller Bearings," *Technical News Bulletin*, no. 100 (August 1925): 3.

156 J. Walter Drake, Assistant Secretary of Commerce, to N. E. Wahlberg, The Nash Motors Company, March 14, 1925, in RG 40, File 67009/80.

157 *SPR No. 67: Roller Bearings* (1928), 6.

158 "Official Proceedings: Conference on Simplified Practice," 9. An agenda item prepared for the DSP's Planning Committee was adamant that the 144 SPRs to date had all been initiated by industry, "as the records will show": Agenda for Meeting of the Planning Committee

of the Division of Simplified Practice . . . [to be held] December 16, 1932, 16, in RG 40, File 67009/80. During World War II, the Office of Production Management's conservation division was authorized to initiate projects: U.S. Department of Commerce, National Bureau of Standards, "Simplified Practice and the Defense Program," *Technical News Bulletin*, no. 295 (November 1941): 95–6. In 1970, Commerce Department procedures were changed to allow the Commodity Standards Division to initiate projects: Congressional Research Service, Science Policy Research Division, *Voluntary Industrial Standards in the United States: An Overview of Their Evolution and Significance for the Congress* [Committee Print] (Washington, DC: Government Printing Office, 1974), 25.

159 "The Trend toward Simplification," 41.

160 Clements, "Herbert Hoover and Conservation," 71.

161 Hoover's use of publicity as Secretary of Commerce was modeled on his experience as U.S. Food Administrator during the war. "He assembled at the Department of Commerce," Stephen Ponder notes, "the most elaborate publicity apparatus yet established in the executive branch in peacetime": Ponder, *Managing the Press: Origins of the Media Presidency, 1897–1933*, 131. On the U.S. Food Administration's publicity drive during World War I, see Tunc, "Less Sugar, More Warships," 193–216; and Jeansonne, *Herbert Hoover: A Life*, 114–15.

162 Quarterly Report on the Activities of the Division of Simplified Practice, June 30, 1923, 8–14, in RG 40, File 67009/80.

163 Mr. Durgin, Memorandum to Mr. Hoover, November 1, 1922, in RG 40 – Department of Commerce, General Correspondence, 1918–1922, File 82341, National Archives II (hereafter cited as RG 40, File 82341).

164 Mr. Durgin, Memorandum to Mr. Hoover, November 1, 1922, in RG 40, File 82341.

165 Quarterly Report on the Activities of the Division of Simplified Practice, June 30, 1923, 15, in RG 40, File 67009/80. For bibliographies, see "A Bibliography of Articles on Simplification," *Factory* 32, no. 3 (March 1924): 318–20, reprinted in U.S. Department of Commerce, *Simplified Practice: What It Is* (1924), 27–33; Priest, *A Primer of Simplified Practice*, 48–54; and U.S. Department of Commerce, *Simplified Practice: What It Is* (1928), 59–67.

166 *SPR No. 9: Woven-Wire Fencing* (1923), 6; Durgin, "Alice in Modernland," 14; *SPR No. 30: Terneplate* (1925), 4; *SPR No. 51: Die Head Chasers (For Self-Opening and Adjustable Die Heads)* (1926), 8.

167 Priest, *A Primer of Simplified Practice*, 3; U.S. Department of Commerce, *Simplified Practice: What It Is* (1928), 18–19.

168 The FSB was created in the new Bureau of the Budget: Cochrane, *Measures for Progress*, 257–9. On the federal government's stature as a consumer, see A. A. Stevenson, "Significance of Standardization to American Industry and the Federal Government," *Mechanical Engineering* 44, no. 3 (March 1922): 185; George K. Burgess, Director, Bureau of Standards, to Chief Clerk, Department of Commerce, May 12, 1923, [copy] in File: SP, April–May 1923, RG 167.3 – National Bureau of Standards, General Correspondence, 1923, National Archives II; Priest, *A Primer of Simplified Practice*, 34; A. H. Erck, "Standardization of Purchase Procedure for the Federal Government," *Annals of the American Academy of Political and Social Science* 137, Standards in Industry (May 1928): 202.

169 U.S. Department of Commerce, *Eleventh Annual Report of the Secretary of Commerce* (Washington, DC: Government Printing Office, 1923), 17–18; U.S. Department of Commerce, Bureau of Standards, *National Bureau of Standards: Its Functions and Activities*, 2nd ed., Circular No. 1 (Washington, DC: Government Printing Office, October 29, 1925), 86; Priest, *A Primer of Simplified Practice*, 34. An excerpt from Hoover's address to a conference of state purchasing agents that he convened in 1923 was reprinted as Hoover, "Industrial Standardization," 189–96.

170 U.S. Department of Commerce, *National Bureau of Standards*, 86; Cochrane, *Measures for Progress*, 258.

171 U.S. Department of Commerce, Bureau of Standards, *National Directory of Commodity Specifications: Classified and Alphabetical Lists and Brief Descriptions of Existing Commodity Specifications*, Misc. Pub. No. 65, August 28, 1925 (Washington, DC: Government Printing Office, 1925); U.S. Department of Commerce, Bureau of Standards, "National Directory of Commodity Specifications," *Technical News Bulletin*, no. 101 (September 1925): 7–8. Subsequent editions were published in 1932 and 1945. See also two companion volumes: U.S. Department of Commerce, National Bureau of Standards, *Standards and Specifications in the Wood-Using Industries: Nationally Recognized Standards and Specifications for Wood and Manufactures Thereof Including Paper and Paper Products*, Misc. Pub. No. 79 (Washington, DC: Government Printing Office, October 5, 1927); U.S. Department of Commerce, National Bureau of Standards, *Standards and Specifications for Nonmetallic Minerals and Their Products*, Misc. Pub. No. 110 (Washington, DC: Government Printing Office, April 1930).

172 Herbert Hoover, *The Memoirs of Herbert Hoover*, vol. II: *The Cabinet*

and the Presidency, 1920–1933 (New York: MacMillan Company, 1952), 68. See also Hoover, "Industrial Standardization," 192; Priest, *A Primer of Simplified Practice*, 35; T. T. Craven, Chief Coordinator, Federal Coordinating Service, To the Heads of All Departments and Establishments, Subject: Procurement: Simplified practice recommendations and their application to Government purchases, September 17, 1931, available in ProQuest Congressional/Executive Branch Documents, SuDoc No. T51.7/5:63, https://about.proquest.com/en/products-services/ProQuest-Executive-Branch-Documents-1789-1932.

173 Tanner, "Secretary Hoover's War on Waste," 13–14; Barber, *From New Era to New Deal*, 14.

6 Diffusing Mass Production

1 Mr. Durgin, Memorandum to Mr. Hoover, November 1, 1922, in RG 40, File 82341.

2 Cecil Chisholm, "What Is Simplification in Industry?" *System* (British ed.) 41, no. 4 (April 1922): 270–1; Chisholm, "'Simplification' in United States: America's New Industrial Policy: I. – Genesis of the Movement," 131; Cecil Chisholm, "'Simplification' in the United States: What the Movement Is Achieving: II. – Operation in Individual Businesses," *The* [London] *Times Imperial and Foreign Trade and Engineering Supplement*, May 6, 1922, 151; Cecil Chisholm, "'Simplification' in United States: Is It Applicable in Great Britain? III. – What Some Firms Are Doing," *The* [London] *Times Imperial and Foreign Trade and Engineering Supplement*, May 13, 1922, 171; [Cecil Chisholm], "'Simplification' in the United States: Progress of New Industrial Policy: Groups Using Commerce Department's Service," *The* [London] *Times Imperial and Foreign Trade and Engineering Supplement*, December 9, 1922, 301. Chisholm was identified as editor of the British *System* in Cecil Chisholm, "Teaching Workers to Think 'Production,'" *Factory* 26, no. 1 (January 1, 1921): 40, and in U.S. Department of Commerce, Division of Simplified Practice, *Monthly News Bulletin*, no. 28 (July 15, 1927): 9.

3 Victor S. Karabasz, "Simplification and Standardization in Europe," *Annals of the American Academy of Political and Social Science* 137, Standards in Industry (May 1928): 25–31; Thomas Wölker, *Entstehung und Entwicklung des Deutschen Normenausschusses 1917 bis 1925*, vol. XXX, DIN-Normungskunde (Berlin: Beuth, 1992); Egbert Klautke, *Unbegrenzte Möglichkeiten: "Amerikanisierung" in Deutschland und Frankreich (1900–1933)* (Stuttgart: Franz Steiner, 2003); Yates and

Murphy, *Engineering Rules*, 78–80, 110–13. The German equivalent of "simplified practice" was *Typisierung*. See, for example, Karl Bücher, "Spezialisierung, Normalisierung, Typisierung," *Zeitschrift für die gesamte Staatswissenschaft* 76 (1922): 427.

4 Hoover, "'No Imposition of Government in Business,'" 536. See also Feiker, "The Trend of 'Simplification,'" 156; Stevenson, "Significance of Standardization"; Ray M. Hudson, "The New Conservation – I," *Scientific American* 127, no. 6 (December 1922), 400, 446; Franklin D. Jones, *Trade Association Activities and the Law: A Discussion of the Legal and Economic Aspects of Collective Action through Trade Organizations* (New York: McGraw-Hill, 1922), 93; Hudson, "The New Conservation – II," 72; Ray M. Hudson, "The New Conservation – III," *Scientific American* 128, no. 2 (February 1923): 98.

5 Quoted in "International Industrial Digest: Some German Progress in Simplification," *Factory* 29, no. 4 (October 1922): 460. The conference concerned standardization of ball bearings. See also Jones, *Trade Association Activities*, 86–7, 93; Stevenson, "Significance of Standardization," 185; Hudson, "The New Conservation – III," 98; U.S. Department of Commerce, "Our Standards or Theirs?" 1–2; U.S. Department of Commerce, "Supplement: British Interest in Simplified Practice," 2–3; U.S. Department of Commerce, Division of Simplified Practice, *Monthly News Bulletin*, no. 10 (January 15, 1926): 2; U.S. Department of Commerce, Bureau of Standards, "Simplification in Germany," *Monthly News Bulletin of Commercial Standards Group*, no. 32 (November 15, 1927): 3. On national standards and competition in international markets in the 1920s, see Thomas Wölker, "Der Wettlauf um die Verbreitung nationaler Normen im Ausland nach dem Ersten Weltkrieg und die Gründung der ISA aus der Sicht deutscher Quellen," *Vierteljahrschrift für Sozial und Wirtschaftsgeschichte* 80, no. 4 (November 1993): 487–509.

6 Chisholm, "What Is Simplification in Industry?" 271.

7 Chisholm, "'Simplification' in United States: Is It Applicable in Great Britain?" 171. On Sweden, see [Chisholm], "Simplification in the United States: Progress of New Industrial Policy," 301; "Steps in Simplification" (August 1922), 146.

8 [Chisholm], "Simplification in the United States: Progress of New Industrial Policy," 301.

9 Quarterly Report of Activities of the Division of Simplified Practice, June 30, 1923, 2–3, 5, in RG 40, File 67009/80.

10 Quarterly Report of Activities of the Division of Simplified Practice, June 30, 1923, 1, 3–4, in RG 40, File 67009/80; U.S. Department of

Commerce, *Eleventh Annual Report of the Secretary of Commerce*, 148; U.S. Department of Commerce, *Simplified Practice: What It Is* (1924), 7–8; U.S. Department of Commerce, American Marine Standards Committee, *American Marine Standards: Lists and Indexes* (Washington, DC: Government Printing Office, 1931).

11 Mr. Durgin, Memorandum to Mr. Hoover and Present Status of Definite Simplification Projects, 1, September 17, 1923, in RG 40, File 67009/80; Quarterly Report of the Activities of the Division of Simplified Practice, September 30, 1923, 7, in RG 40, File 67009/80.

12 [Walter A. Durgin], Memorandum to Secretary Hoover, January 1, 1924, in RG 40, File 67009/80.

13 For a sampling of business opinions, see excerpts from letters solicited by the editor of *Factory* in "Industry's Own Opinions," 538–9.

14 Priest, *A Primer of Simplified Practice*, 43.

15 Quoted in Scranton, *Endless Novelty*, 311.

16 See, for example, U.S. Department of Commerce, *Tenth Annual Report of the Secretary of Commerce*, 140; U.S. Department of Commerce, *Twelfth Annual Report of the Secretary of Commerce* (Washington, DC: Government Printing Office, 1924), 24; Hoover, "'No Imposition of Government in Business,'" 536; Priest, *A Primer of Simplified Practice*, 46; U.S. Department of Commerce, Simplified Practice: Its Purpose and Application [LC-456], 9; U.S. Department of Commerce, Simplified Practice: Its Purpose and Application [LC-590], 10.

17 Ray M. Hudson, "Are There Any Real Obstacles to Simplification?" *Factory* 35, no. 4 (October 1925): 586, 588; Priest, *A Primer of Simplified Practice*, 40–3.

18 Chair of an unidentified company's simplification committee, quoted in "Industry's Own Opinions," 539. On standardization and price competition, see especially Hoyt, "Industrial Combination," 95–104; Hoyt, "Standardization," 271–7; Homer Hoyt, "The Future of Manufacturing in the United States," *The Annalist* 19, no. 478 (March 13, 1922): 320; Brady, "How Government Standards Affect the Ultimate Consumer," 247–52.

19 Hudson, "Are There Any Real Obstacles to Simplification?" 357; Tanner, "Secretary Hoover's War on Waste," 12.

20 U.S. Department of Commerce, *Simplified Practice: What It Is* (1924), 9.

21 Hudson, "Are There Any Real Obstacles to Simplification?" 536.

22 Priest, *A Primer of Simplified Practice*, 19.

23 Hudson, "Are There Any Real Obstacles to Simplification?" 537;

Tanner, "Secretary Hoover's War on Waste," 11–12; Clements, *Imperfect Visionary*, 202–6.

24 According to Ellis W. Hawley, Hoover and President Wilson secured an agreement with the U.S. Attorney General that the war service committees would not be prosecuted under antitrust law: Hawley, "Herbert Hoover and the Sherman Act," 1068–9. See also Hoover, *The Memoirs of Herbert Hoover*, vol. I: *Years of Adventure, 1874–1920*, 247; Sawyer, *American Fair Trade*, 165.

25 Hoyt, "Standardization," 274–5. See also Jones, *Trade Association Activities*, 101–2.

26 U.S. Department of Commerce, *Tenth Annual Report of the Secretary of Commerce*, 29–31; U.S. Department of Commerce, *Twelfth Annual Report of the Secretary of Commerce*, 22–3; Hawley, "Herbert Hoover and the Sherman Act," 1077–8; Sawyer, *American Fair Trade*, 148–95.

27 Himmelberg, "The War Industries Board," 59–74; Himmelberg, "Business, Antitrust Policy, and the Industrial Board," 1–23.

28 *SPR No. 1: Paving Bricks* (1922), 6.

29 On open price plans and antitrust policy, see Hawley, "Herbert Hoover and the Sherman Act," 1072–4; Gerald Berk, "Communities of Competitors: Open Price Associations and the American State, 1911–1929," *Social Science History* 20, no. 3 (Autumn 1996): 391–3; Sawyer, *American Fair Trade*, 180–6.

30 "International Industrial Digest: Associations: Helping to Clear Up the Trade Association Muddle," *Factory* 28, no. 4 (April 1922): 408 (digest of February 1922 editorials in *The Iron Trade Review, Iron Age, The New York Times, The Purchasing Agent*, and *Coal Age*).

31 "International Industrial Digest: Associations," 408; Heckel, *The Paint Industry*, 588–9; Hawley, "Herbert Hoover and the Sherman Act," 1073–4; Russell, *Open Standards*, 83; Sawyer, *American Fair Trade*, 180–2. The Hoover and Daugherty letters were included as an appendix in Jones, *Trade Association Activities*, 324–35. In defense of trade associations, the Commerce Department published a 368-page volume that described their "constructive activities" and featured an introduction by Hoover: Warford and May, *Trade Association Activities*, ii, 1–8.

32 Priest, *A Primer of Simplified Practice*, 32. See also p. 44. The cases were *Cement Manufacturers' Protective Association v. United States*, 268 U.S. 588 (1925); and *Maple Flooring Manufacturers Association v. United States*, 268 U.S. 563 (1925). See Franklin D. Jones, "The Present Legal Status of Open Price Associations," *Annals of the American Academy of Political and Social Science* 139, Stabilization

of Commodity Prices (September 1928): 34–7; Sawyer, *American Fair Trade*, 183–7.

33 See, for example, National Industrial Conference Board, *The Scope of Trade Association Activities in Light of Recent Decisions of the Supreme Court of the United States* (New York: National Industrial Conference Board, Inc., 1925), 3; and Jones, "The Present Legal Status of Open Price Associations," 34–7. After a 1934 case, the DSP changed its acceptance form to avoid legal jeopardy: E. Compton Timberlake, "Standardization and Simplification under the Anti-trust Laws," *Cornell Law Review* 29, no. 3 (March 1944): 323. As the U.S. entered World War II, the Department of Commerce again sought a formal statement from the U.S. Attorney General's office "[t]o ally [*sic*] any fears in the minds of manufacturers that they might run afoul of the anti-trust laws if they took concerted action to reduce the number of styles and sizes in the interest of national defense": [Files, Office of the Chief Clerk], August 14, 1941, and attached copy of Thurman Arnold, Assistant Attorney General, to Wayne C. Taylor, Under Secretary of Commerce, August 12, 1941, in RG 50, File 67009/80. See also P. G. Agnew, "Legal Aspects of Standardization and Simplification: A Discussion from the Point of View of the Lay Worker," *Industrial Standardization* 12, no. 10 (October 1941): 260–4; "The Correspondence between the Attorney General and the Defense Agencies," *Industrial Standardization* 12, no. 10 (October 1941): 264–7. For useful reviews of the antitrust status of standardization, see Timberlake, "Standardization and Simplification under the Anti-trust Laws," 301–29; and Carol Chapman Rawie, "A Guide to Papers Citing Antitrust Cases Involving Standards or Certification," National Bureau of Standards NBSIR 79-1921 (December 1979).

34 R. M. Hudson, Chief, Division of Simplified Practice, to Secretary Hoover, July 1, 1926, Progress in Simplified Practice – Second Quarter, 1926, in RG 40, File 67009/80.

35 U.S. Department of Commerce, *Commerce Yearbook 1930 (Eighth Number)*, vol. I: *United States*, 45.

36 Mr. Durgin, Memorandum to Mr. Hoover, November 1, 1922, in RG 40, File 82341.

37 *SPR No. 42: Paper Grocers' Bags* (1926), 6; *SPR No. 70: Salt Packages* (1928), 2; *SPR R91-29: Glass Containers for Preserves, Jellies and Apple Butter* (1929), 2

38 *SPR No. 13: Structural Slate (for Plumbing and Sanitary Purposes)* (1925), 12; *SPR No. 14: Roofing Slate* (1924), 6; *SPR No. 15: Blackboard Slate* (1925), 6.

39 Mr. Durgin, Memorandum to Mr. Hoover, November 1, 1922, in RG 40, File 82341.

40 *SPR No. 28: Sheet Steel* (1925); *SPR No. 29: Eaves Trough, Conductor Pipe, Conductor Elbows and Fittings* (1925); *SPR No. 30: Terneplate* (1925); *SPR No. 31: Loaded Paper Shot Shells* (1925).

41 U.S. Department of Commerce, *Standards Yearbook 1927*, 361.

42 *SPR No. 4: Asphalt* (1923); *SPR No. 7: Face Brick and Common Brick* (1924).

43 *SPR No. 38: Sand-Lime Brick* (1926), 2.

44 *SPR No. 12: Hollow Building Tile* (1924), 6; *SPR No. 21: Brass Lavatory and Sink Traps* (1925), 6.

45 Hudson, "The New Conservation – II," 28.

46 *SPR No. 11: Bed Blankets: Cotton, Wool, and Cotton and Wool Mixed* (1924), 7. Household bed sheets were not simplified; instead, the American Home Economics Association asked the American Engineering Standards Committee (AESC) in 1927 to develop quality and labeling standards for bed sheets, an initiative that had been "discontinued" by 1940: Agnew, "Work of the American Engineering Standards Committee," 15–16; Edwards, *Product Standards*, 94–6 (quotation, 95). As bed, mattress, and blanket manufacturers limited their production to standard sizes, however, manufacturers of bed sheets may simply have followed suit. On the AESC, see below.

47 *SPR No. 24: Hospital Beds* (1925), 7.

48 *SPR No. 74: Hospital and Institutional Cotton Textiles* (1928); "Editorial: Sheets, Standardization, and Home Economics," 452. See also Katharine A. Fisher, "Sheets: The Part They Play in Bed-Making," *Good Housekeeping*, March 1928, 90.

49 *SPR No. 26: Steel Reinforcing Bars* (1925), 5; *SPR No. 35: Steel Lockers (Single and Double Tier)* (1925), 6.

50 *SPR No. 53: Steel Spiral Rods (For Concrete Reinforcement)* (1926), 4.

51 *SPR R62-37: Metallic Cartridges* (1937), 5.

52 *SPR No. 5: Hotel Chinaware* (1924); *SPR No. 33: Chinaware (Cafeteria and Restaurant)* (1925), 7; *SPR No. 39: Dining-Car Chinaware* (1926), 2, 4; *SPR No. 40: Hospital Chinaware* (1926), 2, 4. On hotel chinaware, see Quinn, "Standardization and Waste Elimination." Quinn chaired the American Hotel Association's Committee on Standardization and Waste Elimination, which set off this chain of simplifications. In 1948, the American Hospital Association initiated the simplification of plastic tableware: *SPR 249-52: Plastic Tableware* (1952), 4.

53 For references to simplification as a movement, see Maddock, "How Simplification Removed Production Difficulties," 612; Thomas,

"Simplification in Industry, II," 715; Mr. Durgin, Memorandum to
Mr. Hoover, November 1, 1922, in RG 40, File 82341; Durgin, "Alice
in Modernland," 14; Louis Sussman, "Why We Cut Our Line from
1,000 to 24 Varieties," *System* 45, no. 5 (May 1924): 623; Hudson, "Are
There Any Real Obstacles to Simplification?" 538; U.S. Department of
Commerce, *Thirteenth Annual Report of the Secretary of Commerce*,
3; U.S. Department of Commerce, *Commerce Yearbook 1930 (Eighth
Number)*, vol. I: *United States*, 44–7.

54 U.S. Department of Commerce, Division of Simplified Practice,
Monthly News Bulletin, no. 11 (February 15, 1926): 4; U.S. Department
of Commerce, Division of Simplified Practice, *Monthly News Bulletin*,
no. 16 (July 15, 1926): 7 (quotation).

55 Hudson and Priest, "Saving through Simplified Practice," 12. The DSP's
1924 pamphlet *Simplified Practice: What It Is and What It Offers*
was produced as a textbook for college courses: Tanner, "Secretary
Hoover's War on Waste," 6.

56 "Die Tagung des Reichsverbandes der deutschen Industrie,"
Dortmunder Zeitung, June 25, 1925, 7; Julius Hirsch, "Das amerika-
nische Wirtschaftswunder: Der Wille zur höchsten Produktivität,"
Berliner Tageblatt und Handels-Zeitung, Morgen-Ausgabe, November
26, 1925, 7; Carl Köttgen, *Das wirtschaftliche Amerika* (Berlin: VDI-
Verlag, 1925), 53–4, 159–62; J. Rousset, "L'Élimination du gaspillage
dans la production par la 'pratique simplifiée' américaine," *Mon
Bureau: Le magazine de l'organisation commerciale et industrielle*, no.
161 (July 1927): 431–3.

57 Chisholm, "Simplification in British Industry: I," 513; Cecil Chisholm,
"Simplification in Industry: II. – Some Examples," *The* [London] *Times
Imperial and Foreign Trade and Engineering Supplement*, August 22,
1925, 561; Cecil Chisholm, "Simplification in Industry: III. – Where
Progress Has Been Made," *The* [London] *Times Imperial and Foreign
Trade and Engineering Supplement*, August 29, 1925, 585; Cecil
Chisholm, *Simplified Practice: An Outline of a New Industrial Policy*
(London: Chapman, 1927).

58 Hudson, "Group Simplification Gains Momentum," 286. See also U.S.
Department of Commerce, *Monthly News Bulletin*, no. 16 (July 15,
1926), 7.

59 U.S. Department of Commerce, Division of Simplified Practice,
Monthly News Bulletin, no. 9 (December 15, 1925): 3.

60 The Russian translation was done by the Russian Agricultural Agency
(RAA): U.S. Department of Commerce, Division of Simplified Practice,
Monthly News Bulletin, no. 10 (January 15, 1926), 2. On the RAA, see

Maria Fedorova, "Bigger than Grain: Soviet–American Agricultural Exchange, 1918–1928" (Ph.D. thesis, University of California, Santa Barbara, 2019), 75–89, https://escholarship.org/uc/item/534899tj. The French translation was published in the bulletin of the Société d'Encouragement pour l'Industrie National: U.S. Department of Commerce, Division of Simplified Practice, *Monthly News Bulletin*, no. 16 (July 15, 1926), 7. The Japanese translation is mentioned in a draft letter attached to George K. Burgess, Director, Bureau of Standards, to Secretary of Commerce, December 15, 1930, [copy] in RG 40, File 67009/80.

61 Hudson, "Organized Effort in Simplification," 8; U.S. Department of Commerce, Bureau of Standards, *The Commercial Standards Service and Its Value to Business, Commercial Standard CS0-30 [Issued March 20, 1930]* (Washington, DC: Government Printing Office, 1930), 16; Brady, *Industrial Standardization*, 157.

62 Chisholm, "Simplification in British Industry: I," 513. See also U.S. Department of Commerce, "Supplement: British Interest in Simplified Practice," 2; Nancy Mitchell, *The Danger of Dreams: German and American Imperialism in Latin America* (Chapel Hill: University of North Carolina Press, 1999).

63 Cochrane, *Measures for Progress*, 254.

64 *SPR No. 34: Warehouse Forms* (1925).

65 *SPR No. 37: Commercial Forms (Invoice, Inquiry, and Purchase Order)* (1925), 11.

66 U.S. Bureau of Standards, The Purpose and Application of Simplified Practice, 16; *SPR R95-28: Skid Platforms* (1929). *SPR R95-28* established vertical and horizontal clearance dimensions for skid platforms. Two years later, the SPR was extended to cover the overall dimensions of skid platforms: *SPR R95-30: Skid Platforms* (1931), 1.

67 U.S. Bureau of Standards, The Purpose and Application of Simplified Practice, 16–17; *SPR R126-31: Set-Up Boxes (Used by department and specialty stores)* (1932); *SPR R127-31: Folding Boxes (Used by department and specialty stores)* (1932); *SPR R128-31: Corrugated Boxes (Used by department and specialty stores)* (1932); *SPR R129-31: Notion and Millinery Paper Bags* (1932). See also U.S. Department of Commerce, *Standards Yearbook 1931*, 247; "Official Proceedings: Conference on Simplified Practice," 3. The thickness of the box board from which set-up and folding boxes were manufactured had been simplified in 1926: *SPR No. 44: Box Board Thicknesses* (1926).

68 *SPR No. 4: Asphalt* (1923), 4. The SPR used "grades" and "varieties" interchangeably. Overall, asphalt grades were reduced from 102 to 10.

69 *SPR No. 16: Lumber* (1924), 10–11.

70 U.S. Department of Commerce, *Commercial Standards Service . . . CS0-30*, 4. See also *SPR No. 48: Shovels, Spades and Scoops* (1926), 1; *SPR No. 52: Staple Vitreous China Plumbing Fixtures* (1927); *SPR No. 61: White Glazed Tile and Unglazed Ceramic Mosaic* (1927), 4.

71 U.S. Department of Commerce, *National Directory of Commodity Specifications*; U.S. Department of Commerce, Division of Simplified Practice, *Monthly News Bulletin*, no. 31 (October 15, 1927): 1.

72 U.S. Department of Commerce, Division of Simplified Practice, *Monthly News Bulletin*, no. 31 (October 15, 1927): 1.

73 U.S. Department of Commerce, Division of Simplified Practice, *Monthly News Bulletin*, no. 31 (October 15, 1927): 1–2; U.S. Department of Commerce, Bureau of Standards, "Broadening of Bureau's Service in the Field of Commercial Standards," *Technical News Bulletin*, no. 127 (November 1927): 14 (quotation); U.S. Department of Commerce, Bureau of Standards, *Standards Yearbook 1928*, Misc. Pub. No. 83 (Washington, DC: Government Printing Office, 1928), 124; U.S. Department of Commerce, *Commercial Standards Service . . . CS0-30*, 4–5.

74 U.S. Department of Commerce, *Commercial Standards Service . . . CS0-30*, 11, 15. For an example of a willing-to-certify list, see U.S. Department of Commerce, National Bureau of Standards, Sources of Supply of Commodities Covered by Commercial Standards, February 15, 1930, Letter Circular LC 277.

75 U.S. Department of Commerce, *Commercial Standards Service . . . CS0-30*, 5, 11, 15.

76 U.S. Department of Commerce, *Monthly News Bulletin of Commercial Standards Group*, no. 32 (November 15, 1927): 1 (masthead); U.S. Department of Commerce, Bureau of Standards, "37. Commercial Standards Group," *Monthly News Bulletin of Commercial Standards Group*, no. 43 (October 15, 1928): 10.

77 U.S. Department of Commerce, "37. Commercial Standards Group," 15; U.S. Department of Commerce, *Commercial Standards Service . . . CS0-30*, 9–16. The latter includes a diagram (p. 12) of the commercial standards procedure.

78 *CS1: New Billet-Steel Concrete Reinforcement Bars* (1927) (printed pamphlet circulated with an acceptance form); U.S. Department of Commerce, Bureau of Standards, *Annual Report of the Director of the Bureau of Standards to the Secretary of Commerce for the Fiscal Year Ended June 30, 1928*, Misc. Pub. No. 88 (Washington, DC: Government Printing Office, 1928), 33; *CS1-28: Clinical Thermometers* (1928).

79 U.S. Department of Commerce, *Commercial Standards Service* ... *CS0-30*, 17–18; *CS2-30: Mopsticks* (1930).

80 U.S. Department of Commerce, *Commercial Standards Service* ... *CS0-30*, 7. See, for example, *CS2-30: Mopsticks* (1930), 2.

81 *SPR R2-30: Bedsteads, Springs, and Mattresses* (1931), 18.

82 U.S. Department of Commerce, *American Marine Standards*, 3–4.

83 U.S. Department of Commerce, *War Work of the Bureau of Standards*, 99–100; U.S. Department of Commerce, Bureau of Standards, "Standardization of Dry Cells," *Technical News Bulletin*, no. 85 (May 10, 1924): 2.

84 U.S. Department of Commerce, *National Bureau of Standards*, 87–8.

85 U.S. Department of Commerce, *Annual Report of the Director of the Bureau of Standards ... 1922*, 249.

86 In U.S. Department of Commerce, Bureau of Standards, *Technical News Bulletin*, see, for enameled ware: "Specifications for Enameled Ware" (title varies slightly), No. 54 (October 8, 1921), 10; No. 56 (December 9, 1921), 3; No. 57 (January 9, 1922), 3; No. 58 (February 9, 1922), 9; and No. 60 (April 8, 1922), 13. For whiteware, see "Standard Specifications for Whiteware Pottery" (title varies), No. 76 (August 10, 1923), 5; No. 77 (September 15, 1923), 4; No. 81 (January 10, 1924), 3; and No. 92 (December 10, 1924), 7.

87 "Official Proceedings: Conference on Simplified Practice," 4.

88 *SPR No. 1: Paving Bricks* (1925), 3; American Engineering Standards Committee, *Year Book* (New York: American Engineering Standards Committee, 1923), 18; U.S. Department of Commerce, *Simplified Practice: What It Is* (1924), 1; Tanner, "Secretary Hoover's War on Waste," 4. Later called the Planning Committee, its membership was expanded to include representatives of distributors, purchasing agents, and retailers. It became the advisory body for the Commercial Standards Group when the latter was formed in 1927: U.S. Department of Commerce, *Thirteenth Annual Report of the Secretary of Commerce*, 19n17; U.S. Department of Commerce, *Fourteenth Annual Report of the Secretary of Commerce* (Washington, DC: Government Printing Office, 1926), 15n13; U.S. Department of Commerce, *Standards Yearbook 1928*, 125; U.S. Department of Commerce, Bureau of Standards, "Committee Member," *Commercial Standards Monthly*, no. 46 (January 15, 1929): 3.

89 U.S. Department of Commerce, *Simplified Practice: What It Is* (1924), 1 (quotation); McCullough, "The Relation of the Chamber of Commerce," 9–12. See also Chamber of Commerce of the United States of America, *A Commercial Tower of Babel*, and articles on simplification by

Chamber employees: Alfred L. Smith, "Standardization of Products: II. As a Trade Economy," *Bulletin of the Taylor Society* 6, no. 2 (April 1921): 59–62; Alfred L. Smith, "Simplification in Industry, V: How Trade Associations Help the Manufacturer Promote Standardization," *Factory* 26, no. 12 (June 15, 1921): 1391–3; Barnes, "Standardization as a Creator of New Advertising," 23–4, 100, 103.

90 Clifford B. Le Page, "Twenty-Five Years – the American Standards Association: 1. Origins," *Industrial Standardization* 14, no. 12 (December 1943): 320–2; Cuff, *The War Industries Board*, 16–20; Russell, *Open Standards*, 61–6. The five societies were the American Society of Civil Engineers, the American Institute of Mining and Metallurgical Engineers, the American Society of Mechanical Engineers, the American Institute of Electrical Engineers, and the American Society for Testing Materials.

91 Agnew, "Twenty-Five Years – the American Standards Association: 2. Development of the ASA," 322. The Bureau of Standards offered strong support for the reorganization. See Edward B. Rosa, "Reorganization of the Engineering Standards Committee [I]," *Engineering News-Record* 82, no. 18 (May 1, 1919): 861–2; Edward B. Rosa, "Reorganization of the Engineering Standards Committee [II]," *Engineering News-Record* 82, no. 19 (May 8, 1919): 916–28.

92 Russell, *Open Standards*, 84. See also Le Page, "Twenty-Five Years – the American Standards Association: 1. Origins," 322; Tanner, "Secretary Hoover's War on Waste," 16–18.

93 Russell, *Open Standards*, 60–1.

94 Russell, *Open Standards*, 60–1, 66–7. In 1919, Agnew served as the Bureau's liaison when the AESC expanded its membership base. His assistant, F. J. Schlink, who later became a prominent consumer advocate, had also worked at the Bureau of Standards during the war: McGovern, *Sold American*, 166. On the standardization movement's emphasis on collaboration and consensus, see Russell, *Open Standards*; and Yates and Murphy, *Engineering Rules*.

95 Cochrane, *Measures for Progress*, 304.

96 U.S. Department of Commerce, *Simplified Practice: What It Is* (1924), 1; Tanner, "Secretary Hoover's War on Waste," 6.

97 Thomas, "Simplification in Industry," 451–3. The quotation is from the cover of the February 15, 1921, issue.

98 Thomas, "Simplification in Industry, II," 715–18, 752, 754.

99 See the covers of *Factory*, February 15, 1921; March 15, 1921; June 15, 1921; September 1921; October 1921; December 1921; and July 1922.

100 Thomas, "Simplification in Industry, II," 715 (quotation); A. W. Shaw, "The Simplification of Business," *System* 40, no. 2 (August 1921): 139.

101 Quarterly Report on Activities of the Division of Simplified Practice, June 30, 1923, 7, in RG 40, File 67009/80. See also Mr. Durgin, Memorandum to Mr. Hoover, November 1, 1922, in RG 40, File 82341.

102 Planning Committee of the Division of Simplified Practice (accompanying the agenda for the committee's December 16, 1932 meeting), in RG 40, File 67009/80; U.S. Department of Commerce, Bureau of Standards, List of Simplified Practice Recommendations, October 1932, Letter Circular 346, [ii].

103 Tanner, "Secretary Hoover's War on Waste," 6.

104 Shaw, "Simplification," 417–27 (quotation, p. 419).

105 "Official Proceedings: Conference on Simplified Practice," 3.

106 Tanner, "Secretary Hoover's War on Waste," 19–20.

107 The breadth of Bureau projects relating to simplification, commercial standards, and specifications may be gauged in the Bureau's publication *Commercial Standards Monthly* and its predecessor, the DSP's *Monthly News Bulletin.* For insights into simplified practice projects from the business side, see "Official Proceedings: Conference on Simplified Practice," 5–12.

108 U.S. Department of Commerce, *Twentieth Annual Report of the Secretary of Commerce* (Washington, DC: Government Printing Office, 1932), xxiii, xxv.

109 U.S. Bureau of Standards, The Purpose and Application of Simplified Practice, Appendix C. The average reduction in product variety is my estimate based on data in Appendix C.

110 U.S. Department of Commerce, Bureau of Standards, *Standards Yearbook 1930*, Misc. Pub. No. 106 (Washington, DC: Government Printing Office, 1930), 7.

111 U.S. Department of Commerce, *Commerce Yearbook 1930 (Eighth Number)*, vol. I: *United States*, 47.

112 Beller, "Economic Effect of Simplification," 72.

113 "Official Proceedings: Conference on Simplified Practice," 11.

114 U.S. Department of Commerce, *Commerce Yearbook 1930 (Eighth Number)*, vol. I: *United States*, 46–47; U.S. Bureau of Standards, The Purpose and Application of Simplified Practice, Appendix B; U.S. Department of Commerce, *Standards Yearbook 1931*, 246; Edwin W. Ely, "Simplified Practice Applied to Paper," *United States Daily* (Washington), June 21, 1932, 8.

115 Report of the Planning Committee (1931), 11. On statewide simplification programs, see also U.S. Department of Commerce, Bureau of Standards, *Standards Yearbook 1933*, Misc. Pub. No. 139 (Washington, DC: Government Printing Office, 1933), 142.

116 U.S. Department of Commerce, *Commerce Yearbook 1930 (Eighth Number)*, vol. I: *United States*, 47.

117 "Official Proceedings: Conference on Simplified Practice," 3.

118 "Official Proceedings: Conference on Simplified Practice," 7.

119 Agenda for Meeting of the Planning Committee of the Division of Simplified Practice ... [to be held] December 16, 1932, 8, 11–22, in RG 40, File 67009/80; National Academy of Sciences, Special Advisory Committee, *The Role of the Department of Commerce in Science and Technology: A Report to the Secretary of Commerce* ([Washington, DC], 1960), 108.

120 The *Standards Yearbook* was published from 1927 to 1933. The *Commercial Standards Monthly* had been introduced in 1925 as the DSP's *Monthly News Bulletin* and retitled in 1927. From 1933 to 1943, it was published by the ASA "with the cooperation of the National Bureau of Standards" as the *Industrial Standardization and Commercial Standards Monthly*. See the publications themselves and Yates and Murphy, *Engineering Rules*, 134.

121 U.S. Department of Commerce, *Twenty-Second Annual Report of the Secretary of Commerce* (Washington, DC: Government Printing Office, 1934), 52–3.

122 National Academy of Sciences, *The Role of the Department of Commerce*, 108. See also Herring, *Public Administration*, 331–2.

123 National Academy of Sciences, *The Role of the Department of Commerce*, 108. See also Herring, *Public Administration*, 331–2.

124 U.S. Department of Commerce, *Twenty-Second Annual Report of the Secretary of Commerce*, 73; U.S. Department of Commerce, *Twenty-Third Annual Report of the Secretary of Commerce* (Washington, DC: Government Printing Office, 1935), 82.

125 National Academy of Sciences, *The Role of the Department of Commerce*, 108.

126 *SPR R62-39: Metallic Cartridges* (1939), 16–17; U.S. Department of Commerce, National Bureau of Standards, *Commercial Standards and Their Value to Business (Second Edition), Commercial Standard CS0-39 (Supersedes CS0-30), Recorded Standards of the Industry* (Washington, DC: Government Printing Office, 1939), 23.

127 Quoted in Shaw, *Enlarging the War Effort*, 3. For a contemporary explanation of the benefits of standardization for federal procurement

in wartime, see Clifton E. Mack, "Standards Aid Efficiency in Federal Procurement," *Industrial Standardization* 14, no. 12 (December 1943): 341–5. Mack was director of procurement in the U.S. Treasury Department.

128 U.S. Department of Commerce, "Simplified Practice and the Defense Program," 95–6; U.S. Department of Commerce, National Bureau of Standards, Variety Reduction Effected by the Application of Simplified Practice, June 4, 1942, Letter Circular LC-693 (Supersedes LC-651), [ii] (quotation).

129 U.S. Department of Commerce, *Thirtieth Annual Report of the Secretary of Commerce: 1942* (Washington, DC: Government Printing Office, 1942), 122; Lyman J. Briggs, "National Bureau of Standards in War Simplification and Standardization Work," *Industrial Standardization* 13, no. 6 (June 1942): 149–50; Howard Coonley, "WPB Drives for Simplified Lines and Standards," *Industrial Standardization and Commercial Standards Monthly* 13, no. 6 (June 1942): 137–41; U.S. Department of Commerce, Variety Reduction, 1; Lyman Briggs, *NBS War Research: The National Bureau of Standards in World War II* ([Washington, DC]: U.S. Department of Commerce, National Bureau of Standards, September 1949), 172–4; Cochrane, *Measures for Progress*, 424–5.

130 Briggs, "National Bureau of Standards," 150.

131 U.S. Department of Commerce, *Thirtieth Annual Report*, 123.

132 Data for 1939 are from *SPR R62-39: Metallic Cartridges*, 16–17; U.S. Department of Commerce, National Bureau of Standards, *Commercial Standards and Their Value to Business (Second Edition), Commercial Standard CS0-39 (Supersedes CS0-30) Recorded Standards of the Industry* (Washington, DC: Government Printing Office, 1939), 23. Data for 1946 are from *SPR R70-46: Salt Packages* (1946), 11–12; *CS15-46: Men's Pajama Sizes – Woven Fabrics* (1946), 10–11.

133 In 1947, the DSP and the Trade Standards Division were merged to form the Commodity Standards Division. Within the Commerce Department, it was transferred to the Office of Domestic Commerce in 1950 and then to the Office of Technical Services in 1954: National Academy of Sciences, *The Role of the Department of Commerce*, 108. In 1963, it was transferred back to the Bureau of Standards, where, as the Voluntary Product Standards Program, it remains today: Mackay, "The Development and Use of National Voluntary Standards," 552; Elio Passaglia, with Karma A. Beal, *A Unique Institution: The National Bureau of Standards, 1950–1969*, Special Publication 925 (Washington, DC: U.S. Dept. of Commerce, Technology Administration, National

Institute of Standards and Technology, 1999), 382; National Institute of Standards and Technology, *Voluntary Product Standards Program*, www.nist.gov/standardsgov/voluntary-product-standards-program.

134 National Academy of Sciences, *The Role of the Department of Commerce*, 113.

135 U.S. Department of Commerce, *Variety Reduction*, 2.

136 Anglo-American Council on Productivity, *Simplification in Industry: Report of an Inquiry in Britain by a Group Appointed by the Council*, Productivity Report (London and New York: Anglo-American Council on Productivity, October 1949), 3–4.

137 U.S. Department of Commerce, *Simplified Practice Recommendations: Alphabetical List Revised to February 1, 1950*; U.S. Department of Commerce, National Bureau of Standards, *List of Commercial Standards, Revised to January 1, 1950*, January 1, 1950, Letter Circular LC978 (Supersedes LC956).

138 On the Marshall Plan's Productivity Program, see Corinna Schlombs, *Productivity Machines: German Appropriations of American Technology from Mass Production to Computer Automation*, Kindle ed. (Cambridge, MA: MIT Press, 2019), chs. 3–5.

139 Anglo-American Council on Productivity, *Simplification in Industry*; Hounshell, *From the American System to Mass Production*, 17–25. The Anglo-American Council also published a follow-up report on simplification in British industry. Anglo-American Council on Productivity, *Simplification in British Industry: Report of an Inquiry in Britain by the Group, Appointed by the Council, Which Made an Investigation of Simplification in the United States of America* (London and New York: Anglo-American Council on Productivity, August 1950).

140 *Vereinfachung der industriellen Produktion: Berichte einer englischen Studienkommission über ihre Erfahrungen in USA und in England*, Schriftenreihe des RKW-Auslandsdienst No. 4 (Munich: Carl Hanser Verlag, 1951).

141 See Economic Cooperation Administration, *Increasing Productivity*; U.S. Department of Labor, Bureau of Labor Statistics, for the Mutual Security Agency, Productivity and Technical Assistance Division, *Cost Savings through Standardization, Simplification, Specialization in Electrically Operated Household Appliances* (Washington, November 1952); and U.S. Department of Labor, Bureau of Labor Statistics, for the Foreign Operations Administration, Productivity and Technical Assistance Division, *Cost Savings through Standardisation, Simplification, Specialisation in the Clothing Industry* (Paris: Organisation for European Economic Co-operation, December 1954).

The latter was one in a series that included pamphlets on containers, the building industry, and materials handling equipment.

142 Economic Cooperation Administration, *Increasing Productivity*, 74; Schlombs, *Productivity Machines*, 107–8.

143 "Achievements of the Marshall Plan: ECA Summarizes European Recovery," *Department of State Bulletin* 26, no. 655 (January 14, 1952): 45; Solidelle F. Wasser and Michael L. Dolfman, "BLS and the Marshall Plan: The Forgotten Story," *Monthly Labor Review* 128, no. 6 (June 2005): 50; Schlombs, *Productivity Machines*, 136–7, 163–4.

144 Betty L. Oberholtzer, *Publications of the National Bureau of Standards, 1966–1967*, U.S. Department of Commerce, National Bureau of Standards, Special Publication 305 (Washington, DC: Government Printing Office, 1969), 41; Betty L. Oberholtzer, *Publications of the National Bureau of Standards, 1970*, U.S. Department of Commerce, National Bureau of Standards, Special Publication 305, Suppl. 2 (Washington, DC: Government Printing Office, 1971), 54–5; U.S. Department of Commerce, *List of Voluntary Product Standards* (1972), 12–16. As SPRs and commercial standards were revised, they were converted to PS numbers. Of the 52 voluntary product standards issued through 1971, at least 22 were conversions. *SPR No. 70* for salt packages, for example, became *PS14-69*, while *CS1* for clinical thermometers became *PS39-70*. The procedure for establishing voluntary product standards was laid out in "Title 15 – Commerce and Foreign Trade, Subtitle A, Part 10 – Procedures for the Development of Voluntary Product Standards," 8349–53. See also Passaglia, *A Unique Institution*, 673, 686–7; Schooley, *Responding to National Needs*, 919, 932–3; "Brief History of Voluntary Standards Published by the U.S. Department of Commerce," NIST Standards.gov, www.nist.gov/standa rdsgov/brief-history-voluntary-standards-published-us-department -commerce.

145 "Department of Commerce, Business and Defense Services Administration, Office of Technical Services, Commodity Standards Division, Statement of Organization," *Federal Register* 20, no. 34 (February 17, 1955): 1028.

146 U.S. Department of Commerce, *List of Voluntary Product Standards* (1972).

147 U.S. Department of Commerce, National Bureau of Standards, *List of Voluntary Product Standards, Commercial Standards, and Simplified Practice Recommendations*, NBS List of Publications 53, Revised February 1977 ([Washington, DC], February 1977), 8–9.

148 E.g., "Notices, Department of Commerce, National Bureau of

Standards, Voluntary Product Standards: Notice of Action on Proposed Withdrawal," *Federal Register* 31, no. 178 (September 14, 1966): 12027 (withdrawing 31 standards); "Notices, Department of Commerce, National Bureau of Standards, Voluntary Product Standards: Notice of Action on Proposed Withdrawal," *Federal Register* 35, no. 244 (December 17, 1970): 19138–9 (withdrawing 43 standards); "Notices, Department of Commerce, National Bureau of Standards, Voluntary Product Standards: Notice of Action on Proposed Withdrawal," *Federal Register* 36, no. 79 (April 23, 1971): 7695–6 (withdrawing 111 standards); "Notices, Department of Commerce, National Bureau of Standards, Notice of Intent to Withdraw Certain Standards," *Federal Register* 37, no. 16 (January 25, 1972): 1130 (citing equivalent ASTM standards); "Notices, Department of Commerce, National Bureau of Standards, Voluntary Product Standards: Notice of Action on Proposed Withdrawal," *Federal Register* 37, no. 86 (May 3, 1972): 8957 (withdrawing 66 standards); "Notices, Department of Commerce, National Bureau of Standards, Voluntary Product Standards: Notice of Action on Proposed Withdrawal," *Federal Register* 37, no. 165 (August 24, 1972), 17072–3 (withdrawing 61 standards); "Notices, Department of Commerce, National Bureau of Standards, Voluntary Product Standards: Action on Proposed Withdrawal," *Federal Register* 39, no. 109 (June 5, 1974): 19972 (citing a trade association's standards as equivalent and up to date); "Notices, Department of Commerce, National Bureau of Standards, Simplified Practice Recommendation, Notice of Intent to Withdraw," *Federal Register* 43, no. 248 (December 26, 1978): 60182 (citing an up-to-date federal specification).

149 Congressional Research Service, *Voluntary Industrial Standards*, 1, 4. On the National Bureau of Standards' new responsibilities in the 1970s and early 1980s, see Schooley, *Responding to National Needs*, 469–71. On the new social regulation, see David Vogel, "The 'New' Social Regulation in Historical and Comparative Perspective," in McCraw, ed., *Regulation in Perspective*, 155–85.

150 Hemenway, *Industrywide Voluntary Product Standards*, 89–90; Passaglia, *A Unique Institution*, 687.

151 "Voluntary Product Standards Program," NIST Standards.gov. See also American Lumber Standard Committee, Inc., "History," http://alsc.org /geninfo_history_mod.htm.

152 Economic Cooperation Administration, *Increasing Productivity*, 11.

Afterword

1 See Geoffrey M. Hodgson, *Conceptualizing Capitalism: Institutions, Evolution, Future* (Chicago and London: University of Chicago Press, 2015); Simon Deakin et al., "Legal Institutionalism: Capitalism and the Constitutive Role of Law," *Journal of Comparative Economics* 45 (2017): 188–200.

2 Historical research suggests that regulation and promotion are interdependent – the government that promotes business is better positioned to regulate it; the government that regulates without the quid pro quo of promotion encounters resistance: Colleen A. Dunlavy, "Mirror Images: Political Structure and Early Railroad Policy in the United States and Prussia," *Studies in American Political Development* 5 (Spring 1991): 1–35. On the distinctive division of policymaking powers between the federal and state governments in the U.S., which weakened the ability of both to regulate business, see David Brian Robertson, *Capital, Labor, and State: The Battle for American Labor Markets from the Civil War to the New Deal* (Lanham, MD: Rowman & Littlefield Publishers, 2000). For a useful conceptual framework for capturing the scope of "industrial policy," see Réka Juhász and Claudia Steinwender, "Industrial Policy and the Great Divergence," National Bureau of Economic Research, Working Paper 31736, Cambridge, MA, September 2023, www.nber.org/papers/w31736.

3 *The Public Statutes at Large of the United States of America, From the Organization of the Government in 1789, to March 3, 1845 . . .* (Boston: Charles C. Little and James Brown, 1845), 24–8 (chs. II and III).

4 For an introduction, see Harry N. Scheiber, "Federalism and the American Economic Order, 1789–1910," *Law and Society Review* 10, no. 1 (Fall 1975): 57–118; William R. Brock, *Investigation and Responsibility: Public Responsibility in the United States, 1865–1900* (Cambridge University Press, 1984); Merritt Roe Smith, ed., *Military Enterprise and Technological Change: Perspectives on the American Experience* (Cambridge, MA: MIT Press, 1985); William J. Novak, *The People's Welfare: Law and Regulation in Nineteenth-Century America* (Chapel Hill and London: University of North Carolina Press, 1996); Heather Cox Richardson, *The Greatest Nation of the Earth: Republican Economic Policies during the Civil War* (Cambridge, MA: Harvard University Press, 1997); Robertson, *Capital, Labor, and State*; David A. Moss, *When All Else Fails: Government as the Ultimate Risk Manager* (Cambridge, MA: Harvard University Press, 2002); Jason Scott Smith, *Building New Deal Liberalism: The Political Economy of Public Works, 1933–1956* (New York: Cambridge University Press, 2006); Brian Balogh, *A Government*

out of Sight: The Mystery of National Authority in Nineteenth-Century America (Cambridge University Press, 2009); Jacob S. Hacker and Paul Pierson, *American Amnesia: How the War on Government Led Us to Forget What Made America Prosper* (New York: Simon and Schuster, 2016); and Lindsay Schakenbach Regele, *Manufacturing Advantage: War, the State, and the Origins of American Industry, 1776–1848* (Baltimore: Johns Hopkins University Press, 2019). The political history of the idea of free enterprise is explored in Lawrence B. Glickman, *Free Enterprise: An American History* (New Haven: Yale University Press, 2019).

5 On industrial policy from the 1980s through the turn of the twenty-first century, see Fred Block, "Swimming against the Current: The Rise of a Hidden Developmental State in the United States," *Politics and Society* 36, no. 2 (2008): 169–206; Andrew Schrank and Josh Whitford, "Industrial Policy in the United States: A Neo-Polanyian Interpretation," *Politics and Society* 37, no. 4 (2009): 521–53. Thanks to Pierre-Christian Fink for pointing me toward this literature.

6 E. J. Dionne, Jr., "Biden, Macron and the End of the Reagan–Thatcher Era," Opinion, *Washington Post*, December 4, 2022, www.washingtonpo st.com/opinions/2022/12/04/biden-macron-end-reagan-thatcher-era.

7 Smith, *Harpers Ferry Armory*; Merritt Roe Smith, "Army Ordnance and the 'American System' of Manufacturing, 1815–1861," in Smith, ed., *Military Enterprise and Technological Change*, 39–86; Schakenbach Regele, *Manufacturing Advantage*.

8 Hartmut Berghoff, *Moderne Unternehmensgeschichte: Eine Themen- und Theorieorientierte Einführung*, 2nd ed. (Berlin, Munich, Boston: Walter de Gruyter GmbH, 2016), 313.

Index

Italics indicate an image.